THE GREAT REVERSAL

THE
GREAT REVERSAL

How America Gave Up on Free Markets

THOMAS PHILIPPON

The Belknap Press of Harvard University Press
CAMBRIDGE, MASSACHUSETTS
LONDON, ENGLAND
2019

Library of Congress Cataloging-in-Publication Data
Names: Philippon, Thomas, author.
Title: The great reversal : how America gave up on free markets / Thomas Philippon.
Description: Cambridge, Massachusetts : The Belknap Press of Harvard University Press, 2019. | Includes bibliographical references and index.
Identifiers: LCCN 2019018624 | ISBN 9780674237544
Subjects: LCSH: Free enterprise—United States. | Free enterprise—Europe. | Free enterprise—Political aspects—United States. | Markets—United States. | Markets—Europe. | Competition—United States. | Competition—Europe. | Lobbying—United States.
Classification: LCC HB95 .P53 2019 | DDC 330.973—dc23
LC record available at https://lccn.loc.gov/2019018624

Contents

Preface

THE QUESTION that spurred me to write this book is surprisingly mundane. It's something that virtually everyone in the United States has probably asked themselves at one point or another: Why on earth are US cell phone plans so expensive? Or, to broaden it a little further, why do consumers in Europe or in Asia pay less for cellular service and, on average, get much more?

Asking this seemingly simple question was my first step on a journey through some of the most hotly debated issues in modern economics. Looking for the answer led me to investigate wage stagnation, corporate lobbying, special interests, governance of large financial funds, money in politics, free trade, technology, and innovation.

It also led to some surprising revelations about the relative prices of goods and services in the US and Europe, overturning common assumptions—including my own—about the status of consumers in the two largest economic markets on the planet.

How did I wind up here? Believe or not, this was not my intention. It's the data's fault. I started with a precise, well-defined question, and then I followed the facts. All the facts. Nothing more, but nothing less. And I'll admit freely that I was as surprised as anyone by the outcome.

My aim is to retrace some of these steps, taking you along with me. If you follow, you'll find out why you're paying an arm and a leg for your cell phone every month, but you'll also learn a lot about economics. In fact, the book could serve as an introduction to modern economics, though in an unconventional format.

A quick note about my approach. Unlike some who write about controversial topics in economics or in other fields, I readily admit that I don't have all the answers. In much of the writing on economics and society today, the tone is certain and prescriptive. The problems are "obvious" and, predictably, so are the solutions.

I would suggest, however, that such prescriptions be taken with a (large) grain of salt. When you read an author or commentator who tells you something is obvious, take your time and do the math. Almost every time, you'll discover that it wasn't really obvious at all.

I have found that people who tell you that the answers to the big questions in economics are obvious are telling you only half of the story. More often than not, they think the answers are obvious either because they have an agenda or because they don't really know what they are talking about.

So be skeptical—always. Most people simply repeat what they have heard without checking the data. In fact, there is often a negative correlation between outward certainty and factual information. The first thing anyone should discover when they research an interesting question is always the limits of their knowledge. Mancur Olson put it eloquently in *The Rise and Decline of Nations*: "The reader should accordingly not accept the argument in this book simply because he or she finds it plausible and consistent with known facts. Many plausible stories have been told before and often also widely believed, yet they failed to stand up."

This brings me to another important note about this book. I plan to enable your skepticism by showing you how the work is done. That research informs much of this book, and where I rely on it to reach conclusions, I provide enough background on the data to allow you to make your own judgment about my findings. I will present all the facts as simply and transparently as possible, refraining from making any claim that is not backed by at least some data. In doing so, I hope to reduce the risk of imposing my own subjective views.

But I am certainly going to fail, at least to some extent, so it is probably useful for you to know a bit about my beliefs, which in economic jargon we call our *priors* to emphasize our willingness to change them if new facts emerge. As John Maynard Keynes is often credited with saying to a critic, "When the facts change, I change my mind. What do you do, sir?"

The best summary of my priors is probably that I am a free market liberal. I believe that free markets work best, provided that we agree on what we mean by "free" markets. I believe that markets are free when they are not subject to arbitrary political interference and when incumbents are not artificially protected from competitive new entrants. Keeping the markets free sometimes requires government interventions, but markets are certainly not free when governments expropriate private property, when incumbents are allowed to suppress competition, or when they successfully lobby to protect their rents.

I am also liberal in the sense that I believe that reducing inequality is a worthwhile goal. I don't believe that inequality is evil. Inequality is necessary to reward success and punish failure, and it would be pointless to argue against that. But I believe that, on balance, there are more forces in our economic system pushing toward excessive, unjust, or inefficient inequality than there are forces pushing toward excessive equality. These are my prior beliefs as I write this book. They should be debated, and they can certainly be challenged. I will try not to let them interfere with my thinking, but I will not ignore the potential value in the belt-and-suspenders approach.

On Data, Anecdotes, and Intuition

"Data! data! data!" he cried impatiently. "I can't make bricks without clay."

ARTHUR CONAN DOYLE,
THE ADVENTURE OF THE COPPER BEECHES

I should like to close by citing a well-recognized cliché in scientific circles: "In God we trust, others must provide data."

EDWIN R. FISHER, PROFESSOR OF PATHOLOGY,
ADDRESSING A SUBCOMMITTEE OF THE
US HOUSE OF REPRESENTATIVES IN 1978

If economists are to be of any use to society—a big "if," some critics might add—then at the very least they should be able to challenge common wisdom, to take a contrarian perspective, and to avoid repeating what everyone else is saying. This is what I find so remarkably refreshing in Robert Gordon's *The Rise and Fall of American Growth*. Contrary to the techno-optimists arguing that innovation has never been faster, Bob argues that our current wave of innovation is not nearly as transformative as previous waves have been. Bob may or may not be right, but he is willing to think coherently about a topic and base his conclusions on data and logic instead of anecdotes and preconceived ideas.

It is also important to emphasize that smart people often disagree, and that is mostly a good thing. In fact, I would argue that we are more likely to learn something interesting precisely when smart people disagree. In a 2014 conversation with James Bennet in the *Atlantic*, Microsoft founder Bill Gates said: "I think the idea that innovation is slowing down is one of the stupidest things anybody ever said." To illustrate his point, he added, "Take the potential of how we generate energy, the potential of how we design materials, the potential of how we create medicines, the potential of how we educate people." Entrepreneurs are "birds-in-the-bush" people, while economists are more "birds-in-the-hand" people. We are certainly interested in the "potential" applications of an idea, but we need to see its impact in the data to be convinced. And so far, we are not convinced by Gates's emphasis on potential. Until the data suggest otherwise, we tend to follow Stefan Zweig and think that "Brazil is the country of the future—and always will be."

It is never easy to change the common wisdom. The idea that US markets are the most competitive in the world has been widely accepted in economics for several decades. Businessmen argue that it's never been easier to start a business, that competition is everywhere, and that the internet allows people to search for the cheapest goods. We certainly live in the most competitive, most breathtakingly innovative society ever. Right? To some extent, these arguments reflect a universal bias in human psyche, namely the idea that we are smarter and more sophisticated than our ancestors, and that everything we do is "unprecedented." This is, in my mind, one of the most bogus claims ever made. In fact, little of what we do is unprecedented.

For example, in the 1990s, the booming stock market was widely believed to be performing at levels never seen previously. Firms were moving from the start-up phase to an initial public offering of stock at record speed. Or so we thought. In fact, Boyan Jovanovic and Peter L. Rousseau (2001) show that the initial public offering market of the 1920s was remarkably similar to the one of the 1990s: IPO proceeds (as share of gross domestic product) were comparable, and firms moved quickly from incorporation to listing. Whatever we were doing in the 1990s with our screens and computers was neither fundamentally different nor fundamentally better than what they were doing in the 1920s without screens and computers.

We should always look at the data first. This is particularly true if we are interested in changes that take place over decades. We cannot trust our intuition, and we certainly should not repeat the conventional wisdom, especially when it happens to coincide with our preconceptions or economic interests. Hence, when you hear a manager arguing that competition has never been tougher, you should put as much faith in that statement as one from a barber who says you really need a haircut. Or, I might add, from a banker who argues that leverage is really, really safe.

There is another example I find striking, and that hits close to home. You have probably heard that the time when a person could expect to enjoy a long career at a single company is long past. Nowadays, we're told, people need to be ready to change careers often. Millennials really just want to hop from one job to the next. Turnover in the labor market, the story goes, is higher than ever. And while that story may feel true, it's not. Data from the Bureau of Labor Statistics show that employees stay a bit longer with a company today than they did thirty years ago. During the 1980s and 1990s, the average employee tenure was around 3.5 years. It started to rise around 2000 to about 4.5 years today. In fact, in almost all developed economies, we observe a decrease in job turnover, which is driven by a steep decline in voluntary separations. Worker flows have declined since the 1990s.* In other words, people are less likely to quit their jobs now than in the past.

When I first saw these numbers, I was reminded of a discussion I had with my own grandfather about being a worker in France in the 1950s and 1960s. Employment protections—in the form of minimum wages, unemployment insurance, severance pay, long-term contracts, and the

---

* The best measure—the Job Openings and Labor Turnover Survey—shows a continuous decline since 2000. The Current Population Survey (Hyatt and Spletzer, 2013) and the Longitudinal Employer–Household Dynamics data show a decline as well. Longer series from Davis and Haltiwanger (2014) show a decline since 1990.

ability to sue one's employer for wrongful termination—were much lower than today. Overall, it certainly looked like firms held more sway over their workers then. I asked him if he felt the pressure as a worker, and he looked at me as if he was surprised by the question. "I guess not," he said: "if the boss or the firm did not treat you well, you simply did not show up the next morning and went to work across the street." That was a Frenchman in the 1950s, not an American millennial in 2019. Let us keep these examples in mind when we review the evidence on the evolution of competition in US markets.

THE GREAT REVERSAL

Introduction

I LANDED AT Logan Airport, Boston, in late August 1999. I was coming to the United States from my native France to pursue a doctorate in economics at the Massachusetts Institute of Technology. This was an incredibly exciting time. I was eager to meet my new classmates and learn as much as I could as quickly as possible.

I was fortunate to be supported by a graduate scholarship. Still, life as a student forced me to pay attention to my personal finances. I studied prices and shopped around for the best deals. As an economist, I would now say that I was "price-elastic."

Figuring out what to do with the scholarship was easy enough. The first thing I needed was a laptop. The second was an internet connection. The third was a place to sleep (priorities!), preferably not in the graduate computer lab because I don't enjoy waking up with a QWERTY keyboard imprinted on my forehead.

I had already agreed to share an apartment with two classmates, so that took care of the detail of putting a roof over my head. I could thus focus on the serious business of studying, buying books, and purchasing a computer. The US was a great place to get a laptop. Computers were so much cheaper that people from other countries would often ask their friends in the US to buy laptops for them, even if it meant dealing with a different keyboard layout. From my own experience, I would say that laptops were at least 30 percent less expensive than in France. Indeed, looking at official statistics (something we will do a lot in this book), Paul Schreyer (2002, fig. 1) shows that the US experienced a steeper decline in its price indexes for computers and office equipment between 1995 and 1999 than France, the United Kingdom, or Germany.

My next task was to get online. When I called around looking for an internet connection to the house, I discovered that access was also a lot cheaper than in Europe. A typical dialup connection via a 56K modem was so slow that you often needed to stay connected for several hours to download a file. In the US, local calls were free, which meant that if your internet service provider (ISP) had a server near your house, you could make a call and stay connected for as long as necessary without paying extra. In France, you were charged by the minute, and it would have cost a fortune. These differences had a large impact on the economy. Nicholas Economides (1999) explained that "one of the key reasons for Europe's lag in internet adoption is the fact [that] in most countries, unlike the US, consumers are charged per minute for local calls."

Having secured a roof, a computer, and an internet connection, my next goals were to attend conferences and to explore this amazing country. I quickly realized that air travel was also easier and cheaper in the US than in Europe. Back in Europe, I would fly maybe once a year, usually in the summer. In America, plane tickets were cheap enough that I could afford them fairly often, even as a student.

Durable goods, transport, and most services were surprisingly cheap in the US. Wages, on the other hand, were rather high, which meant that workers had solid purchasing power. None of this happened by chance, although I was blissfully unaware of it at the time.

The Land of Free Markets

Let us consider air transport first. Before 1978, the Civil Aeronautics Board regulated airlines in the US, controlling the fares they could charge and the routes they could fly. The Carter Administration argued that customers would benefit from deregulation because it would encourage competition among existing carriers as well as entry of new airlines. And it did. The Airline Deregulation Act of 1978 phased out the government's control over prices and routes. Over the following fifteen years, from 1979 to 1994, the average fare per passenger mile decreased by about 9 percent at airports in small communities, 11 percent at airports in medium-sized communities, and 8 percent at airports in large communities, as documented by the Government Accountability Office in its 1996 report. Lower prices led to a sustained increase in the number of passenger-miles flown each year. In recent years, however, most people have had frustrating experiences with differentiated fares, hidden fees, and crowded planes. It seems that the gains achieved in the 1980s and 1990s were not sustained. I will explain how that happened.

A similar process of deregulation took place within the telecommunications industry. As the economists Steven Olley and Ariel Pakes write in their influential 1996 paper, "For most of the twentieth century, American Telephone and Telegraph (AT&T) maintained an exclusive monopoly in the provision of telecommunication services and, through their procurement practices, extended that dominant position into the equipment industry." The landmark antitrust lawsuit *United States v. AT&T* was filed in 1974. The Department of Justice (DoJ) claimed that AT&T had monopolized the long-distance market. In January 1982, Charles Brown, CEO of AT&T, and Assistant Attorney General William Baxter agreed to settle the government's decade-long antitrust suit against the Bell System, and the "Baby Bells" were carved out in 1984. They owned local infrastructures and remained regulated monopolies within their regions. The new AT&T competed with other phone companies, and prices of long-distance phone calls fell dramatically. Much of the initial decrease came from lower access charges, but competition in long distance was also a success. The average revenue per minute of AT&T's switched services declined by 62 percent between 1984 and 1996, and as more competitors entered the market, its market share fell from above 80 percent in 1984 to about 50 percent in 1996, to the clear benefit of US households.

As in the case of airlines, however, later policies have been less successful. The Telecommunications Act of 1996 was intended to foster competition but also led to a merger wave. We will discuss mergers in Chapter 5, the lobbying activities of telecommunications firms in Chapter 9, and the revolving door issues at the Federal Communications Commission in Chapter 10.

These two examples of air travel and telecommunication illustrate three important characteristics of competition policy at that time, all of which we will revisit often in this book. The first feature is that antitrust was largely a bipartisan affair. Airline deregulation happened under a Democratic president, Jimmy Carter, and the breakup of AT&T under a Republican president, Ronald Reagan.

Second, regulation and technology are deeply intertwined. Technological change creates a permanent, and often beneficial, challenge to existing regulations. In the telecom industry, the cost of transmission and information processing declined thanks to integrated circuits and computers. The open architecture of the network and its digitization encouraged entry and competition while improvement in software allowed the sharing of information at a scale that was previously unimaginable. Microwave transmission was a major breakthrough that allowed competition in long distance. Transmission through satellite and through optical fiber followed suit.

As we will see, this interaction of technology and regulation is both a blessing and a curse. It is a blessing because it forces regulation to evolve and regulators to pay attention. It is a curse because it makes it harder to disentangle the consequences of policy choices, and therefore harder to agree on what is a good regulation and what is a bad regulation. Lobbyists know how to use this to their advantage by creating smoke-and-mirrors arguments to push for regulations that hurt consumers but are often difficult to disprove.

A third lesson that I take away from these historical cases is that regulators make policy decisions under a great deal of uncertainty. It is rarely obvious at the time a decision needs to be made whether antitrust actions are a good idea or a bad idea. Journalist Steven Coll wrote about AT&T: "Whether the break of American Telephone & Telegraph Company will be remembered decades from now as one of the more spectacular fiascoes of American industrial history, or whether it will be recalled as a seminal event in the emergence of a great global information age, or whether it will be forgotten altogether, is a matter that was impossible to predict intelligently in 1985." This has an important implication. We must be able to let the government make some mistakes. Sometimes it will be too lenient. Sometimes too tough. It should be right on average, but it is unlikely to be right in every single case. Tolerating well-intentioned mistakes is therefore part of good regulation, provided that there is due process and that there is a mechanism to learn from these mistakes. Unfortunately, this kind of tolerance has become a rare commodity in recent years.

The Reversal

When I landed in Boston in 1999, the US was a great place to be a student or, as far as I could tell, a middle-class consumer. Over the next twenty years, however, something utterly unexpected happened. Each one of the factors I have mentioned has reversed. Access to internet, monthly cell phone plans, and plane tickets have become much cheaper in Europe and in Asia than in the US. Computers and electronic equipment sell for about the same price in Europe as in the US, although comparisons are complicated by differing tax regimes.*

Consider home internet access first. In 2015, the Center for Public Integrity compared internet prices in five medium-sized US cities and five comparable French cities. It found that prices in the US were as much as three and a half times higher than those in France for similar service. The analysis also showed that consumers in France have a choice between a far greater number of providers—seven on average—than those in the US, where most residents can get service from no more than two companies.†

The US used to be a leader in ensuring broad access to the World Wide Web for its citizens, but this leadership has slipped over the past two decades. According to data on broadband penetration among households gathered by the Organisation for Economic Co-operation and Development (OECD), the US ranked fourth in 2000 but dropped below fifteenth place in 2017.

In 2017, market research company BDRC Continental together with Cable.co.uk compared the prices of over 3,351 broadband packages around the world. Table I.1 provides a snapshot of their results. In most advanced economies, consumers pay around $35 per month for broadband internet connections. In the US, they pay almost double. How on earth did that

---

* US prices are quoted before taxes, whereas prices in France always include VAT. There are also specific taxes. For instance, France levies a tax on iPhones and iPods to pay artists and composers. The extra cost is around 10 euros for iPhones with 16GB of memory, and up to 18 euros for 64GB iPhones.

† Center for Public Integrity, "US internet users pay more and have fewer choices than Europeans," April 1, 2015, updated May 28, 2015.

TABLE I.1

Broadband Prices, Selected Countries, 2017

Rank	Country	Average monthly cost ($US)
37	South Korea	$29.90
47	Germany	$35.71
54	France	$38.10
...		
113	United States	$66.17

Data source: Cable.co.uk; https://www.cable.co.uk/broadband/deals/worldwide-price
-comparison/

happen? How did the US, where the internet was "invented," and where access was cheap in the 1990s, become such a laggard, overcharging households for a rather basic service?

As Susan Crawford at Harvard Law School argues, "New York was supposed to be a model for big-city high-speed internet." Instead, it has become yet another example of expensive and unequal access to services. "When the Bloomberg mayoral administration re-signed an agreement with Verizon in 2008, it required that the company wire all residential buildings with its fiber service, FiOS . . . the presence of Verizon's fiber product would end the local monopoly of Time Warner Cable." Unfortunately, "a 2015 city audit showed that at least a quarter of the city's residential blocks had no FiOS service. About a third of Bronx residents and more than 60 percent of New Yorkers without a high school education don't have a wire at home."*

Returning to the question that launched this book, we see the same pattern with cell phone plans. Economists Maria Faccio and Luigi Zingales (2017) have studied the global mobile telecommunication industry. They argue that procompetition policies can reduce prices without hurting the quality of services or investments. In fact, they estimate that US consumers would gain $65 billion a year if American mobile service prices were in line with German ones.

---

* Susan Crawford, "Bad internet in the big city," *Wired,* February 28, 2018.

And finally, airlines are probably among the worst offenders. The *Economist* noted in 2017, "Airlines in North America posted a profit of $22.40 per passenger last year; in Europe the figure was $7.84."* Around 2010, the net profit per passenger was similar in both regions, but since then, prices have increased more in the US than in Europe.

You might reasonably wonder, where's the outrage? If prices are indeed so different, why don't we know about it? First, it is actually quite difficult to compare prices across countries, even for supposedly similar goods and services. We will discuss this issue in Chapter 7, and in the process learn about the price of haircuts and Ferraris around the world. Second, the increase has been gradual, and so it has attracted little attention.

How to Boil a Frog

Price hikes are rarely so clear that consumers notice them. Sometimes headline prices remain unchanged but hidden fees increase. Sometimes prices drift so slowly that it takes several years to notice any significant difference. Stealth, however, can allow harm to go unnoticed.

According to the fable, if a frog is thrown into hot water, it will jump out, but if the frog is put in tepid water, and the temperature is slowly raised, the frog will not perceive the danger until it is too late. In a way, that's what happened to me in my experience with the changing US economy. (And yes, as a Frenchman, I get the irony.)

In the twenty years following my arrival in the US in 1999, most domestic US markets lost their competitive edge. I did not notice any of these changes as they were happening. I was not aware of the trends until I stumbled upon the facts in my own research. Why? Because the changes were very gradual, and because a lot of things are always

---

* "Air fares are higher per seat mile in America than in Europe. When costs fall, consumers in America fail to enjoy the benefits. The global price of jet fuel—one of the biggest costs for airlines—has fallen by half since 2014. That triggered a fare war between European carriers, but in America ticket prices have hardly budged." "A lack of competition explains the flaws in American aviation," *Economist*, April 22, 2017.

happening at the same time: the internet bubble, 9 / 11, the war in Iraq, the housing bubble, the financial crisis of 2008–2009, the eurozone crisis of 2010–2012, oil price volatility, the rise of populism, the risk of trade wars, and so on. Throughout this tumultuous history, oligopolistic concentration and markups have increased slowly but steadily. And it's only now, looking back, that a clear picture emerges.

Notice that I am talking about US markets, not US firms. US firms do very well in global markets. In that sense, they are competitive. But US domestic markets have become dominated by oligopolies, and US consumers pay higher prices than they should. How did it happen, why did it happen, and what does it mean for US households, consumers, and workers? In answering these questions we will visit many of the important debates in economics and political science.

Here are some of the specific questions we will address:

- Do these higher prices affect all industries, or are airline and telecommunications industries special?
- How did Europe, of all places, become more of a "free market" than the US?
- Isn't it better if firms make profits rather than teeter on the verge of bankruptcy?
- Is big beautiful? Can concentration be a good thing? What, if anything, sets Google, Apple, Facebook, and Amazon apart?
- Should we worry more about privacy or about competition? Or are they perhaps two sides of the same coin?
- What are the implications of market power for inequality and for growth, wages, and jobs?
- Why are free markets so fragile? How did lobbyists end up wielding so much power?

This list may seem like an implausibly wide array of topics to cover. It's important to understand, however, that while the questions we're considering are varied and complex, the underlying forces are few. I hope to convince you that economic analysis can shed light on all of them. After all, science aims at reducing complex problems to a few fundamental issues.

An Economic Approach

Economics is the science that studies the allocation of limited resources among individuals or among groups of individuals. The unit of analysis may be a firm, a family, a city, a country, or many countries. The manner in which allocations are determined also varies a great deal. There could be one centralized market, such as a stock exchange, many markets, such as for local services like barbers or dry cleaners, or no market at all, as in the case of internal promotion within a firm.

The goal of the allocation might be efficiency (maximizing the productive use of resources to increase growth) or justice (limiting unfair inequality, redistributing income toward the poorest members of the group). The important point in all of this is that the resources are *limited*. Hence the economic system, no matter how it is organized, must make choices. Tough choices.

In the end, the big debates in economics are about growth and inequality: How did they come about, and what should be done about them?

Where We Go from Here

The book makes three main arguments.

One: Competition has declined in most sectors of the US economy. Measuring competition is easier said than done, for we can find only imperfect proxies. We will look at prices, profit rates, and market shares. None is perfect, but together they can form a convincing picture.

Two: The lack of competition is explained largely by policy choices, influenced by lobbying and campaign finance contributions. We will look at the dollars spent by every US corporation over the past twenty years to lobby their regulators, their senators, their congressmen, and members of key committees, as well as to finance federal and state elections. We will show how these efforts distort free markets: across time, states, and industries, corporate lobbying and campaign finance contributions lead to barriers to entry and regulations that protect large incumbents, weaker antitrust enforcement, and weaker growth of small and medium-sized firms.

Three: The consequences of a lack of competition are lower wages, lower investment, lower productivity, lower growth, and more inequality. We will examine how the decline in competition across industries has effects that reach into the wallets and bank accounts of everyday Americans. We will also demonstrate why lower competition leads to less of the sort of thing that we traditionally associate with growing economies: investment, technological advancement, and rising wages.

Are you ready? Let's begin.

ONE

THE RISE OF MARKET POWER IN THE UNITED STATES

Let us start by exploring the evolution of the US economy over the past twenty years. In doing so, we'll investigate how economists think about competition, concentration, and antitrust. You will learn about the impact of China's entry into the World Trade Organization, about initial public offerings and mergers, and about the growth of young firms. We will introduce the fundamental law of investment, the concept of intangible assets, and the evolution of productivity.

CHAPTER 1

Why Economists Like Competition . . .
and Why You Should Too

THE BIG DEBATES in economics are about growth and inequality. As economists, we seek to understand how and why countries grow and how they divide income among their citizens. In other words, we are concerned with two fundamental issues. The first issue is how to make the pie as large as possible. The second issue is how to divide the pie.

Economists study those choices because they want to understand the factors that foster growth and the factors that influence the distribution of income among individuals. At least since Adam Smith, we have understood that one of these factors is competition.

Growth

An economy can grow in exactly two ways: its labor force can expand, or its output per worker can increase. From the Roman Empire to the Industrial Revolution, population growth was slow and productivity growth was nil. The Industrial Revolution earned its name by unleashing unprecedented productivity growth. The First Industrial Revolution began in Britain in the eighteenth century and moved the economy from agriculture toward manufacturing. It involved new machines (the spinning jenny), new energy sources (coal, steam), and a new division of labor in large plants. As countries became richer and agriculture became more productive, populations also grew. Thus, after 1700, population growth and productivity growth both contributed to overall economic growth.

Which rate of growth should we consider: overall, or per capita? There is no simple answer; it depends on the issue at hand. If we are interested in measuring the global clout of a country—its gross domestic product (GDP), for example—then overall growth is what matters. For instance,

TABLE 1.1

Growth Rate of Real US GDP per Capita

Decade	1950s	1960s	1970s	1980s	1990s	2000s	2010–17
Average growth	2.4	3.1	2.1	2.1	2.0	0.8	0.6

Data source: FRED, real gross domestic product per capita, continuously compounded rate of change

when comparing the relative worldwide influence of the US and China, we would want to use total Chinese GDP versus total US GDP. But if we want to understand how the average Chinese consumer feels, we would want to use per-capita GDP estimated at purchasing power parity (PPP). Chapter 7 explains how PPP exchange rates are computed and how to use them. And sometimes GDP itself is not the right measure. In the case of Russia, for instance, there is a large discrepancy between its semiglobal influence and its relatively small economy because of the hypertrophy of its armed forces.

If we are interested in happiness and standards of living, however, then per-capita growth is what matters. Per-capita growth is also usually the right way to analyze the consequences of economic policies and regulations. This will be our focus in this book.

The rate of per-capita economic growth in the US has declined over the past two decades. Table 1.1 shows the rate of growth of gross domestic product per capita for the US economy. GDP measures the value of all the goods and services produced within the borders of a country in a year. Dividing America's GDP by its population highlights broad changes in the standards of living of US households.

US growth has been around 2 percent per year in the second half of the twentieth century. The 1960s stand out as a period of faster than average growth. Over the past eighteen years, however, growth has been substantially lower.

There is a lively debate among economists regarding the causes of the decline in the growth rate. Much of the debate has focused on three factors: employment, education, and technological innovation. On the question of employment, the US Bureau of Labor Statistics has been tracking the decline of the employment rate among prime-age workers (aged 25–54 years) (Krueger, 2017). After peaking in the late 1990s at nearly 85 percent, the rate fell to below 81 percent as recently as 2015. That may seem like a small change, but it represents the loss of millions of workers from the economy. Bottom line: when fewer people work, growth slows down.

Data collected by the Department of Education show that high school graduation and college completion rates rose rather slowly from the 1970s to the 1990s and have remained virtually flat since 2000 (Goldin and Katz, 2008). One in ten Americans under age 30 have no high school diploma, and nearly half have no post-secondary degree of any kind, which suggests that there is still room for improvement in education. Slower improvements in education have also contributed to the decline in overall growth since education makes workers more productive.

But the major contributor to long-term growth is technology—and that contribution is slowing down. When we say that technological progress has slowed, we are simply saying that, on average, businesses are not as good as they used to be at reducing the unit cost of production or at coming up with higher quality products. To assess the rate of technological progress, economists construct total factor productivity (TFP) growth, which measures the extent to which we can do more with less (or with the same). In other words, it measures how we can expand output for given levels of capital and labor inputs. Economic theory shows that this kind of technological progress is the only sustainable source of growth in the long run. The slowdown in TFP growth started in 2000 and is now widespread among rich countries. The Great Recession of 2008–2009 has probably reinforced this negative trend, but it has not created it (Cette, Fernald, and Mojon, 2016).

Robert Gordon, an economist at Northwestern University, argues that the remarkable growth in productivity from 1870 to 1970 is unlikely to repeat itself. The benefits of the Second Industrial Revolution, associated with electricity and the internal combustion engine, were deep and wide. In his view, computers and communication technologies are simply less important. Of course, it's not as if people are standing idle instead of working hard. The pace of innovation is still rapid, but the impact of innovation on the broad economy is smaller. To be sure, there are techno-optimists who think that artificial intelligence is going to change our lives—and we will return to this debate later in the book—but it's fair to say that we are still waiting to see real, tangible, and widespread gains.

Another important factor behind disappointing productivity growth is the lackluster rate of investment in the corporate sector. Technological innovations often need to be embodied in new equipment and new software. But US firms, despite high profits and low funding costs, have not upgraded their capital much in recent years. This is a puzzle that we will explore in Chapter 5.

Inequality

In addition to a slowdown in growth, inequality has risen over the past forty years. Broadly speaking, income inequality can grow between the middle class and the poor, or between the rich and the middle class. Or both, as it turns out, but not always at the same time. In the 1970s and 1980s, we observe mostly an increase in inequality between the middle class and the poor. This inequality goes hand in hand with the wage gap between college graduates and those without post-secondary degrees, a factor known as the college premium.

As we can see from Table 1.2, education wage premia rose rapidly in the 1980s and 1990s. In 1980, workers with a college degree earned 40 percent more than those with only a high school degree. In 2000 they earned almost 70 percent more. If we compare the more extreme cases (graduate degrees versus no degrees), the premium almost doubled, from 92 percent to 179 percent. Since 2000, however, education premia have been almost flat.

In the 1990s and 2000s, we also observe an increase between the rich (and super rich) and the middle class. Thomas Piketty and Emmanuel Saez (2006) estimate that the share of income earned by the top 1 percent has more than doubled, from less than 10 percent in the late 1970s to around 20 percent today. (The top 1 percent in the US includes well-paid professionals, like doctors or lawyers earning about $400,000 a year. The top 0.01 percent, the one percent of the one percent, includes the extremely wealthy, like LeBron James or Oprah Winfrey.)

TABLE 1.2

Labor Earnings, Education, and Inequality

	1980	1990	1992	2000	2010	2015
Evolution of real hourly wage by education (2015 $)						
No degree	14.19	12.84	12.47	13.03	13.22	13.56
High school	16.33	15.99	15.87	17.2	17.77	17.98
Some college	18.8	19.29	19.16	20.84	21.47	21.59
Four-year college	22.85	25.32	25.18	28.98	30.49	30.93
Graduate degree	27.27	31.43	31.66	36.4	39.7	39.48
Education premia						
College / high school	40%	58%	59%	68%	72%	72%
Graduate / no degree	92%	145%	154%	179%	200%	191%

Data source: Valletta (2016)

Inequality and growth are best discussed together, for various reasons. First, and most obviously, we want to know if everyone benefits from growth. When growth is slow and inequality rising, it is possible for the standard of living of the lower middle class to stagnate or even decline in real terms. This has happened in the US in recent years. Table 1.2 shows that the real income of workers without much education has barely improved over the past forty years. For some, it has decreased.

But the most important reason to analyze growth and inequality together is that they are not independent and unrelated phenomena. They interact, sometimes feeding on each other, sometimes canceling each other out. Growth can reduce inequality, inequality can be necessary for growth, or inequality can hinder it.

The debate on growth versus inequality hinges on the idea of incentives. When economists talk about incentives, they mean a motivation for material (monetary) gains. People work hard because they expect that their efforts (their investment) will increase their income. For the economic system to work, there needs to be a connection between (ex-ante) effort and (ex-post) income. Does that mean that some degree of inequality is necessary? Does that mean that more inequality always creates better incentives? The answers are probably yes and no, but the link between incentives and inequality can be subtle.

The children's story of Goldilocks can figure in the theory of incentives. Money needs to be hard to get, but not too hard. If money is too easy to get, people become lazy. If you earn a lot without working hard, you may not bother to try harder. But if money is too hard to get, people become discouraged.

If we apply this idea to workers within a firm, we see that it justifies performance-based compensation. And as long as performance varies across workers, this will lead to inequality. But it does not necessarily justify high degrees of inequality. Even if we take for granted that people work for money, this does not mean that more money always means more effort. What matters is the correct balance of incentives.

But how do we know that a given degree of inequality is justified? How do we know that it is not excessive? The answer, of course, is that we can never know for sure. Understanding incentives in a modern economic system is quite complicated. There is, however, one critical factor that can give us some confidence, and that factor is competition.

Competition and Growth

Economists like competition for several reasons. The first reason is that competition pushes prices down, since the most direct way for a company to increase its market share is to offer a lower price than its competitors. When a firm lowers the price of the good that it sells, this has two beneficial consequences. The first and most obvious one is that consumers save money, which they can use to buy more of the same good, or more of some other goods. In practice, they tend to do both. If health insurance becomes cheaper, you might purchase a plan with better coverage, and also buy an extra toy for your kids. The second, indirect, effect is that increased demand encourages businesses to produce, invest, and hire. In general, if we compare two economies, the one with more competition will have lower prices, higher production, higher employment, and higher investment. Competition therefore increases our standards of living.

Prices are not the only thing people care about. The quality of services matters a great deal too. If we look at the American Customer Satisfaction Survey, we see some striking patterns. Internet service providers seem to be the most disliked companies in the US. We have already noted that this industry is highly concentrated and charges higher prices than in most other developed countries. This is certainly not by accident.

In a competitive market, firms seek to attract customers not only by reducing prices, but also by offering a wide menu of quality goods and services. Competition leads to more choices for consumers as businesses cater to different segments of the population and as they try to differentiate their products from those of their competitors.*

One of my favorite examples of the positive impact of competition comes from taxis in Paris. First, about the prices: I grew up in the suburbs, and my friends and I would always go into the city by train or metro on Friday or Saturday nights. On the way home, however, we sometimes missed the last metro, typically at 1 or 2 AM. And yet we never took a taxi. If we missed the subway, we would walk—for miles. Taxis were hard to find and expensive: we were priced out.

Second, about innovation in the service industry: when incumbent taxi companies were forced to compete with new platforms, they suddenly discovered that clients appreciated bottles of water and the ability to charge a cell phone, and that basic politeness did not cost that much. These were not high-tech innovations, but they certainly improved the experiences of clients. Uber and its ilk may have many downsides (noncompliance with labor laws, an increase in traffic congestion), but they also illustrate the basic virtues of competition: nothing improves customer service quite like the threat of a new competitor.

Competition encourages investment and pushes businesses to innovate, either to improve the quality of goods and services they sell or to

---

* Bundling and competition can have surprising effects. Gregory S. Crawford, Oleksandr Shcherbakov, and Matthew Shum (2018) find an overprovision of "quality" in cable television markets. They argue that it results from the presence of competition from high-end satellite TV providers: without the competitive pressure from satellite companies, cable TV monopolists would instead engage in quality degradation. Quality overprovision implies cable customers would prefer smaller, lower-quality cable bundles at a lower price.

find ways to reduce the cost of providing these goods and services. From an economic perspective, higher quality and lower cost are two sides of the same coin, and both count as technological progress. In advanced economies, however, the link between competition and innovation is complex and depends on property rights, patents, and market structure. This is why we need to build good theories and to study the data carefully, as we will do in the next chapters.

Competition and Inequality

Competition encourages growth and probably equality too. It encourages growth because it leads to higher output and employment.* It also reduces inequality because competition increases wages and decreases profit margins. Hence, in a competitive economy, payouts (dividends, shares buybacks) are small relative to labor income. Since financial capital (ownership of financial claims, mostly stocks and bonds) tends to be more unequally distributed than human capital (your labor and your education), it follows that a more competitive economy is also likely to be less unequal.

Before discussing the more complicated connections between competition and inequality, it makes sense to pause for a moment to define the term *rent* as it applies to economics. A rent is a payment received by the owner of an asset (human or physical, material or immaterial) in excess

---

* I write "growth" because this is what most people have in mind when they think about a country becoming richer, but this needs some clarification. In the standard economic model competition has an impact on the level of GDP but not on its long-term rate of growth. Imagine a change in policy that leads to an increase in competition in domestic markets. This leads to a temporary increase in the rate of growth of the economy. Afterward, GDP remains permanently higher than it would have been without the policy change, but it eventually grows at the same rate as before because the long-term rate of growth of income per capita depends only on technological progress. Competition can have a permanent impact on growth if it encourages technological innovation. This is a hotly debated issue. The evidence suggests that competition induces more innovation, but there is no consensus on the size of this effect. We will discuss the links between competition, investment, and productivity in Chapter 4.

of the cost of reproducing or re-creating that asset. For instance, if a good that can be produced for $10 is sold for $15 because it is protected by a patent, then the rent to the patent holder is $5.

Some rents are protected by artificial restrictions. For example, draconian occupational licensing laws that restrict entry into certain professions protect those who already hold licenses from competition, allowing them to charge higher prices. When economists talk about "rent-seeking," they refer to the attempt by individuals or by groups to tilt public policy in a way that establishes or increases those artificial advantages in their favor. This term does not necessarily have a moral connotation. It is rational for people to protect their rents. That does not make them bad people. But it often leads to bad policies.

The interplay between rents and inequality means that competition does not always reduce inequality. Competition can make some income-sharing agreements more difficult to sustain. For instance, a business might agree to share some of its rents with its workers. Competition can lower these rents and indirectly hurt some workers. Similarly, competition for talent can push the earnings of some groups to very high levels.

Overall, however, it is difficult to come up with convincing examples of domestic competition that hurts the poor and the middle class, and it is easy to come up with many examples (low-cost retail and airlines, competition in telecoms, among others) where competition is clearly beneficial. Broadly speaking, this is because domestic competition creates efficiencies, and these efficiencies are redistributed among the citizens of the country. It is true that domestic competition leads to reallocations of rents, to gains for some and losses for others. Competition destroys and creates jobs at the same time, but in different places or different communities. My key point, however, is that within a country there are mechanisms to spread both the gains and the losses. This does not guarantee that domestic competition improves the welfare of everyone, but it makes it more likely to be true, at least after some time.

Foreign competition is an altogether different issue. Foreign competition benefits domestic consumers, but it can hurt domestic producers and their employees. Standard economic theory shows that the gains from trade outweigh the losses, so in principle, there should be a way to make everyone better off. In practice, it does not always work so well. Foreign competition might benefit domestic consumers more than it disrupts local businesses and employees, but there is no natural way to redistribute these gains and losses. Countries have experimented with all kinds of trade adjustment programs, but most have been rather ineffective. In addition, competition across countries to attract talent and capital can lead to more regressive tax systems. This is exactly the opposite of what we would need in order to accommodate the impact of trade shocks.

Two of my colleagues at New York University, Spencer G. Lyon and Michael E. Waugh, have provided some fascinating new insights on this issue in a 2018 paper. We know that exposure to trade creates winners and losers. Lyon and Waugh study how society can mitigate the losses while preserving the gains from trade. They find that a progressive tax system is very helpful and that the optimal level of progressivity increases with the exposure to trade. What is the mechanism? As we have explained, trade benefits consumers through lower prices and increased variety of available goods. The picture is more complicated for workers. Most of them are not affected by trade, but those who compete directly with foreign workers are strongly affected. This unequal exposure is at the core of the public debate surrounding international trade. Lyon and Waugh show that an effective way to compensate workers for reduced earnings and lost employment opportunities is through a progressive tax policy.

Why Free Markets Are Fragile

We started this chapter by explaining that economics is concerned with the allocation of *limited* resources. At some abstract but intuitive level, we can see the deep connection between the fact that economic resources are limited and the value of competition. Since resources are limited, it would be damaging to waste them. So how can we make sure that resources are used effectively? One answer is to let people and organizations compete for these resources, ensuring that the resources end up in the hands of those who value them the most. The price system at the core of modern economies is one way to organize this competition. Conversely, when competition weakens, capitalism loses much of its appeal.

More broadly, we can argue that competition increases economic freedom. In a competitive labor market, workers have the freedom to quit and find a better job. When employers compete, they offer more options to workers: different jobs, different hours, and different benefits. Labor market competition is the best defense against employers abusing and bullying their employees.

Should we worry about the loss of competition? After all, if competition is so wonderful, why would it be threatened? Shouldn't we all agree that competition is beneficial and team up to defend it?

Writing more than fifty years ago, Mancur Olson (1971) explained why a spontaneous defense of competition is unlikely. Before Olson, the common wisdom was that if we all shared a common interest, we would act collectively to achieve it. Unfortunately, there is a flaw in that argument. To understand the logic of collective action, we first need to ask who gains and who loses. In the case of competition, it is rather clear. Competition destroys rents and is therefore the enemy of rent seekers.

The key point about rents is that they are usually concentrated. When a dominant firm lobbies to prevent entry by competitors, it is protecting its own rents and perhaps the rents of a couple other dominant firms. The winners are few, and they have a lot to protect. On the other hand, the set of economic actors who are likely to get hurt if lobbying succeeds in limiting competition is widely dispersed. The consumers who buy from the industry are directly affected. Moreover, since high prices lower consumers' real disposable income, they are less able to spend on other goods and services. Most other industries are therefore indirectly affected. These costs, however, are hidden and diffuse. Consumers may never know that entry was restricted, and the indirect costs are small, so it does not pay for anyone to pick up the fight. As a result, the households and other businesses that are hurt by rent seekers are unlikely to create their own lobby to fight back. They would certainly be happy if someone else made the effort to lobby in favor of free entry. But as individuals, they have little incentive to do it themselves. This is Olson's central argument: concentrated special interests are likely to organize and fight to protect their rents, while diffuse majority interests are trumped. The essence of the problem is free-riding and the fact that free-riding incentives grow with the size of the group.

The astute reader might recognize that the same argument applies to free trade among nations. International trade also creates diffuse winners and concentrated losers. Job losses and factory closings are salient facts that are likely to be picked up in the media. Lower prices are much harder to identify and job creation from trade is spread over many locations and industries. This is why free trade needs to be protected.

But, as I have argued above, the argument for domestic competition is stronger than the argument for free trade because the benefits from free trade are more difficult to share among citizens. When trade shifts production overseas, these jobs are literally gone. The same is not true with domestic competition.

To conclude, I would argue that the case for free competition within a country is as strong as any case one can make in economics. Unfortunately, the virtue of competition—that its positive effects are widespread—is also its downfall: the winners are dispersed, and the losers are concentrated. This is why we see a lot of lobbying aimed at restricting competition and little advocacy to protect it. We will delve deeper into this topic in the second half of the book.

But for now, let's figure out how to measure competition.

CHAPTER 2

Bad Concentration, Good Concentration

To assess the degree of competition in an industry, economists look at three main variables: the degree of concentration (that is, whether there are lots of small firms or whether the industry is dominated by a few large firms); the profits that these firms are making, and the prices that customers pay. Each one of these variables contains useful information, but none is a perfect indicator. Taken together, however, they can give us a fairly clear picture of what is happening.

Concentration is a bit like cholesterol; there is a good kind and a bad kind. The bad kind occurs when incumbents in an industry are allowed to block the entry of competitors, to collude, or to merge for the primary purpose of increasing their power over market-wide pricing. The good kind is when an industry leader becomes more efficient and increases its market share. In economics, concentration is often a bad sign, but not always. As an indicator of competition, it should always be taken with a grain of salt. And it should always be considered together with profits and prices.

We are going to start by discussing the concept of market power. We will then review a few examples of deregulation where all the indicators move in the same direction. We will then study cases that are more difficult to interpret and discuss the expansion of Walmart and Amazon.

Market power plays a central role in this book. My central argument is that there has been a broad increase in market power across the US economy, and that this increase has hurt US consumers. We therefore need to understand the causes and consequences of market power. To do so we are going to look at a couple of examples representing stylized markets.

Market Power Versus Demand Elasticity

Market power is a key concept in economics. It measures the ability of a firm to raise its price and increase its profits at the expense of its customers. Clearly, that can happen only if the customers in question do not have readily available alternatives. If they did, they would react to any price increase by switching to another producer. In economics, we say that market power depends on the elasticity of demand.

To understand the relationship between market power and the elasticity of demand, consider the following example. Suppose that you want to fly from *A* to *B*. Suppose the average cost of flying one person from *A* to *B* is $200. This cost covers the wages of pilots, fuel, take-off and landing rights, airport and screening fees, and the wear and tear on the airplane. What should be the price of the ticket? If there are several airlines competing on this route, it should be close to $200. It cannot be less, at least in the long run; otherwise the airlines would lose money. It should be a bit more because airlines need to recoup their fixed costs. Let's say this requires a 5 percent margin. Then the competitive price would be $210, and the average profit per passenger for this route would be $10.

Now imagine that there is only one airline offering a direct flight. It would certainly try to charge more than $210. But how much more? It depends on how quickly it loses passengers when it raises its price. It can lose passengers in one of three ways. People could switch to another airline that offers connecting flights; they could decide to drive or to take the train; they could decide not to travel at all. The speed at which the airline loses customers when it raises its price is called the *elasticity of demand.*

If the number of passengers decreases by 2 percent when the airline increases its prices by 1 percent, then we would say that the elasticity of demand is 2. This elasticity depends on the outside options of the passengers. If they can find cheap and convenient connecting flights, their elasticity of demand is high, and the monopoly airline will not be able to charge much more than $210 for the direct flight. If there are no convenient connecting flights, the elasticity of demand is low, and the monopoly airline can charge much more than $210 for the direct flight.

Market Power and Welfare

Now let's extend the argument to show the relationship between market power and welfare, beginning with a competitive industry. In Figure 2.1a, prices are plotted on the vertical axis and quantities on the horizontal axis.

The demand curve measures consumers' willingness to pay. Imagine this is the market for a car, and you are ranking consumers from the most eager to the least eager to buy. The price pins down the marginal buyer—the person who is indifferent about buying the car at that price. As shown in Figure 2.1a, all of the consumers to the left of the marginal buyer would be willing to pay more, but of course they are happy to pay less. The ones to the right of the marginal consumer decide to pass. The price is just too high for them.

You can also imagine that the good is chocolate, and there is only one consumer. She likes chocolate and would be willing to pay a relatively high price to get some chocolate instead of none. As the quantity goes up, her cravings are gratified, and her willingness to pay for an extra ounce goes down. From our perspective, it is equivalent to think of many consumers buying one unit of a good (such as one car) or one consumer buying several units of the good (ounces of chocolate, for example). Either example creates the same downward-sloping demand curve with which we can perform the same welfare analysis, so you can pick your favorite example. For simplicity, I will continue with the car metaphor.

The next step is to figure out what the price is going to be. Clearly, that will depend on how firms compete to supply the goods. If the industry is competitive, the price must equal the marginal production cost—the price to build one extra car or to produce one extra ounce of chocolate. Why? Because if the price was above the cost, at least one firm would have an incentive to lower its price and attract new customers. Firms would keep undercutting each other until the price equals the cost. At that point they would break even and would not lower the price further. This is what we mean when we say that the industry is competitive. At that competitive price, we can figure out how many people want to buy by looking at the demand curve. We find the marginal buyer, and

A.

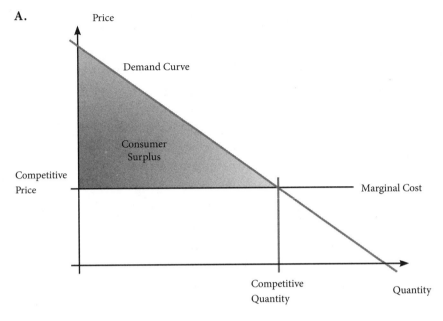

B.

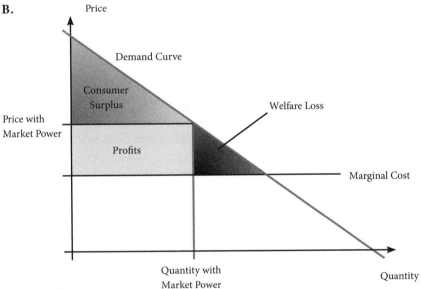

FIGURE 2.1 Industry equilibrium. (*a*) Competitive industry; (*b*) Industry with market power.

we can read the quantity on the horizontal axis. This is the competitive quantity.

The gray triangle in Figure 2.1a measures the consumers' surplus. It should be relatively easy to see why. Each point on the demand curve shows the buyer's willingness to pay; it measures how much she values the car. When her value is above the price, she earns a surplus, measured exactly by the distance between the demand curve and the price. The triangle is the sum of all the surpluses of all the buyers to the left of the marginal one. Naturally, the marginal buyer has a zero surplus, which is the same as saying that she is indifferent to buying and not buying the car at the current price.

To keep things simple, in this example we have assumed that the marginal cost does not depend on the quantity produced: we have drawn a horizontal line for the marginal cost in Figure 2.1a. When the price equals the cost per car, firms make no extra profits, so there is nothing to count on their side. Consumer surplus is the correct measure of total welfare in this economy. You can imagine more realistic cases in which the marginal cost first decreases and then increases without changing the main points of our analysis.

Figure 2.1b shows the same economy when firms have market power. The price is now above the marginal production cost. Fewer people buy cars, and the quantity is lower than in the competitive market. Consumer surplus is measured by the smaller triangle. You can see that it's a lot smaller than the previous one. Our marginal buyer and a few to her left have been priced out, and everyone else is paying a higher price.

The entire difference between the two triangles is not a welfare loss, however, because the light gray rectangle indicates the firms' profits. These were zero in the competitive case, but now they are positive. These profits are not lost. They are paid to shareholders and recycled in the economy. Of course, the profits accrue to shareholders while the high prices are paid by consumers, and these are not necessarily the same people. As I was writing this book, I exchanged some emails with Howard Rosenthal, a political scientist at New York University. In one of them he wrote something that perfectly captures this issue: "When I look at my telecom bills here and what they were when I had a place in Paris, the difference is obvious. But I love my dividend checks from AT&T and

Verizon." We will have to think more about the distributive impact of higher prices. We will return to this theme later in the book, but for now the important point is that the efficiency (or welfare) loss is represented only by the small black triangle.

Since competition is good for welfare, the obvious question is this: How do we move from Figure 2.1b to Figure 2.1a? What does it take to make an industry more competitive? And do we see gains for consumers? Let us study some specific industry cases.

The Deregulation of Airlines and Telecoms

In the Introduction we discussed the deregulation of airlines and telecoms. The Carter administration began the deregulation of airlines. Lower prices led to a sustained increase in the number of passenger-miles flown each year. The "Baby Bells" were carved out of AT&T in 1984. As with the airlines, increased competition in long-distance service resulted in significant benefits for consumers. Prices of long-distance phone calls decreased dramatically. AT&T's market share fell from above 80 percent in 1984 to about 50 percent in 1996 as more competitors entered the market.

The deregulation of telecoms happened much later in Europe. The case of France provides a striking example of the virtue of competition. Free Mobile is the wireless service provider of the Iliad group, a telecom company founded by French entrepreneur Xavier Niel. It obtained its 4G license in 2011 and became a significant competitor for the three large incumbents. The impact was immediate. Until 2011, French consumers had to pay between €45 and €65 per month for their smartphone plans, with limited data and a few hours of talk time. Free Mobile offered unlimited talk, unlimited SMS and MMS messages, and unlimited data for €20. The number of Free Mobile clients grew quickly, from about 2.6 million in the first quarter of 2012 to over 8.6 million in the first quarter of 2014. Free's current market share is around 20 percent, and it aims to achieve 25 percent.

The benefits to consumers spread far and wide: incumbents Orange, SFR, and Bouygues reacted by launching their own discount brands and by offering €20 contracts as well. In about six months after the entry of

Free Mobile, the price paid by French consumers had dropped by about 40 percent. Wireless services in France had been more expensive than in the US, but now they are much cheaper. Quality also improved, as anyone who has made calls in both countries can attest.

These cases are relatively clear cut and easy to interpret: an action taken by the government (deregulation and an antitrust suit) leads to increased competition, and all the indicators move in the same direction. We observe lower prices, lower profits, and lower concentration, at least initially.

There are other examples, however, in which our three indicators (concentration, prices, and profits) do not all move in the same direction. For instance, when search and transport costs decrease, consumers can more easily buy from low-cost producers, and concentration can increase even though the market is competitive. Chad Syverson (2004), an economist at the University of Chicago, documents this effect in his study of plants that produce ready-mixed concrete. He finds that "when producers are densely clustered in a market, it is easier for consumers to switch between suppliers . . . Relatively inefficient producers find it more difficult to operate profitably as a result." Competitive pressures force inefficient producers to exit, and the market share of efficient firms increases. In this case, therefore, competition leads to higher concentration.

Efficient Concentration: Walmart in the 1990s

Let us consider the case of retail trade, and specifically the expansion of Walmart. Walmart had a large impact on the US retail sector in the 1990s, and improvements in the retail sector had a large impact on overall economic growth during that period, driving as much as one-third of the improvement in economic efficiency between the first and second halves of that decade.*

---

* Olivier Blanchard (2003) explains in his discussion of Basu et al. (2003), "fully one-third of the increase in TFP [total factor productivity] growth from the first to the second half of the 1990s in the United States came from the retail trade sector." A study by the McKinsey Global Institute (Lewis et al., 2001) focused on the factors behind US TFP growth in the 1990s. In general merchandise

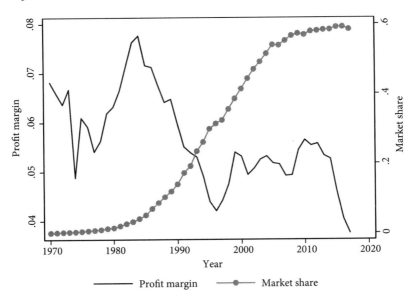

FIGURE 2.2 The growth of Walmart

Figure 2.2 shows the market share and profit margin of Walmart. The *market share* is simply the ratio of Walmart's sales (revenues) over the total sales of the retail sector. Note that we need to define what we mean by "retail sector." The graph shows the market share of Walmart within the category of general merchandise stores. If you want to understand how economists classify firms into industries, you can look at the first section in the Appendix, where I explain everything you always wanted to know about industry codes but were afraid to ask. Walmart's market share grew dramatically in the 1990s, from less than 5 percent to almost 60 percent. The *profit margin* is defined as profits over sales. If the profit margin is 5 percent, it means that when Walmart sells $1 of goods, it makes a profit of 5 cents. Walmart's margin went down a little bit over

(representing 16 percent of the TFP growth acceleration), the study found that "Wal-Mart directly and indirectly caused the bulk of the productivity acceleration through ongoing managerial innovation that increased competitive intensity and drove the diffusion of best practice." Similarly, the wholesale trade sector contributed a lot to productivity growth after 1995. In pharmaceuticals wholesaling, the study found that "half of the acceleration was driven by warehouse automation and improvements in organization."

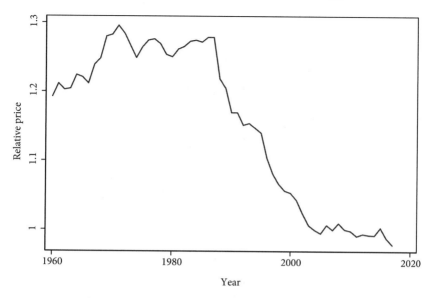

FIGURE 2.3 Retail price index relative to consumer price index. *Data sources*: BEA, GDP by Industry; FRED, PCE index

the period, from 6–7 percent to 4–5 percent. The slight decline in margin can be explained by the astonishing increase in its revenues. The profit margin is an average, and the expansion presumably entailed increasing sales of relatively lower margin products.

The growth of Walmart led to concentration in the retail industry. Was this good news for the consumer? Figure 2.3 shows the evolution of the price of retail trade services relative to the general consumer price index. If buying goods in a local supermarket becomes cheaper, then this index drops. There is a remarkable decline in the price of retail services over a period of twenty years, from the mid-1980s to the mid-2000s, that coincides with the expansion of Walmart. The decline means that US households saved about 30 percent on their retail shopping costs.

It would be tempting to jump to the conclusion that this trend represents a clear improvement for the US economy. But if there is one lesson that economics teaches us, it is that there is always some confounding factor. In this case, it is the decrease in the federal minimum wage during the 1980s. A significant fraction of retail workers earn wages at or below the local minimum wage (up to a quarter in grocery stores, for instance) and the retail sector is the second largest employer of minimum wage workers in the US. As a result, when the minimum wage decreases, we can expect retail prices to decline. Economists spend time and effort measuring precisely these effects. Tobias Renkin, Claire Montialoux, and Michael Siegenthaler find in a 2017 paper that a 10 percent change in the minimum wage changes retail prices by about 0.2 percent to 0.3 percent. The real (that is, inflation-adjusted) minimum wage decreased by about one-third between 1979 and 1995. This would predict a decrease of only 1 percent in retail prices, which is small compared to the relative price decline that we observe in Figure 2.3.

What accounts for the bulk of the decline in retail prices in this period? The retail industry had clearly become more efficient, and the cost savings were passed on to consumers. Walmart's advanced supply chain management system was a key contributor to this evolution. Through its vendor-managed inventory system, manufacturers are responsible for managing their own inventory in Walmart warehouses. Vendors can directly monitor the inventory of their goods in Walmart stores and send additional items when the stocks are low in a particular store. This technology lowers the cost of inventory management, and the efficiency gains are passed on to consumers in the form of lower prices. Economists Ali Hortaçsu and Chad Syverson argue in a 2015 paper that superstores and e-commerce have increased productivity in the retail industry.

The growth of Walmart provides us with an example of efficient concentration. Its profit margins remain stable or even decline, and most important, prices go down. Consumers benefit from Walmart's expansion. It is fair to debate and challenge Walmart's labor and management practices, but there is little doubt that Walmart has been good for US consumers.

As I write these lines, Sears has filed for bankruptcy, showing that the US retail sector has remained competitive. Suzanne Kapner in the *Wall Street Journal* reported, "For much of the 20th century, Sears Holdings Corp. defined American retailing with catalogs and department stores that brought toys, tools and appliances to millions of homes." When Sears filed for bankruptcy in mid-October 2018, it had 687 stores and about 68,000 workers. "Decades earlier, it had been dethroned by Walmart Inc. as the biggest U.S. retailer. Then it was crippled by a chief executive with unorthodox strategies, and Amazon.com Inc., an endless online catalog that sucked profits out of the business."*

The US retail industry shows that concentration alone is not a reliable indicator of competition. It needs to be complemented by other measures, such as profits and prices. Later on, we will also look at hiring and investment.

Measuring Concentration with Several Large Firms

How do we assess the concentration of an industry when there are several large firms? In Figure 2.2 we consider only the market share of Walmart, and it's easy because we draw one line. But in an industry dominated by several large firms, this would not work. We could plot all their market shares, but that would be a rather messy figure. It would be nicer to summarize concentration with one number, even when there are many firms. This is what the *Herfindahl-Hirschman index* (HHI) does (see Box 2.1).

Let's take another look at the airline industry. Figure 2.4 shows the national concentration index (HHI). It decreases with entry of new airlines in the 1980s and increases with mergers in the 2000s. It has historically been around 0.1, but increased to 0.14 following a wave of mergers in the 2000s. The top four domestic airlines are American (18.6 percent of the domestic market between July 2016 and June 2017), Southwest (18.4 percent), Delta (16.8 percent), and United (14.8 percent). The fifth, JetBlue (5.5 percent), is a lot smaller.

Figure 2.4 shows US airlines' HHI at the national level. But is this the relevant market to consider? People fly from one city to another; they do not fly between averages of various cities. In the airline industry the natural definition of a market is a route between two cities. Since airlines fly only a subset of all routes, concentration at the route level is higher than at the national level. But how much higher?

A 2014 report by the Government Accountability Office (GAO) splits routes into quintiles from high to low traffic, using data from 2012. The

---

* Suzanne Kapner, "Sears reshaped America, from Kenmore to Allstate." *Wall Street Journal,* October 15, 2018.

Box 2.1. Measuring Concentration with the Herfindahl-Hirschman Index

The Herfindahl-Hirschman index (HHI) is a measure of market concentration. Imagine an industry with N firms. The market share of the first firm is s_1, of the second firm s_2. HHI is then computed as the sum of the squared market shares.

$$HHI = (s_1)^2 + (s_2)^2 + \ldots + (s_N)^2$$

Why squared? The simple sum of market shares would always be one, by definition, so that would not be informative. If all the firms have the same market share s, then you can see that $HHI = s$. An industry with 10 identically sized firms has an HHI of 0.1. More generally, $1/s$ would be the number of firms and $1/s \times s^2 = s$, so the HHI is always s when the firms are identical. When the firms are different, squaring the market shares means that we put more weight on the larger firms, which makes sense since we are interested in market power.

Let us consider an example. First, a monopoly (one firm with $s = 1$) has an HHI of 1. That is the maximum value. An industry with one large firm controlling one half of the market ($s = 0.5$) and a bunch of tiny firms producing the rest would have an HHI close to 0.25. This would be the same HHI as with 4 identical firms. HHI therefore allows us to compare industries with different configurations.

If you read legal documents, you will see an HHI of 0.25 written as $HHI = 2,500$. That's just because we often measure HHI in basis points by multiplying the natural value (0.25) by 10,000. So instead of saying $HHI = 1$, we often say $HHI = 10,000$.

For purposes of antitrust enforcement, the US Department of Justice defines a competitive market as one with an HHI score of 1,500 or lower. When the HHI is between 1,500 and 2,500, the market is classified as moderately concentrated. Above 2,500, the DoJ considers a market highly concentrated. Naturally, antitrust concerns are greatest in highly concentrated markets, and the DoJ sees any merger that increases the HHI in a highly concentrated market by more than 200 points to be a potential violation of antitrust regulations. (Now you see the convenience of the basis points scale: it's easier to say 200 points than 0.02.)

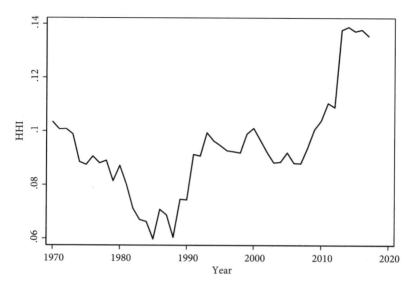

FIGURE 2.4 HHI in US air transport industry. *Data source:* US firms in Compustat

GAO study took place after several high-profile mergers but before the merger of American and US Airways. There were about 410 million passengers in 2012, so each quintile has about 82 million passengers. The first quintile (high traffic) includes only thirty-seven city pairs, but they all correspond to heavily traveled routes between busy airports, such as New York to Los Angeles or Washington, DC, to Boston. The third quintile (medium traffic) has 237 city pairs. The fifth quintile (low traffic) includes 9,379 city pairs and many tiny airports. HHI in the first quintile was around 0.32. HHI in the third quintile was around 0.40. If we compare it to the national HHI in Figure 2.4, which was around 0.11 in 2012, we see that the relevant HHI, at the local level, is about three times higher than the national one.

As explained in Box 2.2, this means that we need to be careful when we interpret national concentration indexes. This is an old controversy in the branch of economics that studies industrial organizations. Carl Shapiro (2018) is unconvinced by industry-level evidence: "it is extremely difficult to measure market concentration across the entire economy in a systematic manner that is both consistent and meaningful." The problem of estimating HHI at the correct level of granularity is a difficult one. As we saw with the airline industry, Shapiro argues that many industry

Box 2.2. What Is the Relevant Market?

If we consider the US retail sector, we see concentration rising from 1995 to 2008. At the national level, HHI increases from 0.03 to 0.06. As far as competition is concerned, however, the US retail sector is not one market. It is made of many local markets that correspond to the places where people actually go shopping. Clearly, the concentration of retail stores in downtown Chicago is irrelevant to the shopping experience of households in Tampa.

Imagine a country with two regions and four independent retailers, two in each region, with equal market shares. Imagine also that people shop only in the region where they live. Clearly, then, the region is the right market to consider. Each region has two equally sized retailers, so each has an HHI of 0.5. The national HHI is 0.25, however, accounting for all four equally sized retailers. This national measure is not meaningful, and the correct HHI is 0.5, the regional one. Now suppose that one retailer of the first region merges with one in the second region. Local competition does not change because the merger happens between firms that did not compete in the first place. Each region still has an HHI of 0.5. The national HHI, however, increases to 0.375 since there is now one firm with a share of 0.5 and two firms with shares of 0.25. Looking at the national index, we could wrongfully conclude that market concentration has increased.

sectors that economists treat as participants in a national marketplace are often local (think of restaurants, supermarkets, wired telecommunications, and hospitals). Shapiro argues that the rise in concentration might simply "reflect the fact that large, national firms have captured an increasing share of overall revenue during the past 20 years."

That's a fair criticism. Antitrust economists need to work with extremely granular data because they need to overcome a difficult burden of proof. We should take their concerns seriously. On the other hand, we cannot simply stop because we do not have a perfect measure. My approach in this book will be never to draw conclusions from only one measure. If we find signs of rising concentration, we will immediately look at other indicators, such as profits and prices. There are additional criticisms of concentration measures that we will discuss later in the book, notably when we consider foreign competition.

For instance, when we look at Figure 2.4, we see a sharp increase in concentration in the airline industry after 2010. That is enough to trigger our interest, but not enough to conclude that competition has weakened. We must first check that concentration has also increased at the route level. We find that it has. We can further show that it came together with higher prices and higher profits. We can then conclude that this concentration was probably bad for US passengers. Even that is not entirely obvious, however, because—in theory—the quality of services could have improved so much as to justify the price increase. Most readers will laugh at this idea in the case of airlines (I am also laughing as I write these lines), but there are other industries where this could happen. Another explanation could be that safety regulations have increased fixed operating costs. That could also explain a rise in concentration. In that case, however, we can look at what happened in Europe, where safety regulations are just as tight, but there we do not see higher concentration or higher prices. In short, the case of US airlines is a rather straightforward example of weak antitrust with negative consequences for consumers, and this discussion might sound overly cautious. As a rule, however, it is healthy to consider alternative explanations.

Amazon vs. Walmart

Let us now return to the retail sector and focus on the growth of Amazon. We have seen that, as Walmart's market share increased, retail prices decreased sharply. But the improvement stops in 2005. This coincides with the development of online shopping, and in particular with the growth of Amazon. When we think about the retail industry now, we still think of Walmart, Home Depot, and Target, but we also think of Amazon.

The growth of Amazon coincides with constant prices. This means that Amazon's expansion is not about cutting prices. Instead, Amazon is all about improving the shopping experience. This can lead to higher or lower effective prices, so how can we compare prices in the world of Amazon?

Suppose you want to buy a tool for $50. You can drive to your local hardware store and get some expert advice before buying. You could buy similar tools for $45 on Amazon, but you are not sure which one would be best for you. If you are indifferent between these two options, it means that you value the expertise of the sales people in your local store at $5. Equivalently, the store is not selling just the tool, it is selling a bundle of tool and expert advice. The price on Amazon is not really cheaper because Amazon is not selling the bundle.

It can also go the other way. If you prefer to buy a $20 toy from Amazon instead buying it for $17 in a brick-and-mortar store, you could ask yourself: how low would the price have to be at the store to convince me to drive there? Let's say it would have to be $15. That means that you value the convenience and the time that you save at $5. In that sense, Amazon effectively saves you $5, and it's equivalent to being able to buy the toy in the store for $15. Since the store sells it at $17, one could argue that Amazon is in fact $2 cheaper than the brick-and-mortar store.

These examples illustrate a complicated issue in the measurement of prices. It is difficult to compare prices because goods vary in quality and come with add-ons. Box 2.3 explains how statistical agencies construct quality-adjusted prices.

Digital platforms create new challenges in measuring prices because they often provide some services for free (for example, Google Maps). Of course, these services are not really free; they are simply part of a new bundle, where the most valuable component is the acquisition of personal data. As they say in Silicon Valley, "If you are not paying for it, you're not the customer; you're the product being sold."

If we adjust prices for the convenience of shopping online, it is likely that Amazon has also contributed to lower prices. There are differences, however, in how these gains are shared. Walmart created more value for lower-income consumers. Amazon is more valuable for upper middle-class households whose disposable income and opportunity cost of time are relatively high. In our previous example, the quality adjustment would be the amount of time saved multiplied by the hourly wage. A team of economists has recently quantified the gains from e-commerce (Dolfen et al., 2019). E-commerce spending reached 8 percent of consumption by 2017. The researchers estimate that gains from e-commerce are

Box 2.3. Adjusting Prices for Quality Changes

Economists love prices. We love to estimate them, compare them, and bundle them into indexes.

Why do we care so much about price *indexes*? Because they are supposed to tell us about the evolution of the cost of living. If both your income and your cost of living go up by 10 percent, you really have not experienced any improvement in your living standards, no real growth.

Constructing accurate price indexes is a surprisingly important job. Any number of widely used (and expensive) government programs use price indexes as a guide to setting budgets and payment rates, from Social Security to Medicare to the per-mile reimbursement for employee travel. If we mess up the computation of price indexes, we draw the wrong conclusions and implement the wrong policies.

In 1996, the Boskin Commission concluded that the US Consumer Price Index (CPI) overestimated inflation by about 1 percentage point, notably because of quality changes and the introduction of new goods. Considering that the annualized rate of inflation at the time was 2.9 percent, this was a rather large mistake. Why is it so hard to construct price indexes?

The CPI is constructed by the Bureau of Labor Statistics (BLS). The BLS collects prices every month on tens of thousands of goods and services in thousands of retail outlets. It then computes an "average" price change. This is relatively easy to do when the goods available this month are the same that were available last month. We can compute the percentage change in the price of each good and take an average, weighted by the share of spending on each good. But what happens when a new product appears? Or when an old one disappears? Or when an existing one changes significantly?

The accurate measurement of quality changes is a difficult task. The idea behind the CPI is to compute over time the cost of buying the same basket of goods and services. If you paid $100 for a particular basket last month, and you would have to pay $101 for the same basket this month, then inflation is 1 percent. In reality, products disappear, products are replaced with new versions, new products emerge, and often you cannot buy exactly the same basket.

The CPI can be slow at incorporating new products: automobiles only entered the index in 1935, air conditioners in 1964, and cell phones in 1998, long after their prices had fallen significantly. The issue is that the CPI misses the (big) initial introduction effect and overestimates inflation.

When BLS data collectors cannot obtain a price for an item in the CPI sample (for example, because the outlet has stopped selling it), they look for a replacement item that is closest to the missing one. The BLS then adjusts for changes in quality and specifications. It can use manufacturers' cost data or hedonic regressions to compute quality adjustments. *Hedonic regressions* are statistical models to infer consumers' willingness to pay for goods or services. When it cannot estimate an explicit quality adjustment, the BLS imputes the price change using the average price change of similar items in the same geographic area. Finally, the BLS has specific procedures to estimate the price of housing (rents and owners' equivalent rents) and medical care. (The medical care component of the CPI covers only out-of-pocket expenses.)

Where are we today, a little more than two decades after the publication of the Boskin Commission report? We can probably say that the glass is half full. The BLS has improved its process of quality adjustments and pays close attention to new goods, but some of the methods that the BLS uses to assess replacement goods work well with relatively small changes in quality or characteristics but less well when an innovative new product significantly disrupts consumer behavior. It is therefore possible that we still overestimate inflation.

This issue is particularly severe in the case of "free" goods and services provided by internet platforms such as Google and Facebook. Fortunately, top-notch economists like Chad Jones (2017) from the University of Chicago have looked into that problem and have given us some ways to think about it. Estimation of inflation is tightly connected to the measurement of productivity growth, and we will continue the discussion in Chapter 5. For now, let's just note that the mismeasurement is not large enough to materially change our conclusions about the slowdown in productivity.

equivalent to a 1 percent permanent boost to consumption, which represents about $1,000 per household. Some of the gains arose from saving travel costs. Higher income cardholders gained more, as did consumers in more densely populated counties.

Clearly, Amazon is great for busy, high-earning households.

Another relevant point is that Amazon's profit margins do not appear to be particularly high. Amazon's profit margin is in line with the average in retail. If anything, it appears to be a bit lower. And more important, Amazon invests a lot. We will discuss investment in greater detail later, but it's important to point out immediately that when competition is weak, investment incentives are also weak. The fact that Amazon invests a lot is clearly a good sign as far as competition is concerned.

Does this mean that there is nothing to worry about? Not quite. Amazon's pricing decisions are dynamic, not static. Amazon charges low prices to build its market share. The fear, as Lina M. Khan of the Open Markets Institute has explained, is that it is willing to forego profits only to establish its dominance in many markets and then exploit its market power (Khan, 2017). But do we have any evidence that this is happening?

Two concepts from industrial economics shed light on the issue: loss leader pricing and predatory pricing. *Loss leader pricing* is the strategy of a firm that sells a product at a loss in order to attract customers and stimulate the sales of other, more profitable goods and services. It is a common strategy in retail. *Predatory pricing,* on the other hand, happens when a firm sets low, unsustainable prices in order to drive its competitors out of business. If you think about it, you quickly realize that, in practice, it is hard to distinguish one from the other.

Khan discusses the case of the e-commerce company Quidsi, owner of Diapers.com and a few other sites. Amazon expressed interest in acquiring Quidsi in 2009, but Quidsi rejected the offer. Soon after, Amazon engaged in a price war with Quidsi by cutting the price of diapers and other baby products on Amazon.com and by offering steep discounts in its new Amazon Mom program. Quidsi did not have a war chest to match Amazon's, and eventually Quidsi's owners decided to sell the company. They received offers from both Walmart and Amazon, and accepted Amazon's offer at the end of 2010. The Federal Trade Commission reviewed the deal under Section 7 of the Clayton Act. The deal clearly raised some red flags, but the FTC decided not to pursue the case. A year later, Amazon rolled back its discounts.

This can plausibly be described as predatory pricing. But is it harmful for consumers? It is not obvious since we do not know if prices are now higher than they would have been without the acquisition. This illustrates the difficulty of judging cases of predatory pricing. It also clearly shows that regulators must remain vigilant.

Concentration Is Not Always Bad

We have seen some of the standard tools that economists use to study competition: market shares, concentration, profits, and prices. We have seen that none of them is perfect. Concentration raises legitimate concerns of market dominance, but it can also reflect the increasing efficiency of market leaders. Efficient firms are profitable, but sustained abnormal profits are a bad sign. Low prices are almost always a good sign, unless they involve predatory pricing.

When we look at antitrust actions, we hope to see lower prices. Can we then conclude that the antitrust actions were beneficial? The answer is that it's likely, but it's not entirely obvious because competition can be excessive, at least in theory. This can happen when investment and innovation decline after competition increases. When we look at episodes of deregulation, we hope to see entry by new firms. Does this mean deregulation was a good idea? Again, the answer is probably yes, but we can also construct examples where there are too many entrants, and the decline in profits exceeds the gain for consumers. These are delicate empirical questions, and we will need to look at a broad set of economic indicators. You guessed it: we need data, more data!

In Chapters 3, 4, and 5 we will review the broad trends in the US economy over the past twenty years, looking at entry and exit of businesses, market shares, mergers, profits, stock buybacks, and investment.

CHAPTER 3

The Rise in Market Power

IN 1998 JOEL KLEIN, who ran the antitrust operation at the US Department of Justice, declared in a January 29 address before the New York State Bar Association that "our economy is more competitive today than it has been in a long, long time." That statement was true, but unfortunately for US households, it was not prescient. This is not a critique of Klein. He could not have foreseen the evolution of US markets. And the history of economics is replete with more embarrassing predictions. The well-known Yale economist Irving Fisher gave a speech at the monthly dinner of the American Purchasing Agents Association where he argued that "stock prices have reached what looks like a permanently high plateau." As a general statement about stock prices, it is rather silly. The more unfortunate point, however, is that he made that claim on October 15, 1929.*

In Chapter 2, we described various ways to measure competition. We understand their meaning, usefulness, and limitations. Let's put them to work.

Concentration of Market Shares

It is natural to start with concentration. There are two basic measures of concentration: one is the market share of the top firms, either of a single firm (concentration ratio CR1) or of the top five or top eight firms in the industry (CR5 or CR8); the other is the Herfindahl-Hirschman index (HHI) that we dicussed in Chapter 2. Using both measures, we are going to show that concentration has increased in most US industries.

---

* The account of the dinner discussion published in the *New York Times* on October 16, 1929, is well worth reading.

The US Census Bureau provides estimates of revenue concentration by industry. In April 2016, the Council of Economic Advisers, chaired by President Obama's chief economist Jason Furman, pointed out that "the majority of industries have seen increases in the revenue share enjoyed by the 50 largest firms between 1997 and 2012" (Council of Economic Advisers, 2016). Figure 3.1 replicates and extends these results. It shows the rise in concentration in the US economy using CR8 computed from Census data separately for manufacturing and nonmanufacturing industries. We have more granular data for the manufacturing sector, where we can perform the analysis with 360 manufacturing industries (NAICS level 6; NAICS levels are explained in the first section of the Appendix). In manufacturing, the top eight firm concentration ratio (CR8) increased from 50 percent to 59 percent. For nonmanufacturing industries, we can perform the analysis at NAICS level 3, which has a few more than seventy industries. With this wider definition the CR8s are smaller, but the increase is large, from 15 percent to 25 percent.*

The Census includes the universe of US firms, so it represents the most comprehensive data source. It has some limitations, however. It does not contain financial information, and it is based on establishment accounting. An alternate data source is Compustat, a database of firm-level financial information from S&P Global Market Intelligence. Compustat, unlike the Census, gives a partial coverage of the economy: it includes only large firms that are (or have been) publicly traded. Its coverage is smaller than that of the Census, but it has more historical depth, and it contains a wealth of financial information consolidated at the firm level. Compustat allows us to check the robustness of our results and to expand them. With my co-authors Matias Covarrubias and Germán Gutiérrez

---

* Figure 3.1 uses data from the US Census Bureau (available from their website). David Autor and his co-authors (2017) extend these data by accessing detailed files from the US Economic Census, which is conducted every five years and surveys all establishments in selected sectors. They collect data over the period 1982–2012 for six sectors (manufacturing, retail trade, wholesale trade, services, finance, and utilities and transportation) and perform a consistent analysis of 388 manufacturing and 288 nonmanufacturing industries, computing the CR4 and CR20 across these industries as well as HHI. They document a clear increase in concentration in all industries.

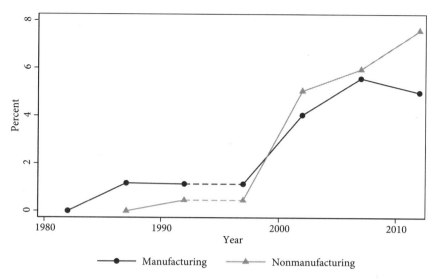

FIGURE 3.1 Concentration using top eight firm Census shares, cumulative change in CR8. Annual data. The concentration ratio is defined as the market share (by sales) of the eight largest firms in each industry. See Autor et al. (2017) for concentration time-series under a consistent segmentation, which exhibit similar trends. *Data sources:* US Concentration Ratios (CRs) from Economic Census, based on SIC segments before 1997 and NAICS segments after 1997. Data for manufacturing are reported at NAICS level 6 (SIC 4 for 1992) because it is available only at that granularity in 1992. Data for nonmanufacturing are based on NAICS level 3 segments (SIC 2 for 1992).

(2019) we show that the rise in concentration is similar in Compustat and in Census data, and whether we measure concentration using HHI scores or CR8.* Gustavo Grullon, Yelena Larkin, and Roni Michaely (forthcoming) were the first to point out the increase in concentration in the Compustat data set. They found that concentration had increased in more than three-quarters of US industries. In addition, they showed that firms in concentrating industries experience rising profit margins. We are going to study profits later in the chapter.

---

* The broad increase in concentration after 1995 is clear in both data sets, but the timing varies. In the Census data it occurs mostly in the 1990s, but in Compustat it occurs mostly in the 2000s. HHI declines in the early 1990s in Compustat. This reflects the quick increase in the number of listed firms.

In Chapter 2 we discussed some caveats when using industry concentration as an indicator of competition. One caveat is that the relevant market concentration might not be correctly captured by industry-level measures (recall our example of routes versus national average for airlines). A second caveat is that concentration might signal changes in industry dynamics that are not directly related to market power, such as an increasing efficiency gap between industry leaders and laggards (Walmart in the 1990s) or consolidation in declining industries.

Spelling Out the Hypotheses

Although the rise in concentration has been well documented, there is little agreement about its causes and even less about its consequences. Jason Furman, when he was chair of the Council of Economic Advisers, argued that the rise in concentration suggested "economic rents and barriers to competition." David Autor, David Dorn, Lawrence Katz, Christina Patterson, and John Van Reenen (2017) have argued almost exactly the opposite, namely that concentration reflects "a winner take most feature" explained by the fact that "consumers have become more sensitive to price and quality due to greater product market competition."

Measures of concentration are suggestive, but they cannot by themselves tell us that competition has indeed decreased. To continue our inquiry and deepen our understanding, it is useful to articulate several hypotheses. This is, after all, the usual process in scientific research. So here is a list of six hypotheses to interpret the data:

- *Hypothesis of Much Ado about Nothing*
  Industry concentration measures are meaningless because industry codes are too coarse and because markets are local (an argument of antitrust specialists).
- *Hypothesis of Decreasing Domestic Competition*
  Competition has declined in many US industries (the argument of this book).
- *Hypothesis of the Rise of Superstar Firms*
  Concentration reflects the increasing productivity of industry leaders.

- *Hypothesis of Lower Search Costs*
  The internet makes price comparisons easier, and this leads to winner-take-all outcomes.
- *Hypothesis of Globalization*
  Foreign competition leads to domestic consolidation.
- *Hypothesis of Intangible Assets*
  The growth of intangible assets explains the evolution of concentration, profits, and investment.

It might seem strange at first to entertain the *Much Ado about Nothing* hypothesis as an explanation, but I think it is healthy to keep in the back of our mind the possibility that we might simply be creating more background noise. I am reminded of this issue every time I listen to pundits discuss the stock market. They always have a view about where the market is going and why. They can argue passionately about the meaning of a particular pattern and come up with theories to rationalize fluctuations that are essentially random. The lack of knowledge has rarely prevented human beings from discussing the news, so let us entertain this hypothesis as a way of keeping our overconfidence in check. Under it, measures of industry concentration should be treated as noise, and they would neither predict nor explain real outcomes.

The remaining five hypotheses are not mutually exclusive. It is obvious that foreign competition (from Mexico, China, and Japan) has affected some industries. It is also obvious that some firms have amazing intangible assets. We have already discussed Amazon. We will study Apple, Facebook, Google, and Microsoft in Chapters 13 and 14. In all likelihood, therefore, the truth is a mix of these hypotheses with varying relevance across industries and time periods. There could be other hypotheses, but I think they would boil down to a combination of these five.

The *Rise of Superstar Firms* hypothesis is the story of Walmart in the 1990s, which is discussed in Chapter 2. According to this view, concentration is good news and should be linked to faster productivity growth. The hypothesis of *Lower Search Costs* is related to the superstar firms hypothesis, but it is conceptually distinct. It argues that consumers have become more price-elastic thanks to online shopping tools. Notice that this hypothesis implies that ex post competition has increased and that profit margins (earnings over sales) have decreased. Sales concentration increases because, with lower margins, firms need to be larger in order to recoup their fixed entry costs. In their well-known 2017 paper, Autor, Dorn, Katz, Patterson, and Van Reenen argue that the rise of superstar firms explains the fall in the labor share of income that we see in most US industries and in the aggregate. We will come back to this point.

The *Decreasing Domestic Competition* hypothesis argues the opposite position, that barriers to entry have increased and that this has given incumbents more market power, thereby decreasing domestic competition. This is the interpretation that I am promoting in this book for most—but not all—industries. If correct, it invites the next question: why?

Globalization is not really a hypothesis. Globalization is a fact. Rather, the question is a quantitative one: Does it explain much of what we see or only a little? Are there industries where globalization is the main driving force, and others where it is not? Under the *Globalization* hypothesis, we expect foreign competition to put downward pressure on profit margins, forcing domestic firms to exit or to merge. It is clear that some manufacturing industries such as textile manufacturing have followed this pattern. Trade economists Robert Feenstra and David Weinstein estimated in a 2017 paper the impact of globalization on mark-ups and concluded that mark-ups generally decrease in industries affected by foreign competition. Another important fact to keep in mind is that globalization is a two-way street. The flip side of foreign competition is that successful domestic firms can expand globally and become large relative to their home countries. A perfect example is the rise of the Finnish telecom company Nokia in the 2000s. At its peak, it accounted for about two-thirds of Helsinki's stock exchange market capitalization, almost half of corporate research and development, and about 20 percent of Finnish exports.* We should be careful, then, when comparing consolidated firm revenues (including foreign sales) to domestic GDP.

---

* Nokia is actually older than Finland. Nokia was founded in 1865. Finland only attained its independence in 1917 after over 700 years of Swedish rule and 109 years of Russian rule.

Finally, the *Intangible Assets* hypothesis contains several ideas. Intangible assets are nonphysical in nature. They include intellectual property, like patents and copyrights, but extend to vague or fuzzy assets, such as brand recognition. Economists Nicolas Crouzet and Janice Eberly (2018) argue that industry leaders are often firms that are very good at producing intangible assets. In fact, they argue that this is how they became leaders in the first place. The attractive feature of a theory of intangible assets is that it can explain concentration both through increasing productivity (superstar firms) and through decreasing domestic competition since intangible assets can create barriers to entry. To test this idea, we will look carefully at intangible investments across firms and industries in Chapter 5. Network effects and increasing differences in the productivity of information technology could also increase the efficient scale of operation of the top firms, leading to higher concentration.

Persistence of Market Shares

Economists who specialize in industrial organization and antitrust rightfully complain about the use of industry-level HHIs to measure concentration. Indeed, we have pointed out the limitations of HHI in Chapter 2 and discussed cases where they can lead to misleading conclusions about the state of an industry. On the other hand, it makes no sense to completely ignore industry-level market shares because there are many cases in which they do provide useful information.

Matias Covarrubias, Germán Gutiérrez, and I consider an alternative, more dynamic measure of competition: instead of looking at the concentration of market shares at a point in time, we look at the persistence of market shares *over* time.

Our intuition is that in a competitive industry, the leaders should be challenged. To make the point, imagine an industry with five firms. In any given year, one firm dominates and has a market share of 60 percent, while the other four firms have only 10 percent each. This looks like a concentrated industry. It has an HHI of 4,000, clearly above the "highly concentrated" threshold of 2,500. But now imagine that every two years or so, the leader is replaced by one of the followers. This might be because these five firms are constantly trying to innovate and out-smart each other, and one succeeds on average every two years. This dynamic turnover would radically change the picture. We would say that this industry is in fact quite competitive, because the dominance of the leader is temporary. Its large market share is transient. There is turn-over at the top.

Gutiérrez and I computed two measures to get at this idea: one mea-sure captures turnover at the top, and the other measure captures the re-shuffling of market shares. Our first measure works as follows: given that a firm is at the top of its industry now—among the top four by profits or by market value—how likely is it that it will drop out over the next three years? Figure 3.2 shows the results of our calculations. You can see that the likelihood of being replaced was about 45 percent in the 1990s. At that time, the chance of remaining a top dog for more than three years was barely more than fifty-fifty. Today the likelihood of being replaced within three years is only 30 percent. Leaders have less to worry about today than twenty years ago.

Our second measure captures a similar idea, that of reshuffling. We rank firms by market value or by revenue in a particular year. We com-pute their rank again five years later. Then we compute the correlation of the two rankings. If the correlation between the two ranking series is one, it means that the relative position of firms has not changed at all over five years. If it is zero, it means that there has been a complete reshuf-fling within the industry. We can therefore define reshuffling as one minus the rank correlation. Figure 3.3 shows that reshuffling has de-creased over the past twenty years. Market shares have become more persistent. You can more easily predict who will be on top five years from now. The answer is: the same firms as today.

The conclusions we draw from Figures 3.2 and 3.3 are not consis-tent with what most people think of as competition. If we go back to our six hypotheses, we can say that Figures 3.2 and 3.3 rule out lower search costs as an explanation because this hypothesis predicts the opposite pattern. Under the *Lower Search Costs* hypothesis, small changes in productivity or innovation lead to large swings in market shares. Instead we see increased persistence and stability of market shares.

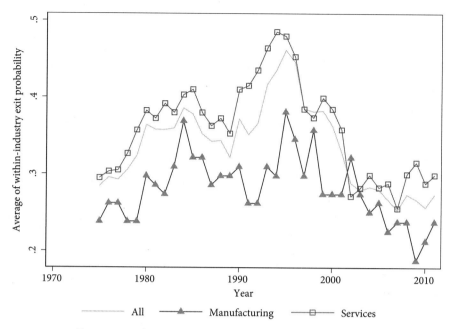

FIGURE 3.2 Turnover at the top. See text for details.

Figures 3.2 and 3.3 are consistent with decreasing domestic competition. They are also consistent with the hypotheses of the rise of superstar firms and the role of intangible assets if we assume that the comparative advantages of leaders have become more persistent. Why that would be the case is unclear, however. I have often heard arguments that intangible assets are subject to higher increasing returns to scale than tangible assets, but I have not seen convincing evidence that this is the case. In fact, I will show later that standard estimates of returns to scale have not changed much over the past twenty years. But at this point we can simply acknowledge that Figures 3.2 and 3.3 could be consistent with a rising persistence of stardom.

Let us continue our investigation by looking at profits. The *Rise of Superstar Firms* and *Decreasing Domestic Competition* hypotheses predict rising profits. *Globalization* predicts decreasing profits for firms exposed to global competition. The *Much Ado* hypothesis predicts no systematic relationship between concentration and profits. Looking at profit margins can thus help us to parse out these hypotheses.

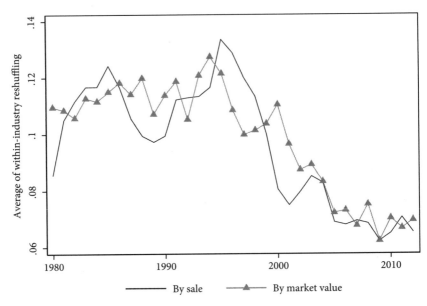

FIGURE 3.3 Reshuffling. See text for details.

Profits Margins and Payouts

Let us now scrutinize the profits of US firms. As usual, there are several measures and several sources to construct them: profit margins versus profit rates, and national accounts versus firm-level accounts. Box 3.1 explains the key concepts.

Figure 3.4 computes the ratio of after-tax corporate profits to GDP using the US national accounts. The profit share of GDP varies with the business cycle, and you will notice a trough during most recessions, such as in the fourth quarter of 2000 or the fourth quarter of 2008. But you can also see that over fifty years the profit share remains stable—stationary, to use the technical term—around 6 percent or 7 percent, from the end of World War II to the end of the twentieth century. Over the past two decades, however, profits have outpaced economic growth, and the after-tax profit share has increased to around 10 percent. This suggests that something fundamental has changed. We reach a similar conclusion if we compute profit margins from firm-level data. Using merged data from Compustat and the Center for Research in Security Prices, Gustavo Grullon, Yelena Larkin, and Roni Michaely (forthcoming) show that the

Box 3.1. Profits, Margins, Dividends, and Share Buybacks

Consider the following stylized example of a firm. The firm starts the year with a capital stock (assets) of $100. Its annual revenues are $150 and its gross operating profits (income) are $15. In the course of doing business, the capital depreciates by 5 percent. The firm invests $7, $5 of which serve to replace the depreciated capital.

Assets	Revenues	Income	Depreciation	Taxes	Gross Investment	Dividends
$100	$150	$15	$5	$3	$7	$5

The *gross profit margin* of the firm is 10 percent. It is the ratio of two flows: the flow of income ($15) over the flow of revenues ($150). Income net of depreciation is $10. The net margin is 6.67 percent.

Gross profit margin	$15 / 150 = 10\%$
Net profit margin	$(15-5) / 150 = 6.67\%$
Net profit rate	$(15-5) / 100 = 10\%$

The *profit rate* of the firm is 10 percent. It is the ratio of income net of depreciation (10) over the stock of capital at the beginning of the year (100). The firm pays a 30 percent tax rate on net income. It is thus left with $7 of income after taxes and depreciation.

After paying taxes and replacing the depreciated asset, the firm must decide what to do with the leftover money. It can either invest it to grow its capital stock, or it can pay it out to its owners, the shareholders. The firm decides to pay out $5. The *payout rate* of the firm is 5 percent. It is the ratio of the flow of dividends (5) over the stock of capital (100). Shareholders can be paid in one of two ways. They can receive a dividend— basically, the firm writes a check to each shareholder. If our notional firm has 100 shares outstanding, each share receives 5 cents. Shareholders often prefer to avoid cash payments. For various tax and accounting issues, they tend to favor capital gains. Instead of sending 100 checks for 5 cents each, the firm could spend $5 to buy back its own shares. The value of the shares would rise and shareholders would get exactly the same payouts. In our simple example there is no difference between dividends and share buybacks. In more complex and realistic cases (with stock options granted to managers, for instance), there are some differences, but it is always useful to start from the premise that dividends and buybacks are basically equivalent.

Finally, the firm invests $2 in addition to the replacement of depreciated assets of $5. Its gross investment is $7 and its net investment is $2. The *net investment rate* of the firm is 2 percent. This means that the capital stock of this firm will grow by 2 percent and its assets at the beginning of next year will be $102. With more assets, it should be able to hire and produce more next year. This net investment rate is clearly crucial for real economic growth, as we discuss in Chapter 4.

ratio of operating income after depreciation (but before tax) over sales was around 10 percent from 1970 to 2000, and then increased to 12 percent after 2000.

The other natural way to look at profits is to compare them to assets. We can further refine our profit measure by looking at the share of profits that is paid out to investors. Figure 3.5 shows the total payout rates for US-incorporated firms included in our Compustat sample, both dividends and share buybacks. The payout rate has increased substantially, primarily driven by share buybacks. The increase is so large that firms are now repurchasing as much as 3 percent of the book value of their assets each year.

We now have two sets of facts: market shares have become more concentrated and more persistent, and profits have increased. The natural next question to ask is whether the two sets of facts are connected: do we see higher profits precisely in industries where we see more concentration? The answer is yes. The increase in profits is systematically linked to the increase in concentration, as shown by Grullon, Hund, and Weston (2018) and Gutiérrez and Philippon (2017): firms in concentrating industries experience rising profit margins; firms in stable industries do not. This means that our concentration measures, despite all their flaws and limitations, are capturing something real, and it rules out the *Much Ado about Nothing* hypothesis.

What about international trade? Figure 3.5 is inconsistent with globalization being the dominant force for the entire US economy. Simply put, businesses struggling with foreign competition and forced to consolidate would not increase payouts to their shareholders. The fact that

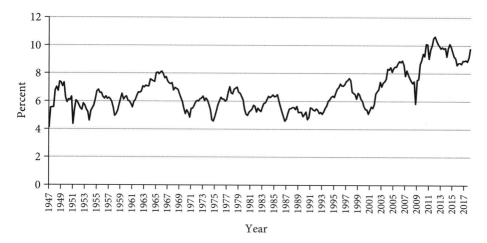

FIGURE 3.4 Corporate profits over GDP. Corporate profits after tax with inventory valuation adjustment and capital consumption adjustment, quarterly, seasonally adjusted. *Data source*: FRED

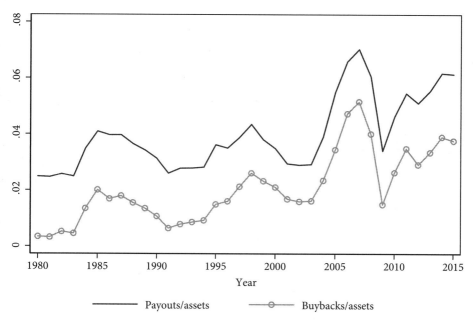

FIGURE 3.5 Share buybacks and payouts. Annual data for all US-incorporated firms in our Compustat sample. Results are similar when including foreign-incorporated firms. The SEC instituted in 1982 rule 10b-18, which allows companies to repurchase their shares on the open market without regulatory limits. It was followed by a large increase in buybacks.

payouts have increased suggests that many firms feel like they have a lot of cash to spare. This of course does not mean that globalization is not crucial in some industries, particularly those heavily exposed to foreign competition from China.

The China Shock

Industry HHIs are national measures focused on domestic firms. They can be criticized both for being too broad or too narrow. We have already discussed the critique that industry HHIs are too broad when markets are in fact local. A more interesting critique is that domestic HHIs are too narrow in a globalized world. When foreign competitors wipe out domestic firms, competition clearly increases, but domestic measures of concentration, computed with surviving firms, may very well increase. This is a serious issue.

A prime example is what economists now refer to as the China shock. China became a member of the World Trade Organization on December 11, 2001. It marked the end of lengthy negotiations as well as a significant step toward the integration of China into the world economy. Daron Acemoglu and his co-authors (2016) estimate that import competition from China was a major force behind reductions in US manufacturing employment during the 2000s.

Imports from China to the US had risen since the early 1990s and experienced a very rapid rise in the 2000s. This growth affected different US industries in different ways. One effect is particularly interesting for us. Before 2000, China was not considered to be a market economy. Under the Smoot-Hawley Tariff Act of 1930, nonmarket economies are subject to a relatively high tariff, known as a nonnormal trade relations (non-NTR) tariff. From 1980 onward, US presidents began granting NTR tariff rates to China, but these waivers had to be reapproved each year by Congress. If Congress failed to renew the waiver, the tariffs would jump back up to levels set in the 1930s. This introduced substantial uncertainty around future tariff rates that limited investment by both US and Chinese firms, as explained in an influential paper by Justin R. Pierce and Peter K. Schott (2016). Some industries were more affected because their 1930s reset tariffs were particularly high. We say that these industries faced high NTR gaps—gaps between the rolled-over NTR tariffs and the reset values.

In 2000, permanent normal trade relations (PNTR) were granted to China, which took effect in December 2001. The granting of PNTR removed uncertainty around tariffs, which was particularly beneficial for industries with large NTR gaps. Indeed, Pierce and Schott (2016) show that industries with larger NTR gaps experienced larger increases in Chinese imports and larger decreases in US employment.

Let us now study the impact of China's import competition across US manufacturing industries. We split our industries according to their exposure to the China shock, defined by import penetration from China. Figure 3.6 shows the normalized number of firms in industries with high and low Chinese import penetration. Chinese competition leads to a strong replacement effect. Both groups have the same pre-existing trends, including during the dot-com boom, but start to diverge after 2000. By 2015 the number of firms in manufacturing industries with low exposure to China is about the same as it was in 1991. In manufacturing industries with high exposure to China, it is 40 percent lower.

Figure 3.6 focuses only on the manufacturing sector, which employs a relatively small (and decreasing) share of the population. But it clearly shows that *Globalization* is a valid hypothesis in this limited field. We therefore need to take it into account.

Our ideal competition measure should cover the whole economy and should consider foreign competition.* Once we control for foreign competition, we find that concentration has remained stable in US manufacturing (see Covarrubias, Gutiérrez, and Philippon, 2019). For the economy as a whole, we still find an increase in concentration, but it is more muted when we take into account foreign competition.

---

* For manufacturing, Feenstra and Weinstein (2017) construct such a measure. They use Census HHIs for the US and import data for foreign countries. We extend Feenstra and Weinstein's data over time (until 2015) and outside the manufacturing sector. Outside manufacturing, neither Census nor foreign HHIs are available—so we have to use Compustat. We start with the "raw" HHIs from Compustat and adjust them to account for the domestic coverage of Compustat as well as the share of imports. The detailed calculations are described in Covarrubias, Gutiérrez, and Philippon (2019).

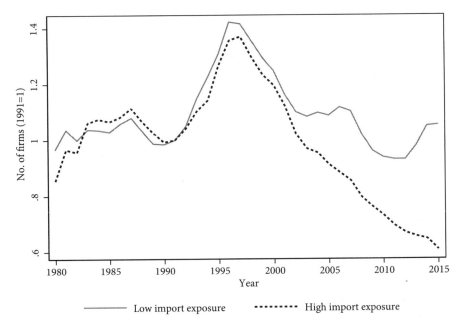

FIGURE 3.6 The China shock: The number of active US firms in manufacturing, by exposure to China, normalized to 1 in 1991. Annual data. Manufacturing industries only are split into "high" (above-median) and "low" (below-median) exposure based on import penetration from 1991 to 2011. *Data sources*: Firm data from Compustat; import data from UN Comtrade

Trade and competition interact in many fascinating ways. In Chapter 5 we will see how foreign competition is sometimes used to justify dubious domestic mergers.

Concentration, Entrenchment, and Profits

We have shown two important and related sets of facts. In most US industries, market shares have become more concentrated and more persistent. Industry leaders are less likely to be challenged and replaced than they were twenty years ago. At the same time, their profit margins have increased.

We have classified the various theories into several broad hypotheses. The data that we have analyzed so far allow us to narrow our focus down to three hypotheses: consolidation driven by foreign competition, increasing efficiency of leaders, perhaps driven by intangible assets, or decreasing domestic competition. We have shown that globalization is a powerful explanation of the trends observed in the manufacturing sector, and in industries exposed to foreign competition more broadly. In the rest of the economy, however, we are left to consider star firms, decreasing domestic competition, and intangible assets as the leading theories.

Two hypotheses can explain increasing concentration and increasing profit margins—the *Rise of Superstar Firms* and *Decreasing Domestic Competition*. They have opposite predictions for growth and welfare. How can we tease them apart? We are going to do it in two steps. In Chapter 4 we will look at investment and employment. In Chapter 5 we will look at entry, exit, and mergers to understand how concentration took place.

The Decline of Investment and Productivity

IN CHAPTER 3, we demonstrated that since 2000, US industries have become more concentrated. Leaders' market shares have become more persistent and their profit margins have increased. This pattern holds in all industries that are not heavily exposed to foreign competition, that is, most of the economy minus about half of the manufacturing sector.

We have argued that there are two leading explanations. One possible explanation is that industry leaders have become increasingly more efficient. This might explain why their market shares and their profits have grown. According to this view, which we called the *Rise of Superstar Firms* hypothesis, concentration is good news. The other explanation is that domestic competition has decreased and that leaders have become more entrenched. Their market shares are not threatened, and therefore they can charge high prices. According to this view, which we have called the *Decreasing Domestic Competition* hypothesis, concentration is bad news.

The two explanations are not mutually exclusive, in the sense that leaders can become more efficient and more entrenched at the same time. But they have opposite implications for efficiency, growth, welfare, and policy. The data that we have considered so far do not allow us to distinguish one explanation from the other. We must bring new data to bear. In this chapter, I will argue that the firms' investment decisions offer clues about the driving forces behind rising concentration and profits.

Under the optimistic explanation, concentration is the consequence of increasingly efficient leading firms. To transmit this individual success to the broad economy, successful businesses should draw in more resources. They should hire and invest more. Do they?

Business Investment Has Been Low

Figure 4.1 shows that in recent years investment has been low relative to firms' profits. Figure 4.1 shows the ratio of net investment (investment expenditures minus depreciation) to net operating surplus (gross surplus minus depreciation). Net investment is what matters for economic growth because it measures the change in capital from one year to the next.

There is a lot going on in Figure 4.1, so let us use the example from Chapter 3 to explain what these numbers mean. Recall that we imagined a firm with the following accounting information:

Assets	Revenues	Income	Depreciation	Taxes	Net investment	Dividends
$100	$150	$15	$5	$3	$2	$5

For this firm, we concluded that gross operating surplus (income) is $15. Depreciation is $5, so net operating surplus is $10. Gross investment

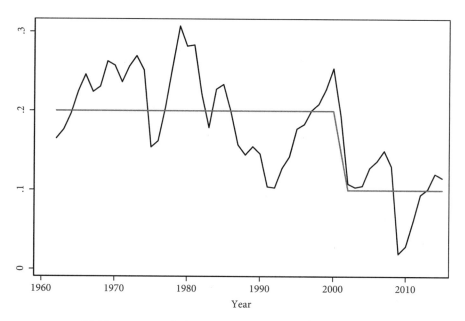

FIGURE 4.1 Net investment relative to net operating surplus

TABLE 4.1

Flow of Funds to Business Sector in 2014

| Name | Value in 2014 ($ billions) | | |
	Corporate (1)	Noncorporate (2)	Business (1+2)
Gross value added (*PY*)	$8,641	$3,147	$11,788
Stock of fixed capital (*K*)	$14,857	$6,126	$20,983
Consumption of fixed capital (CFK)	$1,286	$297	$1,583
Net operating surplus (*PY*–Wages–Tax–CFK)	$1,614	$1,697	$3,311
Gross fixed capital formation (*I*)	$1,610	$354	$1,964
Net fixed capital formation (*I*–CFK)	$325	$56	$381

Note: Stock of fixed capital is measured at replacement cost.

is $7, and net investment is $2. Net investment over net operating surplus is 20 percent.

We can apply the same logic to the entire US economy. Table 4.1 summarizes the current account of the business sector in 2014. The starting point is gross value added, which means revenues minus the cost of intermediate inputs (materials) and energy (cost of electricity and so on). The gross value added of the US business sector in 2014 was $11.8 trillion, with a contribution of $8.6 trillion from incorporated businesses. Let's call this gross value added *PY*: it is the product of the average price of goods and services (*P*) and the quantity of goods and services sold (*Y*), the letter used to denote real value added or real GDP in economic textbooks. To create this value added, the business sector uses a capital stock (*K*) of $21 trillion. This is measured at "replacement cost," which means that it would cost $21 trillion to replace all the plants, warehouses, computers, vehicles, and equipment in the US business sector. Production wears out equipment, structures, and vehicles. Equipment and software can also become obsolete and be discarded. The sum of this wear and tear and obsolescence is called *consumption of fixed capital* (CFK), or more simply, depreciation. Replacing the depreciated capital at the end of the year costs $1.6 trillion. Finally, businesses spend money on employees' wages and benefits. They also pay taxes on production. This leaves them with a net operating surplus of about $3.3 trillion. They use $381 billion to increase their capital stock. This figure is what we refer to as *net investment.*

In 2014, the ratio of net fixed capital formation ($381 billion) over net operating surplus ($3,311 billion) was 11.5 percent. As you can see from Figure 4.1, the average of this ratio between 1962 and 2001 is 20 percent. The average of the ratio from 2002 to 2015 is only 10 percent. In other words, over the first period, firms took 20 cents of each dollar of profits and plowed them back into their businesses by growing their capital stock.

In our simple example, with a net investment of 2 and starting from a capital stock of 100, the firm will have a capital stock of 102 next year. The growth rate of capital is 2 percent. This growth rate is important. When the capital stock grows, workers become more productive, and both labor demand and wages increase. In the long run, GDP and the capital stock tend to grow at the same rate.

In recent years firms have been plowing back into investment only a bit more than 10 cents for each dollar of profit. As a result, the growth of productive capital has been slow. Using the fixed asset tables from the Bureau of Economic Analysis (table 4.2 on the BEA website), we see that the growth rate of the capital stock of corporate businesses was 3.7 percent on average between 1962 and 2001, but only 1.9 percent on average between 2002 and 2012. You can see the trend decline in Figure 4.2.

How can we interpret this fact? Is this necessarily bad news? Perhaps firms are simply responding to market signals telling them the economy does not need more capital right now. Can we tell? Yes, we can, but first we need some theoretical background.

Why Do Firms Invest?

The goal of investment is to create (or replace) a long-lived valuable asset. This is in fact the exact definition of investment used in economic statistics.* Firms invest when they think that they need more long-lived

---

* Net investment. In a stationary environment (constant profits, constant wages, no growth), firms replace the depreciated capital each year. That would be

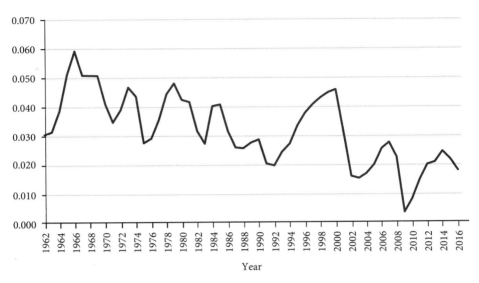

FIGURE 4.2 Declining growth of capital: growth rate of corporate businesses' capital stock

assets. This can happen for two reasons: because firms perceive growing demand for their products, and because they want to innovate.

When demand grows, firms usually start by increasing overtime: employees work longer hours, and the utilization rate of equipment increases. When the growth in demand is sustained, firms need to hire more capital and more labor.

Firms invest to expand their production capacity and satisfy a growing demand. Firms also invest to improve the range and quality of their products. In both cases, investment allows firms to increase their profits in the future. But what about the cost today? How can we compare uncertain future profits with current, known expenditures? This is where finance comes in.

Investment trades off future profits against current expenditures. The cost of financing the investment therefore plays a crucial role. Investment, by its very nature, is an intertemporal decision. You must decide how

---

between 5 and 10 percent, depending on the industry and the kind of capital. In Table 4.1, the depreciation rate in 2014 was 1,583 / 20,983 = 7.5 percent. Although important, this is not what we are interested in. We want to understand why and how firms grow. We therefore focus on net investment.

much to spend today in the hope of reaping uncertain benefits in the future. To assess the value of investment, you need to discount uncertain future payoffs. The financial markets allow you to do just that.

Consider the following example. You can invest in a project by buying an asset for $100 today. You think it will generate $12 in annual profits and depreciate by $6 each year. After the first year, for example, you pay $6 to replace the depreciated part, and you have a net income of $6. You do the same thing in the second year. The asset generates $6 year after year. The yield of this investment is 6 percent per year. Should you invest in this project? This depends on your funding cost. Imagine that you borrowed the $100 to buy the asset. If the interest rate on your loan is less than 6 percent, then it is a positive investment. Imagine that the interest rate on your loan is 5 percent. You repay $5 per year, and your net income after interest is $1 per year. At the rate of 5 percent, we say that the net present value (NPV) of this investment is positive. A perpetual income of $6 discounted at 5 percent is worth $6 / 0.05 = $120. The NPV is $120 − $100 = $20. The NPV is subject to the funding cost. If the funding cost was 7 percent instead of 5 percent, the NPV would be negative. A perpetual income of $6 discounted at 7 percent is worth $85.7. The NPV would be −$14.28, and you would not invest.

Making an investment decision therefore requires a complicated discounting of uncertain future cash flows and a comparison with the current cost of buying new capital. How can these decisions be made for the whole economy, with thousands of businesses, hundreds of billions of dollars of cash flows and investment costs? How can predictions be made not only one year ahead, but two, five, ten, or twenty?

It sounds like a daunting task, and it is. But if you think about it the right way and make some assumptions, you can see that accountants, together with stocks and bonds traders, *have* done it for us. This was the brilliant insight of Nobel Prize winner James Tobin. The measure that "looks at it the right way" is called Tobin's q and is explained in Box 4.1.

Tobin's insight is that the market value of the firm encodes all we want to know about the firm, at least as far as classical investment decisions are concerned. If accountants do their job properly, then we can measure the replacement cost of the firm's fixed assets. If investors do their job properly, then we can measure the market value that the firm creates

Box 4.1. Tobin's q and the Fundamental Law of Investment

Let us return to our simple example of the firm with a stock of capital, measured at replacement cost, of $100. The firm pays out $5 this year and spends $2 on net investment. Imagine that the firm is financed only with equity: there are 100 shares, and investors value each share at $1.10, so the market value is $110. The shareholders own the capital stock as well as all future profits of the firm.

Tobin's q is the ratio of the market value of the firm ($110) to the replacement cost of its capital ($100). For our firm, we therefore have $q = 1.1$. Tobin's insight is that as long as q is more than one, the firm should invest. When q is more than one, the market values each additional $1 of capital at more than $1. By increasing its capital stock—by investing—the firm creates value.

How fast should the firm invest? Our firm could decide to increase its capital stock to $110 in one year, but that would require a lot of investment and disruption. Installing new equipment is costly and time consuming, so it makes sense to implement the investment plan over several years. In general, the annual rate of investment should follow this formula:

net investment rate $= (q - 1) /$ *investment time*

This equation is the *fundamental law of investment*. The firm in our example uses an investment time parameter of five years. Since $q - 1 = 0.1$, with a five-year parameter, it chooses an investment rate of $0.1 / 5 = 2$ percent. Our firm will grow slowly. It does not want to incur large adjustment costs.

It will invest 2 percent in the first year. Next year (assuming no news), its q will be $110 / 102$, so it will invest $0.08 / 5 = 1.6$ percent. The year after that, its q will be $110 / 103.6$, and it will invest 1.2 percent. It will take a few more than four years to reach a book value of 105. It will never actually reach 110, but it will get closer each year.

We have assumed so far that the firm has only issued stocks, but Tobin's insight also applies when the firm is financed with both stocks and bonds. In that case you need to add the value of the stocks and the value of the bonds to get the total market value of the firm. Imagine, then, that our firm has issued some bonds, and the value of the outstanding shares is $80 and the value of the outstanding bonds is $30. Bondholders and stockholders jointly own the capital and the future profits generated by the firm. The total value is still $80 + $30 = $110 and Tobin's q is still 1.1.

How successful is Tobin's q at explaining investment in practice? It depends on three main issues. First, you must measure capital and investment—in particular, intangible assets—correctly, using the methods of Peters and Taylor (2016), for instance. Second, q assumes that the market is rational, or at least that the managers, who make the investment decisions, and the investors, who price the shares, agree on the correct value for the firm. Bubbles in the market (internet startups in the late 1990s, crypto assets in recent years) disrupt this process. Third, and most relevant here, is the fact that q theory assumes that firms operate in competitive industries. If firms have market power, they will not want to invest until $q = 1$. They will restrict their expansion to maintain relatively high prices, and q will stay above 1. To put it differently, a decrease in competition would show up as an increasing gap in the relationship between q and investment. This is exactly what we see in the data.

from these fixed assets. The difference between the market value and the replacement cost is the NPV of the firm. Tobin's q is the ratio of the market value to the replacement cost. If q is more than one, the firm should scale up because each additional $1 of capital expenditure is worth q dollars. Tobin's q contains a lot of information. In particular, Tobin's q captures expectations about uncertain profits in the future as well as funding costs. The funding cost is directly reflected in the market value. If there is a crisis and investors freak out, you immediately see that funding costs rise, market values tank, and so does investment. If investors are optimistic, you see the opposite.

The Growing Investment Gap

Let us put our theory to work. Figure 4.3 shows q and the investment rate. Tobin's q has been rescaled to fit on the same graph. You can see that, as predicted by the fundamental law of investment, the two series are highly correlated: they move up and down together. But you can also see that after 2000, the investment rate seems to be lower than what one would predict based on q. In fact, if we cumulate the residual difference between

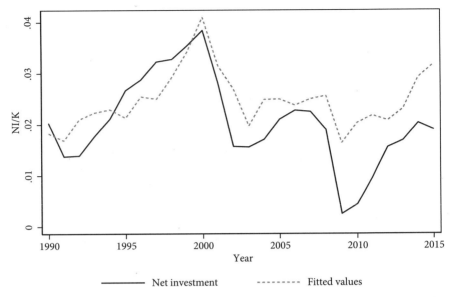

FIGURE 4.3 Tobin's *q* and investment. Tobin's *q* is the market value of nonfinancial private businesses over the replacement cost of capital. Net investment is investment minus depreciation over the replacement cost of capital. Fitted values is investment predicted by *q* at the beginning of each year. *Data source*: BEA

the investment rate and *q*, we find that, by 2015, the capital stock is about 10 percent lower than it should be.*

This fact is interesting for us because this is exactly what the decreasing competition hypothesis would predict. The reason is intuitive. When *q* is above 1 in an industry, it means that there are rents left on the table. If the industry is competitive, these rents should be competed away: either incumbents would expand (as in our example), or new firms would enter. Over time, the capital stock would increase, and *q* would decrease toward 1. On the other hand, if the industry is not competitive,

---

* Gutiérrez and Philippon (2017) test eight possible explanations for the weakness of investment, ranging from measurement errors to financial constraints, and find consistent support for only three: rising concentration in product markets (the hypothesis that domestic competition is decreasing); tightened governance and increased short-term thinking; and rising intangible capital (which itself is a complex explanation involving measurement problems, efficiency gains, and barriers to entry).

then investment would not increase as much, and q would remain above 1. If you believe that domestic competition has declined in the US economy, then you would expect a growing gap between q and investment, exactly as in Figure 4.3. Figure 4.3 supports the hypothesis that the US has experienced decreasing domestic competition.

We see a growing residual between Tobin's q and net investment in the aggregate, but we can go a lot further. As we have discussed in previous chapters, concentration has increased more in some industries than in others. If the decreasing competition hypothesis is correct, then we would expect the investment-q residual to come from concentrating industries.

Figure 4.4 shows that this is exactly what we observe. We split industries into two groups based on the evolution of their HHIs. One group includes the ten industries where HHIs have increased the most; the other group the ten industries where HHIs have increased the least (as it turns out, HHIs are roughly constant in that group). We then es-

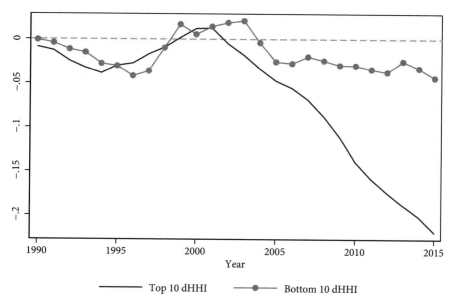

FIGURE 4.4 Concentration and investment gap. Annual data. We use the ten industries with the largest and smallest relative change in import-adjusted HHI indexes. The figure shows the cumulative implied capital gap (as percent of capital stock) for the corresponding industries (Gutiérrez and Philippon, 2017).

timate a fundamental law of investment for both groups of industries, and we compute the residuals. Figure 4.4 plots the cumulative residuals. You can see that the gap is essentially zero for nonconcentrating industries and more than 20 percent for the concentrating ones. On average, this is consistent with a 10 percent aggregate cumulative gap as argued earlier. The key point is that the aggregate gap comes entirely from concentrating industries.

Figure 4.4 is inconsistent with the basic version of the *Rise of Superstar Firms* hypothesis. The historical evidence suggests that successful firms and industries maintain high levels of investment. If concentration was a sign of efficiency, then, we would expect to see more investment in concentrating industries. Figure 4.4 shows that we observe exactly the opposite across industries.

In my work with Germán Gutiérrez, we also uncover a negative relation between concentration and investment across firms. We find that industry leaders' shares of investment and capital have decreased while their profit margins have increased. This is the opposite of what a hypothesis of superstar firms would predict. Under such a hypothesis, as leaders become more efficient, they should draw in more resources. Efficient firms typically expand by hiring more capital and more labor. In recent years, however, they have done the opposite. This is exactly what a decreasing competition hypothesis would predict. It is inconsistent with a hypothesis of superstar firms unless their investment and productivity are both badly mismeasured. Let us consider this possibility.

Intangible Investment

Our discussion so far assumes that we measure investment correctly, or at least that the quality of our measurement has not decreased over time. There are two types of investment: tangible and intangible. In Chapter 3 we noted the hypothesis of Nicolas Crouzet and Janice Eberly, that intangible investment might be partly responsible for the trends that we have discussed so far. Some firms might be really good at accumulating intangible assets. This might give them high profits and isolate them from competition.

Tangible investment is easily measured: more machines, more computers, more workers, more warehouses, more plants, more delivery vehicles. But measuring innovative investment is more difficult. Firms can invest in the development of new products and services or in the systematic improvement of existing ones. Some of these expenditures are captured under the headline "research and development." Many are not.

When we go about measuring investment, we encounter the important distinction between tangible and intangible investment. A significant share of today's capital is intangible. It includes patents, software, chemical formulas, databases, artistic value, special employee training, design, processes, and brand recognition. Intangible assets are not just about information technologies, however. Some intangible assets rely on computers—software and databases—but some are embedded in people, organizations, and brands. Intangible assets are also important in classic, "old-fashioned" manufacturing industries.

Economists are pretty good at measuring tangible investment. Tangible assets are usually purchased from another firm, as opposed to produced internally. If a firm needs a new truck, it buys it from a truck manufacturer; it does not build the truck itself. We therefore have a transaction price readily available to measure the cost of the investment. In addition, we have no difficulty in agreeing that it should be capitalized and not expensed. The purpose of the investment transaction is unambiguous: the truck is a long-lived valuable asset, so it falls clearly under the definition of investment.

Intangible investment, on the other hand, is harder to measure. Consider software. If a firm buys a piece of software, the transaction is similar to the truck example. It's clearly an investment. But if the firm pays its own employees to write the software, then it is formally a labor expense. Statistical agencies are aware of this issue, so they survey firms and construct measures of in-house software investment based on the wage bill of in-house programmers. You can easily imagine why this is not as reliable a measure when compared to an outside purchase.

The impetus for improving our measure of intangible assets came in the early 2000s from a group of economists led by Carol Corrado, Daniel Sichel, Charles Hulten, and John Haltiwanger (2005). Broadly speaking, they divided intangible assets into three categories: computerized information, innovative property, and economic competencies. Computerized information that can be correctly captured as investment includes software and database development, but some database development costs may be missing from the official data. Research and development, patents, mineral exploration, and artistic IP—all falling under the rubric of innovative property—may be captured, but some design and other product development costs may escape official notice. And such economic competencies as employee training, market research, and business processes may not be captured by the data at all.

The quality of our measure of intangible investment varies widely across categories. In the domain of economic competencies, for instance, we measure very little. It is easy to see why: these are mostly in-house efforts whose contributions to the creation of long-lived assets is ambiguous. Computerized information is usually correctly measured, but internal development is difficult to capture precisely.

The data in Table 4.1 and Figure 4.1 include both tangible and intangible investment. The decline in investment applies to the sum of the two types of investment. There has been an important shift in the composition of investment toward intangible assets and away from tangible ones. If we study the two categories separately, we see that both tangible and intangible investments have been weak in recent years, but the weakness is less severe for intangible investment.*

The data suggest that intangible investment rates have declined less than tangible investment rates since 2000. The BEA fixed asset tables show a decline in the growth rate of the intellectual property products (IPP) stock since 2000, as you can see in Figure 4.5. Between 1962 and 2000, the average growth rate of the stock of IPP capital was 6.2 percent. Between 2001 and 2016 it was only 3.9 percent. The corresponding figures for structures are 4.9 percent down to 2.9 percent, and for equipment 2.6 percent down to 0.9 percent.

Intangible investment has not declined as much as tangible investment. Moreover, researchers using broader definitions of intangible capital than the official BEA tables find even weaker declines. It is not likely, however, that this bias would overturn our results. One reason is that sta-

---

* See Haskel and Westlake (2017) for more on intangible assets.

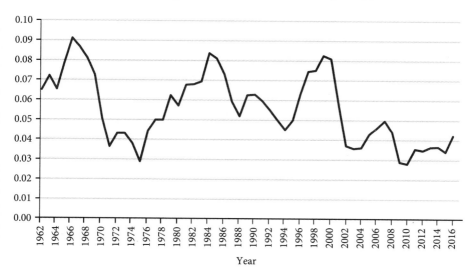

FIGURE 4.5 Growth rate of intangible capital stock: intellectual property products

tistical agencies have been improving their measurement of intangible investment over time. We certainly measure IPP capital better now than twenty years ago. Moreover, if you think that government agencies are too conservative in their treatment of intangible investment, you can choose your own definitions at the firm level. Gutiérrez and I have done that, and even using the most aggressive measures, we still find an investment gap.*

We have thus found support for the *Intangible Assets* hypothesis. There has been a shift toward intangible assets, and the investment gap is smaller for intangible investment than for tangible investment. The great boom of intangible investment, however, was during the late 1990s. In recent years, intangible investment has been weak—perhaps not as depressed as tangible investment but definitely not strong enough to pull the economy forward.

---

* This is consistent with figure 5.6 in Haskel and Westlake (2017): "it turns out that the effect of including previously unmeasured intangibles is to raise the investment/GDP ratio, but not to greatly affect its trend." They conclude that "the mismeasurement of intangible investment does not explain most of the investment problem."

Productivity

Perhaps the most direct prediction of the *Rise of Superstar Firms* hypothesis is that concentration should be linked with strong productivity growth. According to this hypothesis, concentration reflects an efficient increase in the scale of operation. A key prediction, therefore, is that concentration leads to productivity gains at the industry level, as high productivity leaders expand. This has happened before. In Chapter 2 we discussed the example of retail trade during the 1990s. The retail trade industry became substantially more concentrated *and* more productive during that decade.

But the 1990s are long gone. Are rising superstar firms the main driver of concentration over the past twenty years, as hypothesized by David Autor, David Dorn, Lawrence Katz, Christina Patterson, and John Van Reenen (2017)? To test this idea, Matias Covarrubias, Germán Gutiérrez, and I (2019) study the relationship between changes in concentration and changes in total factor productivity (TFP) across industries during the 1990s and 2000s. We use our trade-adjusted concentration measures to control for foreign competition and for exports.

Box 4.2 and its table summarize our results and discuss the interpretation of the various numbers in statistical models. We find that the relationship between concentration and productivity growth has changed over the past twenty years. During the 1990s (1989–1999) this relationship was positive. Industries with larger increases in concentration were also industries with larger productivity gains. This is no longer the case. In fact, between 2000 and 2015, we find a negative (but somewhat noisy) relationship between changes in concentration and changes in productivity.

This pattern holds for the whole economy as well as within the manufacturing sector, where we can use more granular data (NAICS level 6, a term explained in the Appendix section on industry classification). The relationship is positive and significant over the 1997–2002 period but not after. In fact, the relationship appears to be negative, albeit noisy, in the 2007–2012 period.

Box 4.2. Statistical Models

Table 4.2 presents the results of five regressions, that is, five statistical models. The right half of the table considers the whole economy; the left half focuses on the manufacturing sector.

TABLE 4.2

Regression Results

	(1)	(2)	(3)	(4)	(5)
Productivity growth	Manufacturing			Whole economy	
Years	97–02	02–07	07–12	89–99	00–15
Census CR4 growth	0.13*	0.01	−0.13		
	[0.06]	[0.05]	[0.17]		
Compustat CR4 growth				0.14*	−0.09
				[0.06]	[0.07]
Data set & granularity	NAICS-6			KLEMS	
Year fixed effects	Y	Y	Y	Y	Y
Observations	469	466	299	92	138
R^2	0.03	0.00	0.02	0.07	0.09

Notes: Log changes in TFP and in top 4 concentration. Standard errors appear in brackets below the coefficients. 97–02 means that the sample spanned 1997–2002. See Covarrubias, Gutiérrez, and Philippon (2019) for details.

Let us look at the right side and explain all the numbers: (4) means it is the fourth model. It covers the whole economy over the period 1989–1999. The coefficient 0.14 means that, over this sample, a 1 percent increase in the market share of the top four firms is associated with an increase in productivity of 0.14 percent. The number below, in brackets, is the standard error, which measures the precision of our estimate. A standard error of 0.06 for a coefficient of 0.14 means that the effect could really be anywhere between 0.08 (0.14 − 0.06) and 0.20 (0.14 + 0.06). We put a star (*) next to the coefficient when it is more than twice the standard error to signify that we are pretty confident that the coefficient is meaningfully positive. In the jargon of empirical economics, we say that the coefficient is statistically different from zero. In column 2 you see a coefficient of 0.01 with a standard error of 0.05: this means that there is no statistical connection in that sample between concentration and productivity.

The bottom of the table offers more background information, such as the data used and the number of observations. The inclusion of year fixed effects (Y = yes) means that the regression controls for any common shock that would move all the industries in the same direction in any given year. This is important because the US economy was not (and is not) static over this period: there are booms and busts, a stock market bubble, a terrorist attack, a housing bubble, and a financial crisis. We thus want to make sure that our results are driven by the comparison of industries within the US. Finally, the R^2 measures the goodness of fit of the model: 0.07 means that it captures about 7 percent of the changes we see in the data. Not surprisingly, there are many other factors that affect productivity growth beyond concentration, and it is also likely that there is quite a lot of measurement error in the data.

To summarize, the 1990s supported a hypothesis of superstar firms, but the 2000s rejected it. There is, however, one last issue to worry about: Are we measuring productivity correctly?

A popular explanation by techno-optimists for the slowdown of the economy (slowdown in productivity and investment) is that we mismeasure the free goods provided by firms like Google and Facebook, and the intangible investments that sustain them. The story rings true but the evidence suggests that it is a rather small effect. The best available research concludes that mismeasurement is unlikely to be the explanation for our current lackluster economic growth. As Chad Jones (2017) explains, "Byrne et al. (2016) and Syverson (2017) conclude that the slowdown is so large relative to the importance of the 'free' sector that mismeasurement is likely a small part of the explanation."* I would add that nothing is free. Remember the Silicon Valley adage given in Chapter 2: "If you are not paying for it, you're not the customer; you're the product being sold." We will dig deeper into the business models and growth contributions of Apple, Amazon, Google, Facebook, and Microsoft in Chapter 13.

---

* David Byrne, John G. Fernald, and Marshall B. Reinsdorf (2016) explain that "mismeasurement of IT-related goods and services also occurred before the slowdown and, on balance, there is no evidence that it has worsened." Moreover, innovations—such as free internet services—cannot explain the business sector TFP slowdown.

Nonetheless, the measurement of the digital economy is an active area of research, and we are likely to obtain better estimates in the near future. For instance, Erik Brynjolfsson and his co-authors (2019) have recently argued that properly accounting for Facebook's free services could add between 5 and 10 basis points (0.05 to 0.1 percent) to our measure of growth for the US economy.

Weak Investment and Weak Productivity

The pattern of investment and productivity growth is inconsistent with the hypothesis of rising superstar firms, which holds efficiency gains to be the root cause of increasing concentration. If concentration were reflective of increasing efficiency, then we should see more productivity growth in places where concentration increases. We saw some of it during the 1990s, but the opposite happened during the 2000s. The evolution of productivity is consistent with the investment choices that firms make. Industry leaders' shares of investment and capital have decreased, and their profit margins have increased. Given that leaders in concentrating industries do not feel the urge to invest and choose to increase their payouts to shareholders, it is hardly surprising that productivity growth is lackluster.

CHAPTER 5

The Failure of Free Entry

WE HAVE SEEN in previous chapters that, since the late 1990s, most US industries have become more concentrated, industry leaders have become more entrenched, and leaders' profit margins have increased.

But how did this concentration actually occur? Concentration comes from the equilibrium of two main forces: entry and growth of new firms versus exit and mergers of existing firms. The relationship between concentration and entry and exit can be easily explained.

We are going to study these two forces. In doing so, we will continue our analysis of antitrust, in particular of merger reviews. On the entry side, suppose n firms are created each year. On the exit side, suppose a fraction d of existing firms is destroyed each year. Now ask yourself: after the dust settles, how many firms should we observe in this economy? Or in the jargon of economics: what is the number of firms in steady state? The steady state is reached when there are as many firms entering as there are firms exiting in any given period (say, a year). Let's call N the number of active firms in steady state. For entry and exit to cancel out, we must have entry (n) equals exit ($d \times N$). Since balancing entry and exit requires $n = d \times N$, the number of firms in steady state must be $N = n/d$.

Imagine for now that all firms are the same size. Then $\text{HHI} = 1/N = d/n$. This is the simplest relationship we can envision. It says that concentration is the ratio of the exit rate over the number of entrants. An industry can become concentrated because the entry rate falls, because the exit rate increases, or both.

In the simple example above, all firms are identical and concentration only depends on the entry and exit rates. In reality, firms have different sizes and different growth rates, so concentration depends on whether young firms grow quickly and whether large firms exit. The strategy of young firms once they have grown and the type of exit (say, merger versus liquidation) also matter. Nonetheless, entry and exit are the natural forces to study first.

Entry and Exit

A wide range of measures of firms' dynamics points toward a sustained decline in business dynamism in the US. Figure 5.1 shows the entry and exit rates of establishments and firms. An establishment is a store or a factory, and firms often own several establishments, so the head counts differ.

Both entry and exit, the figure indicates, have declined. Ryan Decker, John Haltiwanger, Ron Jarmin, and Javier Miranda (2014) refer to this evolution as a decline in business dynamism. It has been particularly severe in recent years. The same authors show that declining dynamism, which appeared only in selected industries during the 1980s and 1990s, happened in all sectors during the 2000s—including the traditionally high-growth information technology sector (Decker et al., 2015).

You might qualify the importance of these trends by arguing that the nature of the entrants matters. If the decline in the entry rate is due to a decline in new "mom and pop" stores, but there is no decline in the entry

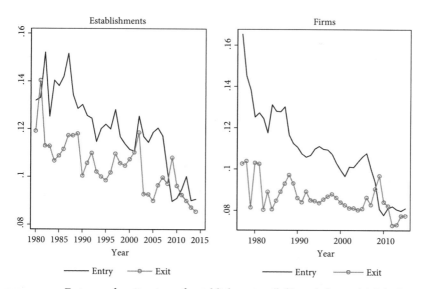

FIGURE 5.1 Entry and exit rates of establishments *(left)* and firms *(right)*. *Data source*: US Census Bureau, Business Dynamics Statistics

rate of ambitious startups, then it might not matter as much for the economy. For this reason, MIT researchers Jorge Guzman and Scott Stern argue in a 2016 paper that the decline in entry is not as bad as we might think. They point out that early-stage financing of new companies has remained strong. Their measure of entrepreneurial quality looks different from the declining entry rate in Figure 5.1. It shows a rise during the 1990s and a sharp decline after 2000, followed by some stability at a level that remains higher than before 1990.

Another factor that may dampen our pessimism is the age of successful entrepreneurs. Among the top 0.1 percent of new firms (the fastest growing out of 1,000 firms), you see that the founder is, on average, forty-five years old (Azoulay et al., 2018). The popular image of the twenty-something tech entrepreneur is not accurate. This is true even in the high-technology sectors and entrepreneurial hubs. Why is this good news? It means that an aging population does not automatically imply fewer successful new firms.

On the other hand, the number of initial public offerings (IPOs) has been low in recent years, as shown in Figure 5.2. There is still a lot of early-stage financing of new companies, but most of them get acquired instead of going public. This has important implications for competition and growth, since buying a startup can be a way for incumbents to preempt future competition. A large incumbent may want to acquire a target and shelve its products. Colleen Cunningham, from the London Business School, and Florian Ederer and Song Ma, from the Yale School of Management (2018), call this a "killer acquisition." They focus on the pre-market acquisition and development of new drugs and find significant anticompetitive effects. A drug project is less likely to be developed when it overlaps with the acquirer's portfolio of existing products, and the pattern is more pronounced when competition is already weak. This has not been the traditional focus of antitrust. Most of the existing research focuses on horizontal mergers of firms with existing products that compete in the same market and largely ignores innovation and premarket products.

To summarize, there has been a decline in both exit and entry, but the decline has been more pronounced for entry. These changes are particularly visible in the average age of establishments. Figure 5.3 shows the

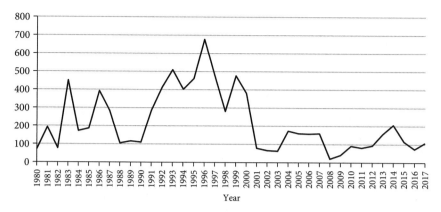

FIGURE 5.2 Number of IPOs per year, 1980–2017 (Ritter, 2019)

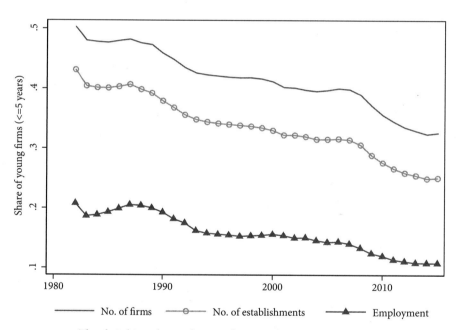

FIGURE 5.3 The shrinking share of young firms in the US economy

aging of US businesses. We define young firms as those less than five years old. In 1980, young firms accounted for half of the number of firms, 40 percent of the number of establishments, and 20 percent of employment. Today, the fractions are much smaller, and young firms employ only about 10 percent of the US workforce.

Mergers and Acquisitions

We saw from Figure 5.1 that exit in the traditional sense (closing an establishment) has actually decreased and therefore has not contributed to the increase in concentration. Mergers, on the other hand, have played a key role in the consolidation of US industries. Mergers are a particular type of exit. Establishments need not close, but the number of independent firms decreases and competition often declines. Figure 5.4 shows the number of merger deals each year from 1950 to 2016.

The increase in mergers and acquisitions (M&As) has several causes and consequences. As the *Economist* reported in March 2016, "since 2008 American firms have engaged in one of the largest rounds of mergers in their country's history, worth $10 trillion. Unlike earlier acquisitions aimed at building global empires, these mergers were largely aimed at consolidating in America, allowing the merged companies to increase their market shares and cut their costs."*

Another immediate consequence is that the number of listed firms has been shrinking (Figure 5.5). High-profile mergers typically involve public firms. The increase in the number of mergers implies a decline in the number of publicly listed companies. On a per capita basis, the US has lost half its firms in forty years. In 1976, the US had 4,943 listed companies (firms listed on US exchanges). By 2016, that number was down to 3,627. As René Stulz points out, "from 1976 to 2016, the US population increased from 219 to 324 million, so the US went from 23 listed firms per million inhabitants to 11."†

The decline in the number of listed firms starts in the late 1990s. Circa 1980, the US had about 5,000 listed firms. Listings peaked in 1997, at about 7,500 companies. Since then the number of listed firms has fallen by more than half, and the main contributor has been the large number of mergers. The decline is widespread: it happens in all industries. And, as Stultz points out, few other countries have experienced such a large decline.

That naturally raises some questions. Are there too many mergers in the US? When and why are they allowed?

---

* "Too much of a good thing," *Economist,* March 26, 2016.
† René Stultz, "The shrinking universe of public firms," *NBER Reporter* 2 (2018).

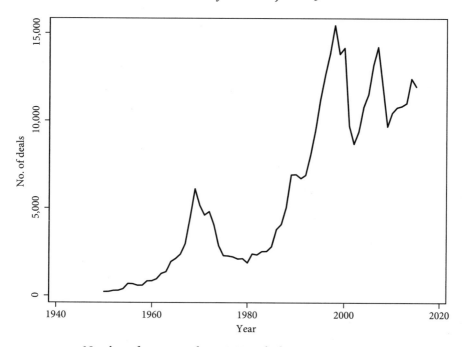

FIGURE 5.4 Number of merger and acquisition deals

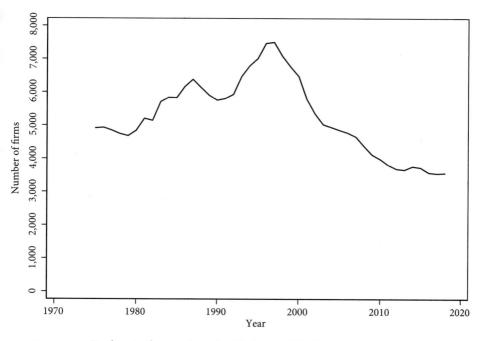

FIGURE 5.5 Decline in the number of publicly listed US firms

Merger Reviews

Mergers and acquisitions between large firms are typically reviewed by the Department of Justice (DoJ) and the Federal Trade Commission (FTC). The parties to the transaction must file forms and wait for thirty days before they can consummate their merger. Depending on the product and industry, either the FTC or the DoJ may review the filings.*
If the transaction appears to pose a threat to competition, the agencies ask for additional information ("Second Request") and extend the waiting period for twenty days.

Merger reviews build on what we call the economics of industrial organization (often simply called IO). This branch of economics allows us to understand how many firms are active in an industry and how they set prices, to predict their behavior after a merger, and to ask questions such as "is competition always good?" or "can there be too much entry?"

Industrial organization began as an intellectual discipline in France in the 1830s. Antoine Augustin Cournot was the first to formalize the behavior of a duopoly—two firms competing in the same market. The Sherman Act, motivated by the growth of large-scale businesses during the Industrial Revolution, incorporated IO into US public policy in 1890. Nearly a quarter-century later, the Clayton Act of 1914 was the first attempt to deal with anticompetitive mergers and acquisitions. It was motivated by large mergers that fell outside the purview of the Sherman Act.† The Clayton Act prohibited any company from buying the stock of

---

* The DoJ is an element of the executive branch, whereas the FTC is a commission made up of presidential appointees from both major political parties. Although their responsibilities overlap somewhat, they work cooperatively and tend to divide their attention in predictable ways. DoJ focuses on financial services, telecommunications, and agriculture. The FTC generally takes the lead in cases involving the defense industry, pharmaceuticals, and retail. State attorneys general and private lawsuits can also challenge potentially anticompetitive behavior.

† One of the most significant ways in which Section 7 of the Clayton Act changed US antitrust policy was by creating a lower standard of proof for anticompetitive effects than the Sherman Act required. Where the Sherman Act required proof that a company had been harmed by anticompetitive practices, Section 7 allowed the government to block mergers when "the trend to a lessening of

another company when "the effect of such acquisition may be substantially to lessen competition." Section 7 of the Clayton Act and the Hart-Scott-Rodino Antitrust Improvements Act of 1976 give authority to the government to review mergers and acquisitions before the merger is consummated. The legislation prohibits mergers and acquisitions that may substantially lessen competition or tend to create a monopoly.

The economic understanding of antitrust has evolved significantly over time. Early lawmakers were interventionist. Their doctrine was supported by the structure-performance-conduct paradigm of Edward Chamberlin and Joan Robinson in the 1930s. It viewed the market as a *structure* influencing the *conduct* of businesses and the *performance* of the industry. This set of ideas and principles came to be known as the Harvard School of antitrust.

The Chicago School brought a counterrevolution in the 1970s which tried to put economic efficiency at the center of antitrust policy. Robert Bork's highly influential book, *The Antitrust Paradox,* marked a shift in policy in 1978. As IO economists John Kwoka and Lawrence White (2014) explain, "the skepticism and even some hostility toward big business that characterized the initial period of antitrust have been replaced by current policy that evaluates market structure and business practices differently." For instance, an idea from the Chicago School is that high concentration does not necessarily imply market power as long as the threat of entry is real, that is, as long as the market is contestable.

These evolutions are reflected in the various vintages of the Merger Guidelines, initially developed by the DoJ's Antitrust Division in 1968. Major revisions to the guidelines took place in 1982 and 2010. The DoJ and the FTC publish the guidelines in order to make the review process fair and predictable. As we have explained in Chapter 2, the DoJ considers a market to be highly concentrated when its HHI is above 2,500. In that

---

competition in a line of commerce was still in its incipiency." Congress was forced to amend Section 7 in the 1950s to close a loophole that had allowed companies to exploit the original law's description of mergers as purchases of "stock." The amendment made companies seeking to effectively merge through asset purchases subject to the law.

case, a further increase by more than 200 points is a potential violation of antitrust regulations.

The review includes the following steps:

1. define the relevant market (product and region) and the firms that compete in it;
2. compute the Herfindahl-Hirschman Index (HHI, defined in Chapter 2);
3. assess the ease of entry by new firms;
4. assess the likely impact of the merger;
5. consider the efficiencies resulting from the merger.*

The consequences of the merger depend on its impact on the market power of the firms, which depends on the elasticity of demand, as explained in Chapter 1.

Market Power versus Efficiency

The regulation of mergers embodies a tradeoff between market power and efficiency, captured in points 4 and 5 in the list above. Even if the merger creates a threat to competition, the agencies have some discretion to determine if the efficiencies outweigh the competitive risks.

---

* To determine the relevant product market, imagine a "small but significant and non-transitory" increase in price. If such an increase would cause buyers to shift to other products and would thus be unprofitable for the monopolist, we expand the market to include the closest substitutes until we find products for which the increase would be profitable. We add next-best substitutes until there are no practicable substitutes to which the consumer may shift. At this point, the product market is defined. To define the area, if a buyer of the product could respond to the price increase by purchasing outside the area, then the area is too narrow. We expand it until we have an area where the seller could maximize profits by increasing the price.

To determine ease of entry, the agencies analyze the timeliness (less than two years to plan entry and have a significant market impact), likelihood (profitability under premerger prices), and sufficiency (adequate knowledge of the market and the financial resources to withstand supracompetitive pricing by a merged firm).

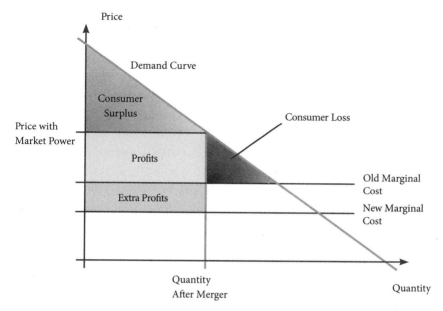

FIGURE 5.6 Merger with efficiency gain

Efficiencies include economies of scale, production spillovers, and sharing of overhead expenses.

Any merger that increases market power is bound to result in losses with regard to consumer welfare. So why would we ever allow them? Mergers are almost always motivated by claims of improved efficiency. To understand the issue, let us go back to the example we used in Chapter 2.

Figure 5.6 depicts the case of a merger with efficiency gains. Imagine that we start from a competitive equilibrium where the price equals the marginal cost, labeled "old marginal cost" in the figure (you might want to review Figure 2.1). In that initial situation, there are no profits and consumer surplus is measured by the large triangle above the price / marginal cost line. Suppose the regulator allows a merger and suppose for now that there are no efficiency gains. Market power increases, and the price goes up. Consumer surplus is reduced to the small gray triangle. Firms make profits, represented by the rectangle. The rise in profits is less than the loss in consumer surplus, and the black triangle in Figure 5.6 indicates a welfare loss for society at large.

Let us finally bring in the efficiency gains. Imagine that the merger lowers the cost of production from the old cost to a new, lower cost. This is the interesting part of the analysis. These extra profits represent efficiency gains and, unlike the previous ones, they do not come from a reduction in consumer surplus. To properly assess total welfare we need to compare the black triangle of consumer losses to the gray rectangle of extra profits. What can we say?

Not surprisingly, the conclusion of our analysis depends on two effects: the markup effect versus the efficiency effect. Suppose we start from an industry with marginal cost c and price p, and thus a markup $m = p - c$. In the figure we assumed initially that $m = 0$, but the industry might not be perfectly competitive in the first place. If we allow the merger, two things happen: the markup increases from m to m', and the marginal cost decreases from c to c'. The new price is therefore $p' = c' + m'$. There are two cases to consider:

- The win / win case: the new price is lower than the old price ($p' < p$). This happens when the increase in the markup is smaller than the efficiency gain: $m' - m < c - c'$. In that case, consumers are better off, and firms' shareholders are better off. This is clearly a good merger.
- The ambiguous case: the new price is higher than the old price despite the efficiency gain ($p' > p$). This happens when the increase in the markup is larger than the efficiency gain: $m' - m > c - c'$. In that case consumers are worse off, but shareholders are better off. The regulator needs to estimate and compare the relative impacts on consumers' surplus and new profits.

The win / win case is rare in practice. In the ambiguous case, a critical issue is what economists call the contestability of the market. If the merger creates efficiencies, this is good for the economy. If entrants can challenge the incumbent in the future, then prices will not increase much, and might even decrease if entrants can realize the same efficiency gains as the merging firms at some point in the future. In other words, the threat of entry might bring us toward a win / win, if not immediately, at least eventually. This highlights the critical role of entry, or more formally, what we call the contestability of markets.

Merger Reviews in Recent Years

There is a lively discussion regarding the role of antitrust enforcement and regulations in the evolution of US markets. On balance, however, one can make the case that merger reviews have become rather lax in the US. Bruce A. Blonigen and Justin R. Pierce (2016) find that, between 1998 and 2006, mergers between rival manufacturing firms led to higher profits without lower costs. Orley Ashenfelter and Daniel Hosken (2010) study five mergers that were close to the investigation threshold (but were not challenged) and find that four led to higher prices. John Kwoka (2015) shows that the FTC gradually reduced enforcement between 1996 and 2008. In recent years, merger enforcement actions by the FTC dropped to essentially zero in moderate-concentration industries, that is, those in which at least five competitors remain after the merger. In effect, the agency seems to have decided that five competitors are enough to ensure adequate competition in most markets.

Based on this evidence, Kwoka criticizes the weakening on merger reviews in the US over the past twenty years. This led to a sharp debate among antitrust experts.* Competition can take many forms, making IO a complicated field in economics. Moreover, as the economy develops, the variety of goods and services expands. A bit more than a century ago, Standard Oil produced a commoditized product, and the antitrust case was relatively simple. In most modern cases of antitrust, however, the product is not commoditized, and market power depends on a host of forces beyond the simple restriction of supply. In the telecom industry, for instance, competition takes place not only with prices but also with the bundling of services (phone, internet, TV) and the quality of the components.

This complexity, together with the lobbying efforts of the industry, makes it difficult for experts to agree, and I expect the debate to continue over individual cases. What is undeniable, however, is that mergers have been allowed to proceed at an unprecedented pace, which has significantly contributed to a rise in concentration in the US.

---

* Vita and Osinski (2018) offer a rebuttal, while Kwoka (2017a) maintains the validity of his original critique.

Trade Talks and Merger Reviews

Trade and competition interact in many fascinating ways. In the second half of the book we will study in detail the political economy of lobbying and campaign finance, but let's enjoy a quick preview of how foreign competition is often used to justify dubious domestic mergers. It also gives me a chance to talk about one of my favorite podcasts.

In their deliciously wonky podcast, *Trade Talks,* Soumaya Keynes and Chad P. Bown discuss economics and trade policy. In January 2018, President Trump imposed tariffs on washing machines and solar panels. The story of washing machines is fascinating, by the way, so after reading this section, I encourage you to put down this book for twenty minutes and listen to *Trade Talks* #20.

Back in the mid-2000s, two manufacturing companies—Whirlpool and Maytag—dominated the US production of washing machines with a combined market share of 60 percent. When they decided to merge, the DoJ was understandably worried. The DoJ eventually approved the deal because it thought that foreign competitors (Korean manufacturers LG and Samsung in particular) would keep market power in check. As the *New York Times* reported on March 30, 2006, "Thomas O. Barnett, the assistant attorney general for antitrust, said yesterday that foreign competitors—although they are primarily supplying more expensive machines now—can still put meaningful pressure on appliance prices. 'It's not a question of whether they will enter the U.S.,' Mr. Barnett said. 'In this case, they're quite credible given that they're already here.'"

A team of economists studied the evolution of prices in appliance markets affected by the merger (Ashenfelter, Hosken, and Weinberg, 2011). They found significant price increases for dishwashers and clothes dryers, but not for washing machines. In that last market, the competition from abroad seemed to keep prices low.

"But then, the competition from abroad that Whirlpool had relied on to get the merger approved became a little bit too tough to handle," as Soumaya Keynes explains. Whirlpool lost market share to LG and Samsung and petitioned for safeguard tariffs. When the government granted the request, the stock price of Whirlpool went up and LG announced it would raise the price of its washing machines. In April 2018, "the price of washing machines increased by 9 percent. The next month they increased by 6 percent. Both are the largest monthly price increases since the Bureau of Labor Statistics began collecting such data in 1977."* This example shows the danger of relying on foreign competition to discipline domestic firms.

The Failure of Free Entry

Let us finally combine the insights from Chapter 4 on investment with those of this chapter on entry. We have described the fundamental law of investment. When q is above 1 in an industry, it means that there are rents left on the table. If the industry is competitive, these rents should be competed away: either incumbents expand (as in our example) or new firms enter.

The fundamental law of investment therefore begets a fundamental law of entry. As industries adapt to various economic shocks, some become more profitable and some less profitable. Economic efficiency requires exit from less profitable industries and entry into more profitable ones. This naturally leads to a q-theory of entry, similar to that for investment. Just as scaling up a high-q firm generates economic value, reallocating firms from low- to high-q industries also generates value. Gutiérrez and I have studied this idea and concluded that free entry has been failing in recent years.

Figure 5.7 shows the elasticity of the number of firms to the industry-median q over the past forty years. This elasticity used to be around 0.5: when the median value of q in a particular industry increased by 0.1 (say from 1.1 to 1.2), the standardized change in the number of firms would be 5 percent higher over the following three years relative to other industries. Firms used to enter more and exit less in industries with larger values of Tobin's q, exactly as free entry would predict. In recent years, however, this elasticity has been close to zero. The decline is consistent across data sources and is stronger outside manufacturing.

What explains the failure of free entry? Several factors have probably contributed, but one is central to the theme of this book. Figure 5.8 shows the rise in federal regulations in the US along with the decline in the firm

---

* B. R. Mayes, T. Mellnik, K. Rabinowitz, and S. Tan, "Trump's trade war has started. Who's been helped and who's been hurt?" *Washington Post*, July 2018.

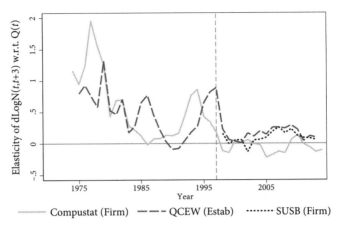

FIGURE 5.7 Declining allocation of entry to high-value industries. The figure plots the coefficient of year-by-year regressions of changes in the log-number of firms / establishments on the industry-median Tobin's q. *Data sources:* Compustat and SUSB series based on the number of firms by NAICS level 4 industry. QCEW series based on the number of establishments by SIC level 3 industry up to 1997 and NAICS level 4 industries afterward. Changes in the number of firms are standardized to have mean zero and variance of one to ensure comparability across data sources. Industry-median q is based on Compustat. See Gutiérrez and Philippon (2019b) for details.

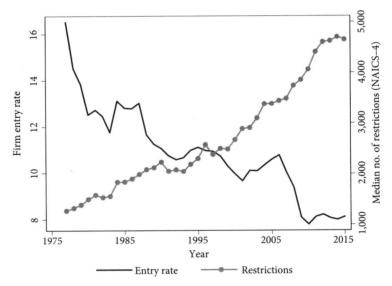

FIGURE 5.8 Regulation index and establishment birth rate. *Data sources:* Establishment entry rates from Census' Business Dynamics Statistics. Regulatory restrictions from RegData. See Gutiérrez and Philippon (2019b) for details.

entry rate. As emphasized by University of Chicago economist Steven Davis (2017), the Code of Federal Regulations has grown eightfold over the past fifty-six years and now consumes nearly 180,000 pages.

We would like to study if and how federal regulations affect industry dynamics. For that we need to build an index of regulations. How does one go about building an index of federal regulations? By using computers to read and classify the data! RegData is a relatively new database—introduced in Al-Ubaydli and McLaughlin (2017)—that aims to measure regulatory stringency at the industry level. It relies on machine learning and natural language processing techniques to count the number of restrictive words or phrases such as "shall," "must," and "may not" in each section of the Code of Federal Regulations and to assign them to industries. RegData represents a vast improvement over a simple measure of page counts.*

Figure 5.8 shows that the decline in entry coincided with the rise of entry regulations, but this does not mean that regulations caused the decline in entry. There are two fundamental theories of regulations: public interest versus public choice. Following the work of English economist Arthur Cecil Pigou (1932), the public interest theory emphasizes corrective regulations to deal with externalities and protect consumers. On the other side are public choice theorists who are suspicious of Pigou's ideas. Famed Chicago economist George Stigler (1971) argues that "as a rule, regulation is acquired by the industry and is designed and operated primarily for its benefit." In our paper, Gutiérrez and I use industry and firm-level data to dig deeper into this issue. We find that regulations drive down the entry and growth of small firms relative to large ones, particularly in industries with high lobbying expenditures. This supports public choice theory over the Pigouvian public interest theory and brings

---

* Goldschlag and Tabarrok (2018) provide a detailed discussion of the database and its limitations, including several validation analyses that, for example, compare RegData's measure of regulatory stringency to the size of relevant regulatory agencies and the employment share of lawyers in each industry. They conclude that "the relative values of the regulatory stringency index capture well the differences in regulation over time, across industries, and across agencies."

another piece of evidence to support the decreasing domestic competition hypothesis.

Concentration from the Top Down and from the Bottom Up

Two main facts emerge when we consider the shifting demographics of US businesses. First, the entry rate of new businesses has declined. Businesses are now older and face fewer new competitors each year. This has led to concentration from the bottom up. Second, agencies and judges have allowed more frequent mergers among large businesses. This has led to concentration from the top down. Together, they account for the rise in concentration that we have observed.

Free entry is a critically important rebalancing mechanism at the heart of market economies. Unfortunately, free-entry rebalancing has diminished in the US economy over the past twenty years. It's not just that fewer firms appear each year; it's also that they do not enter in high-q industries as much as they used to. It also appears that lobbying and regulations explain much of the decline in entry rates over time and across industries. At this point, we have enough evidence to suggest that the rise in profits and concentration in the US reflects a significant increase in rents, but we do not have enough evidence to quantify the harm done to consumers and workers. It's time to broaden our analysis and study what has been happening in the rest of the world.

Our focus so far has been almost exclusively on the US. I will now show you that much can be learned if we compare the US with other regions—Europe in particular.

[TWO]

THE EUROPEAN EXPERIENCE

We have analyzed the evolution of the US economy over the past twenty years. We have formulated and tested various theories. The theory of "star" firms argues that concentration reflects the increasing productivity of industry leaders. The intangible hypothesis argues that the accumulation of intangible assets explains the evolution of concentration, profits, and investment. The decreasing domestic competition theory argues that domestic competition has declined and that, in many industries, firms have been able to exploit their market power. Globalization, on the other hand, has brought foreign competition into some manufacturing industries.

Our detailed analysis of these theories has allowed us to refine our diagnosis of the US economy. We have found evidence of "star" effects during the 1990s, but not in the 2000s. The intangible hypothesis is clearly relevant for the retail and wholesale trade sectors, and globalization is a major force shaping the manufacturing sector.

The overall evidence, however, is that most industries have suffered from weak and declining domestic competition over the past twenty years. Decreasing competition has led to increasing concentration, increasing entrenchment of industry leaders, increasing profits and payouts to shareholders, decreasing investment, and decreasing productivity growth.

At this point, we would like to understand why and how this has happened. Is it because of technology? Is it because of changes in consumers' preferences? Or is it because of regulations and policy choices?

We already have a hint that policy choices are important. Lobbying and regulations predict the decline in entry rates over time and across industries, but we do not have a perfect controlled experiment. The ideal experiment would be to compare similar industries in different regulatory environments. This ideal experiment does not exist, but it turns out that we can go a long way by comparing the United States and Europe. This is what the following chapters will do.

Europe provides a striking comparison to the US, but before diving into policy differences between the US and the EU, it is useful to get one issue out of the way. I do *not* claim that Europe as a whole is doing better than the US, or even that it is doing particularly well. The rise of populism and the growing distrust of established parties and institutions are similar in the two regions. The macroeconomic architecture of the euro area is still incomplete and much less stable than that of the US. European universities still lag behind American universities—there is a reason I am writing this book in New York and not in Paris. European financial markets do not offer the same growth opportunities to ambitious new companies as American markets do. Europe also lags behind the US and China in some new technologies, most notably in artificial intelligence.

If we take a step back, however, we see that the similarities outnumber the differences, especially as far as economic development is concerned. The two economies are roughly the same size. Consumers have roughly the same tastes and buy essentially the same products. Firms use similar technologies in most industries, and identical ones in many. American and European trade patterns are also similar. Similarities in these key dimensions make the comparison between the US and Europe particularly relevant.

Finally, it is not a coincidence that the comparison of Europe and the US will prove to be rich and informative. At least since the end of World War II, European policy makers and entrepreneurs have been inspired by what they saw (and admired) in the US. As we shall discuss, several European institutions were either modeled after the corresponding American institutions or at least heavily influenced by their design.

CHAPTER 6

Meanwhile, in Europe

IN THE PREVIOUS chapters we have shown that, since 2000, US industries have become more concentrated and American firms' profit margins have increased. At the same time, investment has been weak, despite high profit margins and low funding costs. Is this a universal evolution? Is it an unavoidable consequence of globalization? Do we see the same trends in all countries?

I have just explained why there is much to learn by comparing Europe and the US. The two regions are similar enough to make the comparison meaningful but different enough to provide a fertile ground for testing our theories. So, how has Europe been doing?

Is Europe Growing?

The results that I am going to present are usually greeted with a fair amount of skepticism. Some of it is warranted—indeed, I was also skeptical at first. The US has traditionally had better economic policies than Europe. US markets were indeed the most competitive in the world for a long time. It is reasonable to remain attached to this prior assumption. We should ask for more evidence before we change our mind, and this is what we are doing in this book.

In discussing these results, however, I have noticed some unusually defensive reactions, suggesting that some people are simply unwilling to change their minds. Here's one argument I hear frequently: "If you are right, why is the US growing faster than Europe?" Well, to start with, growth obviously depends on many confounding factors. It is possible for Europe to have at the same time good antitrust and data protection policies, inefficient macroeconomic policies, and weak and badly regulated universities. As it happens, I believe all these statements to be correct.

But before we look at the details, let us pause for one second: is it even true that Europe is growing more slowly than the US?

Let us start by looking at the facts about Europe. Map 6.1 shows the groups of countries that make up Europe, including the euro area (EA19), which shares the common currency of the euro, and the European Union (EU28). The why-is-the-US-growing-faster-than-Europe argument seems to play on the idea that the EU is obviously growing more slowly than the US. Well, not so fast (pun intended). Of course, the US has faster population growth. But as we have explained in Chapter 1, what matters for our analysis is growth in living standards, or *per-capita growth*.

Figure 6.1 shows the cumulative growth of GDP per capita over the past eighteen years in the US, in Europe, and for selected European countries. In the Appendix I explain how real growth is computed. All countries' GDP per capita in 1999 are normalized to 1 in the figure, so you can read the axis as showing exactly the cumulative growth in standards of living between 1999 and 2017.

US citizens are about 21 percent richer in 2017 than they were in 1999. Let me add an important caveat here: this is an average. It does not take inequality into account, and therefore it may not represent the experience of the median American household. Still, this is the measure that people have in mind when they think about growth.

The euro area (EA19) has not done as well as the US: the average citizen in EA19 is only 19 percent richer in 2017 than in 1999. The European Union, however, has done a bit better than the US: the average citizen in EU28 is 25 percent richer than in 1999. Why? Because countries like Poland have been catching up, and countries like Sweden have done well. These averages hide a significant amount of heterogeneity inside Europe. Germany is about 25 percent richer. France is only 15 percent richer. Sadly, Italy is slightly poorer.

If we step back and look at the big picture, however, we see that the US and Europe are growing at approximately the same rate on a per-capita basis. This is exactly what standard economic theory would predict. An important but somewhat subtle point is that the decreasing domestic competition hypothesis does not predict permanent differences in growth rates but rather temporary ones. Market power has a negative impact on the level of real GDP. As markups rise, growth will slow

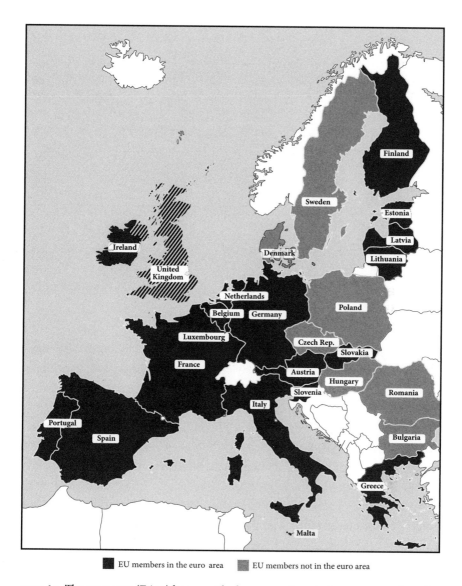

■ EU members in the euro area   ■ EU members not in the euro area

MAP 6.1 The euro area (EA19) began with eleven members in January 1999: Austria, Belgium, Finland, France, Germany, Ireland, Italy, Luxembourg, Netherlands, Portugal, and Spain. Later arrivals were Greece (2001), Slovenia (2007), Cyprus and Malta (2008), Slovakia (2009), Estonia (2011), Latvia (2014), and Lithuania (2015). Members of the European Union (EU28) share a common set of institutions (the European Commission, the European Parliament, a court of justice, and so on) and, most importantly for this book, the Single Market. Cyprus, an EA19 country, is not shown on this map. Brexit negotiations may change the UK's membership status. *Data source*: https://d-maps.com/m/europa/europemax/europemax11.pdf

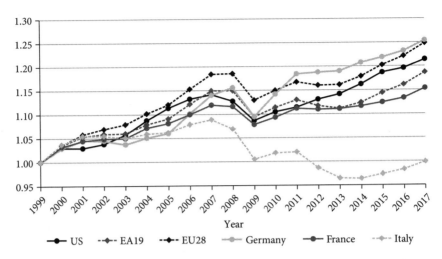

FIGURE 6.1 Cumulative growth of GDP per capita in the US, the euro area, the EU, and selected EU countries. *Source:* OECD

temporarily. If markups stay high in your country, you will be poorer than you would have been otherwise, but your country will eventually grow at about the same rate as before because long-run growth depends mostly on technological progress.

Even if one argues that the lack of competition is also bad for innovation—and indeed, I believe this is the case—that effect by itself does not predict permanent differences in growth rates between regions such as Europe and the US that trade and share ideas. In a globalized world, technology flows across countries, and the average growth rates of productivity tend to be similar among advanced economies. As a result, the long-run growth rate of GDP per capita in a particular country may not depend much on the degree of competition in that country. But when domestic competition is weak, many goods and services not exposed to foreign competition will be too expensive.

Figure 6.1, then, is consistent with the idea that the two regions use more or less the same technologies and therefore enjoy roughly the same per-capita growth rates in the long run. There are success stories (such as Germany) and growth disasters (Italy) because of specialization, comparative advantages, and policy choices. The same is true inside the US: some states grow quickly, some struggle. It is simply not true that the US is growing systematically faster than Europe on a per-capita basis.

Fundamental economic similarities in tastes and technologies make Europe a natural comparison group for the US, so let's analyze Europe in the same way we analyzed the US in Chapters 3, 4, and 5.

Profits and Concentration Are Not Rising in Europe

Figure 6.2 compares profit margins in the US and in the EU. We have seen that this is an important part of the puzzle in the US. Before 2000, the margins are lower in the US than in the EU. After 2000, we see that profit margins increase in the US, while they remain stable or decline in Europe. By the end of our sample, margins are higher in the US than in Europe.

Figure 6.3 shows the evolution of concentration in the US and in the EU over the past fifteen years. The solid line shows increasing concentration in the US. In the EU, concentration is roughly flat, although it appears as slightly decreasing in some data sets and slightly increasing in others.

There is quite a bit of work required to make sure that the data are comparable across regions.* The sample of EU countries includes only ten countries for which we have good firm-level data: Austria, Belgium, Germany, Spain, Finland, France, Great Britain, Italy, Netherlands, and Sweden. Then there is an interesting question: should we treat the EU as one market? Or as ten markets?

If we treat the EU as one market, we get the line with triangles by using one data set and with squares by using another. In these graphs, we start from EU-wide market shares, we compute HHI for each EU industry, and then we take the weighted average of these industry HHIs.

---

* We need to make sure that we have consistent industry classification and that we cover the same sample of firms in both regions. To ensure consistency, HHIs follow segmentation in the EU KLEMS database and are averaged across industries using the US share of sales in each industry and year. We use the top fifty firms in each industry. We use industry data to compute the market shares: share = firm sales / industry sales. We get industry sales from the KLEMS database and firm sales from Compustat for the US and Amadeus for Europe.

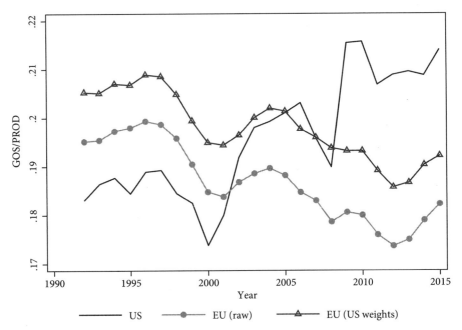

FIGURE 6.2 Profit margins in the US and EU. Shown are profit rates for the nonagriculture business sector, excluding real estate. The line with circles weighs by EU country × industry gross output. The line with triangles first aggregates across EU countries, within industries, using EU country × industry output as weights, then across EU industries using US industry output as weights. *Data source*: OECD Database for Structural Analysis (STAN)

For instance, we compute the market share of Peugeot or Volkswagen in EU car production. Then we compute EU HHI for the car industry. We do the same for the pharmaceutical industry, and so on. Then we take the average of these HHIs, weighted by the size of the industry at the EU level. We use the same process for the US.

If we treat each country as a separate market, we get the line with circles. For example, in assessing the telecom industry in France, we start from the market share of various French service providers: Orange, SFR, Free, and so on. We do the same for business services in France, and then compute French HHIs. We repeat this process for other countries and, finally, take the average across countries. Of course, the level of this measure is higher than that of the previous measures, since it is based on

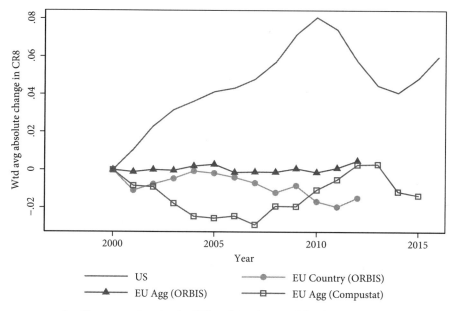

FIGURE 6.3 Concentration in the US and in the EU. The figure reports the real gross-output weighted average of absolute changes in an eight-firm concentration ratio (CR) across industries, from 2000. Country series treat each country as an independent market. Aggregate series treat the EU as a single market. To ensure consistency, all CRs follow the EU KLEMS segmentation and are averaged across industries using the US share of sales in each industry and year. CRs are adjusted for database coverage using gross output from OECD STAN. EU concentration includes Austria, Belgium, Germany, Spain, Finland, France, Great Britain, Italy, Netherlands, and Sweden. See Gutiérrez and Philippon (2018a) for details. *Data sources*: US CR, Compustat. EU CRs, consolidated financials from Compustat (squares) and unconsolidated financials from ORBIS (circles and triangles), using the data of Kalemli-Ozcan et al. (2015)

national market shares instead of EU-wide market shares. But you can see that their evolutions over time are quite similar.

Which line is the relevant one? There is no simple answer. For cars, EU-wide shares are probably more relevant. For personal services, national shares might be more relevant.

Measuring concentration in Europe is more complicated than in the US. Another data set from the OECD suggests mildly increasing concentration in Europe (Bajgar et al., 2019). They take into account that some

TABLE 6.1

Profit Margins and Profit Rates

	US			EU		
	1997–99	2013–15	Δ	1997–99	2013–15	Δ
Operating margin	9%	13%	4%	8%	7%	−1%
Operating profit rate	13%	16%	3%	9%	8%	−1%

Data source: EU KLEMS data for Nonfinancial Corporate Business Sector

firms are part of larger business groups. When they measure concentration at the business group level within two-digit industries they find a moderate increase in concentration in Europe, with the unweighted average CR8 increasing from 21.5 percent to 25.1 percent. In North America, CR8 increases from 30.3 percent to 38.4 percent. Our main conclusion— that concentration has increased in the US more than in the EU— therefore holds regardless of the measure that we use. Moreover, as EU integration progresses, we can expect more intra-Europe competition. Even if national market shares remain constant, the effective concentration is likely to decrease. This would reinforce our conclusion.

There are other data sources and definitions we can use to assess the evolution of competition. Table 6.1 summarizes some of these measures. The profit margin compares profits to sales (revenues). The profit rate compares profits to the stock of capital. These two measures increase in the US between the late 1990s to the present, while they are roughly stable in the EU.

In a paper I co-wrote with Germán Gutiérrez, we presented many more measures as well as adjustments for the cost of capital (Gutiérrez and Philippon, 2018a). In all cases, the indicators point toward an increase of concentration and profits in the US and a stability or a small decrease in the EU.

The Labor Share of Income

This discussion brings us to another controversial topic: the evolution of the labor share. The fundamental idea in economics is that firms combine labor and capital to produce goods and services. Ideas matter as

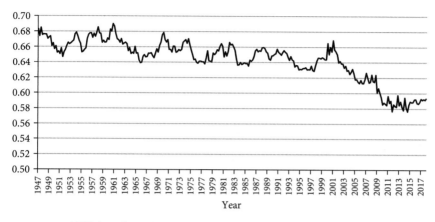

FIGURE 6.4 US labor share. *Data source:* FRED

well, of course, but they are embedded in either physical capital (patents, for instance) or in human capital (people's heads). Firms also use intermediate inputs, but we net them out when we think about value added. For instance, a coffee store needs to buy coffee beans and milk to make cappuccinos. These are intermediate inputs. The value added of the coffee store is the value of cappuccinos minus the cost of milk, coffee, and electricity. The value added is then split between the owners of the capital (machines, tables, real estate) and wages for the baristas. The ratio of wages to value added is called the labor share. If we subtract taxes, it is also 1 minus the capital share.

The labor share is the ratio of the compensation of labor relative to value added.* Over the past fifteen years, labor has lost 5 percentage points in its share of value added in the US. In Europe, by contrast, the labor share has remained roughly constant.

If we focus on the US, we can study the labor share over a long period, from 1947 to today, with consistent data. Figure 6.4 shows labor's share of the value added in the US nonfarm business sector. When we

---

* For workers on payrolls, compensation consists of their wages and salaries plus employer contributions to pension and insurance funds and to social insurance. It's more complicated for self-employed workers since their income includes returns on the business assets that they own. Their labor share is usually imputed assuming that their hourly wage is the same as for payroll employees.

teach economics, we use models in which the theoretical value of the labor share is two-thirds.* You can see why we like these models. The labor share has been fairly close to 0.66 for much of the postwar period. In the 2000s, however, it declined and stabilized around 0.6. Labor has lost about five or six points of value added since 2000.

Broadly speaking, there are two possible interpretations of this evolution. The first interpretation is that the competitive capital share has increased because capital has truly become more important in the production of goods and services. This could presumably be explained by changes in technology, including automation, or by international trade flows. If capital becomes more important, it will be compensated relatively more, and labor relatively less.

The second interpretation is that payments to capital include rents. These rents can reflect market power in the market for goods and services (*monopoly*), or in the market for labor (*monopsony*). Monopsony reflects the idea that employers have discretion in setting wages because employees have few alternatives. Monopoly rents are the ones we have discussed in previous chapters. It is not entirely obvious that monopoly rents increase the capital share. These rents can also be appropriated by key employees. The finance industry and the health care industry provide examples of this. On average, however, we expect monopoly rents to accrue disproportionately to profits, and thus to increase the capital share.

Computing labor's share of value added requires a framework for national accounts. To compute the value added we need to take a stand on what are intermediate inputs (expensed) and what are investments (capitalized). To compute the total compensation of labor we need to estimate the wages of the self-employed. All of the assumptions going into the calculations differ across countries, which makes direct international comparison difficult. Fortunately, the KLEMS database project has created comparable measures.

---

* The slight decrease from the 1950s to the 1980s comes from the decrease in self-employment and the assumption of equal wages. Other methods make the labor share even more stable. The decline after 2000 is clear in all measures. See Elsby, Hobijn, and Sahin (2013) for an excellent discussion.

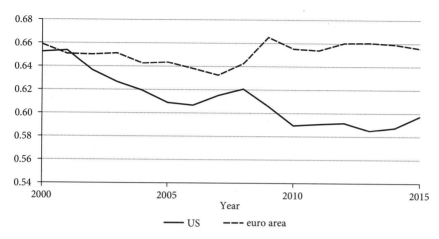

FIGURE 6.5 Labor shares for the market economy. Euro area includes eleven original countries plus Greece. *Data source*: KLEMS

Figure 6.5 compares labor shares of the market economy in the US and the euro area. The figure focuses on the last fifteen years because this is the period when we observe a large decline in the US, and also because the euro area did not really exist before 2000. Over this period, the US labor share has declined by about five points. It has not declined in Europe, however. In fact, it is exactly the same at the beginning and at the end of the sample. The rise in profits, the rise in concentration, and the decline in the labor share are thus phenomena specific to the US. Since they do not happen in Europe, and since Europe broadly uses the same technology as the US, this casts doubt on the technological interpretation. Since Europe also trades with China and other emerging markets, this casts doubt on the international trade interpretation.

Europe Is Different

Europe offers an interesting contrast to the US, casting doubt on the technology and trade explanations for rising profits. In most sectors, technologies are similar in Europe and in the US. Europe is also exposed to the same trade flows as the US. Yet, it does not have the same increase in profits, increase in concentration, and decrease in labor shares. This suggests that we need to look at explanations based on differences in policy, not in technology or external factors.

Before we do so, however, we would like to be more confident with our diagnosis. Are European markets really more competitive than US markets? When I present my results, people are usually more convinced by direct price comparisons. I think this is fair. After all, if I am right, prices should be lower in Europe. Unfortunately, comparing prices across countries is a lot more complicated than asking, say, if a bottle of Coca Cola is cheaper in Atlanta than in New York. Our next chapter, then, is all about comparing prices around the world.

CHAPTER 7

Are US Prices Too High?

ECONOMISTS SPEND of a lot of time comparing prices. We compare prices over time to estimate real growth rates. We compare prices across countries to estimate differences in living standards.

Here, we want to compare prices to see if a relative lack of competition in US markets has led to an increase in what US consumers pay for goods and services. This is a tough question. The data we are going to use are not specifically designed for this purpose. And, of course, we need a comparison group, so we are going to use Europe again.

To improve our analysis of Europe and the US, we would like to be able to directly compare the prices of goods and services in the two regions. Comparing prices across countries, however, is a lot harder than you might think. Should we expect similar goods to be sold at similar prices in different regions? In the field of economics, this is what we call the *law of one price,* or LOOP.

The LOOP says that identical goods sold in different countries must sell for the same price (when those prices are expressed in terms of the same currency and after we take into account shipping and distribution costs). Retail prices naturally depend on distribution costs. We know from the literature on international trade that distribution costs are high and that they depend on local wages (and taxes), so we need to be careful when we compare prices across countries.

Suppose that a pair of shoes costs €50 in Brussels, and that the euro / dollar exchange rate is 1.2 dollars for one euro. Then, according to the LOOP, the shoes should cost $60 in Chicago. Why would the LOOP hold? Let us think about how the law would be enforced. If the price in Chicago was more than $60, then you could buy the shoes in Brussels, ship them to Chicago, and sell them there. The profit would be the price difference minus the transportation cost and the cost of reaching customers in Chicago. You can see the issue immediately. If the transport costs are high, then that would not be profitable.

Imagine that the manufacturing cost for the shoes is €20, the shipping cost to Brussels is €5, the distribution cost is €10, and the profit margin is €15. This adds up to the price you pay in the store: $20 + 5 + 10 + 15 = €50$ in Brussels.

Now imagine that the transport cost to Chicago is $6, the distribution cost is $15, and the profit margin is $18. The manufacturing cost is $24, as before. The cost of the shoes in the store in Chicago is thus $24 + 6 + 15 + 18 = \$63$.

You can see that the retail price of a good has four components: one is the manufacturing cost, for which the LOOP should hold. The other components are transport costs, distribution costs, and profit margins. In our example, the price in the US is higher by $3 because the retail cost is $3 higher, but the profit margin is the same, since at an exchange rate of $1.2 per euro, $18 = €15. In this case the higher cost in the United States reflects distribution costs instead of higher markups.

Of Haircuts and Ferraris

Comparing prices around the world is complicated for two reasons. One reason is practical, the other theoretical. In the Introduction, we discussed the relative prices of cell phone plans and broadband internet between the US and Europe. In doing so we relied on detailed work by industry specialists who worked hard to compare equivalent contracts in various countries. It is not easy to replicate such an analysis for a broad basket of goods and services. That is the practical issue.

But there is another, deeper—and more interesting—issue. If I told you that haircuts cost more in the US than in Cambodia, you would not think that this has anything to do with oligopoly rents in the US. And you would be right. The cost of a haircut basically depends on the wages of hairdressers. According to United Bank of Switzerland (UBS) analysts, who used data from 2015, haircuts for women cost $95.04 in Oslo, Norway; $83.97 in Geneva, Switzerland, but only $4.63 in Jakarta, Indonesia, and $9.27 in Beijing, China. Hairdressers are paid more in rich countries. Hence, haircuts cost more in rich countries than in poor countries. That's pretty obvious, but it has deep implications, as we shall see. It even has a name: the *Balassa-Samuelson effect,* after Hungarian economist Béla Balassa and Nobel Prize winner Paul Samuelson, who described the phenomenon in the 1960s.

Let us now think about the other extreme of the market: luxury goods that are built in one place and shipped around the world, such as luxury cars. All the Ferraris sold around the world are assembled in Italy. And they are so expensive that pure local distribution costs are a relatively small fraction of the ultimate price tag. On the other hand, Ferrari prices are impacted by transportation costs, taxes, and marketing decisions.

The MSRP of a baseline Ferrari 488 GTB in the US is $252,800. The same car costs about €226,039 in France, which in August 2018 was about $262,380, but some taxes are included in France and not in the US. Broadly speaking, then, we can say that the prices are similar, even though the US has a higher per-capita income than France. The 488 GTB also costs about the same in Prague as in Paris, even though per-capita GDP in the Czech Republic is 40 percent lower than in France. This is consistent with basic economic theory. Ferraris are traded goods, and their cost does not depend much on where they are sold. So we can expect to see about the same prices in Prague and in New York City.

Perhaps surprisingly, however, the same car would cost more than twice as much in China, about $550,000. Why? China imposes import duties and complicated taxes. For instance, China imposes higher taxes on cars with an engine capacity of more than four liters (engines mostly found in high-end luxury cars . . . and US gas guzzlers). Probably not by coincidence, the engine of the new 488 GTB is 3.9 liters, just below the four-liter threshold. One has to take these details into account to obtain an accurate comparison of prices. Even after we adjust for taxes, however, prices of Ferraris and other high-end luxury cars are much higher in China than in the US or Europe. The common explanation is that Chinese buyers are more willing to spend large amounts of money on exclusive cars than buyers in Europe or in the US because the effect of owning a status symbol is stronger. In our economic framework, we would say that wealthy Chinese buyers have a high willingness to pay and a low elasticity of substitution. Therefore, as economic theory would predict, markups are high. That's Econ 101, exactly as in Chapter 1, but what is surprising is the sheer magnitude of the difference.

Let us keep these two examples in mind when we compare prices around the world. It is quite clear that the price of a haircut has a lot to do with average local wages, and that the price of a Ferrari has almost nothing to do with local wages or GDP per capita. Most goods and services fall in between these two extreme examples: they are part haircuts and part Ferraris.

Are You Big Mac Richer, PPP Richer, or Market Rate Richer?

Prices matter a lot in economics. In a sense, economics is really the science of figuring out equilibrium prices. In general, the higher the price of something, the less of it one would want to buy. That's what we call a *demand curve*. But that assumes a degree of consumer choice, meaning that the buyer is free to choose to consume less, or to substitute a different good for the one in question. If a consumer does not have access to alternative products and cannot meaningfully reduce her consumption—say on basic staples like food and shelter—then higher prices create higher poverty. In general, higher prices have two effects: they lead to lower demand and to lower standards of living.

As it turns out, however, even seemingly concrete concepts like "getting richer" or "getting poorer" have very different meanings, depending on context.

To compare incomes around the world, we need to convert them from local currencies into a common currency, using either foreign exchange market rates (FOREX) or purchasing power parity exchange rates (PPP). The FOREX exchange rate is the one that you read about in the newspapers or online. It is the rate that says, for instance, that 1 euro equals 1.2 dollars. The PPP exchange rates are more complicated and more interesting. PPP rates are defined in such a way that one unit of currency can purchase the same amount of goods and services everywhere.

Let us illustrate the idea with an example. Pierre is from Bordeaux and earns €50,000 per year. Karen is from Boston and earns $70,000 per year. Who is richer? It depends on their consumption baskets. Suppose they both spend one year living in the Azores. Pierre's income in the

Azores is €50,000. Karen's $70k is worth 70k / 1.2 = €58,333. In the Azores, Karen is clearly richer.

We can compare GDP per capital around the world by converting all incomes into a common currency using FOREX rates. For instance, US GDP per capita in 2017 was about $53,130. France GDP per capita in 2017 was €35,400. Suppose the euro trades at $1.2. France's GDP per capita at market rate was therefore $42,480. In that sense, French people are only 80 percent as rich as American people. That is a good measure of how they would feel as tourists in the same foreign country.

But is that the right way to think about their relative standards of living? It only makes sense to compare people's income at market exchange rates if they live in the same place. If they live in different places instead, we need to consider the fact that they have different *needs* (think of heating costs in Anchorage versus San Juan) and that they face different *local* prices. If Pierre lives in France, he pays $35 per month for his broadband internet connection, and Karen pays $80 per month in the US. With his income, Pierre can buy more internet access than Karen. In that sense, we would say Pierre is richer.

A more useful way to assess who is richer, then, would be to compute income at purchasing power parity (PPP) rates, i.e., income divided by the price of a common set of goods and services. This is easier said than done, as you can imagine. For a start, Pierre and Karen consume many goods and services, not just goods and services accessed on the internet. When we make international comparisons of real income, we need to look at the prices of the items that people actually consume. So how do we proceed?

The first thing we can do is to focus on items that everyone consumes— or at least, that are sold everywhere. In 1986, the *Economist* invented the Big Mac index. It was half a joke and half an attempt to make the theory of PPP more digestible (pun intended). They went around the world and collected prices of the same McDonald's sandwich.

This may seem frivolous, but it is actually quite useful, because McDonald's requires a large degree of consistency in its products, regardless of where they are made and sold. That means all the inputs that go into a Big Mac are virtually identical, whether it's made in Paris or Paducah.

TABLE 7.1

FOREX Rates, Big Mac Prices, and ICP PPP Rates

Year	Market exchange rate €1 = $x	Local price of Big Mac EA19	Local price of Big Mac US	PPP exchange rates, €1 = $x Big Mac	PPP exchange rates, €1 = $x ICP
2000	$0.92	€2.56	$2.51	$0.98	$1.16
2001	$0.89	€2.57	$2.54	$0.99	$1.16
2002	$0.94	€2.67	$2.49	$0.93	$1.17
2003	$1.13	€2.71	$2.71	$1.00	$1.16
2004	$1.24	€2.74	$2.90	$1.06	$1.17
2005	$1.24	€2.92	$3.06	$1.05	$1.17
2006	$1.25	€2.93	$3.15	$1.08	$1.21
2007	$1.37	€3.06	$3.41	$1.11	$1.22
2008	$1.46	€3.37	$3.57	$1.06	$1.24
2009	$1.39	€3.31	$3.57	$1.08	$1.26
2010	$1.32	€3.38	$3.73	$1.10	$1.26
2011	$1.39	€3.44	$4.06	$1.18	$1.28
2012	$1.28	€3.58	$4.33	$1.21	$1.29
2013	$1.33	€3.62	$4.56	$1.26	$1.32
2014	$1.33	€3.68	$4.79	$1.30	$1.33
2015	$1.11	€3.70	$4.79	$1.29	$1.32
2016	$1.11	€3.82	$5.04	$1.32	$1.33
2017	$1.13	€3.91	$5.30	$1.36	$1.33

Source: Economist, OECD

Table 7.1 shows you the Big Mac prices for the US and the euro area. In 2003, a Big Mac cost €2.71 (on average) in the EA19 and $2.71 in the US. Clearly, in terms of Big Macs, the euro and the dollar had the same purchasing power. We would say that the purchasing power parity (PPP) Big Mac exchange rate was $1 per euro. However, in that same year, the currency markets valued the euro at $1.13. In that sense, the euro as a financial asset looked a bit expensive, or "overvalued" as we would say in the language of international economics.

You might reasonably object that the Big Mac index is too narrow. People (thankfully) do not consume only Big Macs. Economists have built other indexes that attempt to do something similar on a larger scale.

The United Nations, together with the University of Pennsylvania, established the International Comparisons Program (ICP) in 1968. The goal of the ICP is to facilitate price comparisons across countries.* They conduct global surveys of prices (in about 150 countries and for 1,000 products) to compute their estimate of PPP exchange rates. In 2003, the ICP PPP was $1.16 per euro. Using this measure, the financial value of the euro ($1.13 in 2003) was about right, even a bit cheap.

In 2007, ICP PPP was $1.22 per euro. Big Mac PPP was only $1.11, and the nominal exchange rate was $1.37. Clearly, these three indexes evolve somewhat independently. The correlations between these three exchange rates reveal an interesting pattern, however.

The two PPP measures—Big Mac and ICP—are both trending up, meaning that, in general, the same amount of money buys more in Europe than it does in the US. The trend is steeper and bumpier for the Big Mac PPP, as one would expect since it is based on only one local good. Still, I would argue that both PPP rates tell roughly the same story.

On the other hand, the market exchange rate has a weak correlation with either PPP exchange rate of only about 0.38. Clearly, the forces that pin down the euro / dollar rate on the FOREX market are different from those that influence the price of the typical consumer's basket.† FOREX prices are much more influenced by financial conditions, interest rates, risk appetites, and so on. Given our long-term perspective and our focus on the real economy, PPP exchange rates are clearly more relevant for our analysis.

---

* The program collects price data for specific goods and then defines an aggregation methodology for each country. For the OECD and the rest of Europe, data for specific goods are collected every three years, and results were reported for 2005, 2008, 2011, and 2014. The level of detail available publicly is at the aggregate good level, which includes, for example, bread and cereals, milk, nonalcoholic beverages, transport, and so on.

† Which method should we use: PPP or market rates? It depends on the issue at hand. Financial flows should clearly be measured at market rates. Economic growth, human development, and poverty are more often assessed at PPP rates. The main drawback of PPP is that it is difficult to measure and is not readily available in real time.

Prices, Marginal Costs, and Markups

Figure 7.1 shows that prices have been going up faster in the US than in Europe over the past eighteen years. ICP PPP went from $1.16 to $1.33, so prices went up by 15 percent more in the US than in Europe over this period. Why?

As we have discussed, we can think of the price of a good as a markup over its production cost:

$$Price = (1 + markup) \times MC$$

MC is the *marginal cost*—the cost of the last unit of production. The marginal cost depends on the cost of labor (higher wages = higher costs) and on productivity (higher productivity = lower costs). The price can also depend on taxes and other input costs beyond labor, such as energy and raw materials. Can higher prices in the US be explained by a combination of the following forces?

- Wages have increased more in the US;
- Markups have increased more in the US;
- Productivity growth has been faster in Europe;
- Taxes or energy costs have decreased more in Europe.

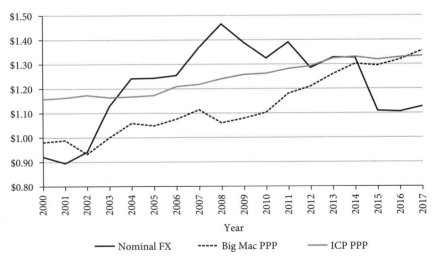

FIGURE 7.1 Nominal euro / dollar exchange rates

I am going to ignore the last explanation for its implausibility. Taxes have certainly not decreased in Europe relative to the US over this period. With respect to energy, the US has benefited from the boom in shale gas extraction, so its internal energy costs must have decreased relative to Europe. And since the nominal exchange rate is the same today as in 2012, oil import prices cannot explain the difference.

Productivity raises a more complex set of issues. In theory, it is clearly better to control for productivity differences. But productivity is hard to measure and requires a host of auxiliary assumptions, so there is the risk of adding noise or even biases if the measurement errors in productivity and prices are not independent.

Fortunately, it turns out that the results hold with or without controlling for productivity. To some extent, this reflects the fact that measures of GDP per capita follow rather similar trends. If anything, the US has done little better than the euro area over the past twenty years in terms of productivity growth. Controlling for productivity therefore only reinforces my point.

We can construct a measure of marginal costs with wages controlling for productivity. This is what economists call *unit labor costs* (ULC), as defined in Box 7.1. Let us compare the evolution of markups in the US and in Europe. Box 7.1 explains how to construct a measure of the change in the markup between year 2000 and any year t afterward for any country i: $DM_{i,t}$. Now we want to compare the *relative* evolution of markups between Europe and the US, so we simply compute the difference:

$$RDM_{i,t} = DM_{i,t} - DM_{US,t}$$

The solid gray line in Figure 7.2 shows the weighted average of $RDM_{i,t}$ across the ten main EU countries for which we can also compute measures of concentration. The line with circles shows the average change in the CR4 (remember, that's the market share of the four largest firms in an industry) in the same EU countries, relative to the US. Over the same period, CR4 has increased by 5 percentage points in the US relative to the EU. In practice, as we saw earlier, concentration has remained constant in Europe but has increased by about 5 points in the US.

Box 7.1. Unit Labor Costs and Markups

Unit labor costs (*ULC*) measure the average cost of labor per unit of output. We compute them as the ratio of total labor costs to real output. In other words, the unit labor cost is:

$$ULC = WL / Y$$

In that equation, Y is real output and WL measures total labor costs. By definition, WL is the product of the average wage (W) times the amount of labor employed (L), which can be proxied either by the number of employees or by the total number of hours worked.

Equivalently, we can think of the unit labor cost as the wage relative to the productivity of labor. We define labor productivity (*LP*) as output per worker (or per hour):

$$LP = Y / L$$

Using this alternative definition, the unit labor cost is also the cost of one unit of labor (the wage) divided by the productivity of that unit of labor. The unit labor cost in country i at time t is then:

$$ULC_{i,t} = W_{i,t} / LP_{i,t}$$

We can define the logarithm of the markup of prices over unit labor costs as

$$M_{i,t} = \log(P_{i,t}) - \log(ULC_{i,t})$$

Differences in the accounting between countries can create persistent differences between measured prices and wages. We can remove these differences by considering the difference from a base year, which we call time 0, set here to the year 2000:

$$DM_{i,t} = M_{i,t} - M_{i,0}$$

$DM_{i,t}$ then gives us the evolution of markups in country i over time.

You can see that markups have decreased by about 14 percent in Europe relative to the US. Remember that the total increase in relative US prices was 15 percent, and the increase in relative wages about 7 percent, so the price / wage markup has increased by about 8 percent more in the

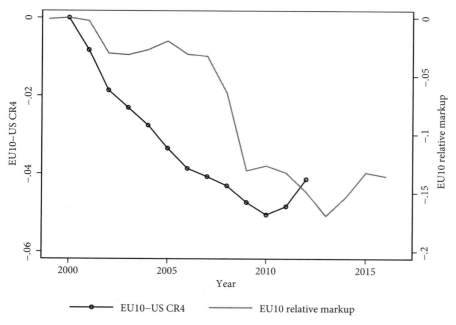

FIGURE 7.2 Markup and concentration in Europe versus the US

US than in Europe. How do we get a 14 percent markup increase? In the industry data that we use for the benchmark, productivity rises by 6 percent more in the US than in Europe. In theory, higher productivity should have led to either lower prices or higher wages in the US. It did not, so that implies an even higher markup of 8 percent + 6 percent = 14 percent. As I have explained above, measuring productivity is tricky, and we need to treat this 6 percent number with a (large) grain of salt. But even if we ignore it entirely, we would still get a relative increase in US markups of about 8 percent.

Figure 7.2 is what we call *time series evidence*: we consider the evolution of two series of data over time. We see concentration going down in Europe relative to the US, and then we see European markups decrease relative to American markups.

Is this a smoking gun? Yes and no. It is pretty convincing because this is direct evidence that prices have increased more in the US than in the EU for the same goods and services. On the other hand, the correlation between markups and concentration might be a coincidence. It's not likely, but it is possible. In a sense, the time series contain only one observation. To have a smoking gun we would have to be sure that nothing was contributing to the disparity in the price/wage markup numbers and concentration at the same time. Given the complexities of these two economies, it is difficult to effectively exclude all other potential explanations.

To gain confidence in our diagnosis, we would like to see this pattern repeated in different samples. We can look inside Europe and ask if we see the same pattern across countries and time periods. Is it true that the change in concentration predicts the change in markups across years and across countries? To run this test, we have what we call a panel data set. It contains data for ten countries over sixteen years. This means we can compare Germany and Italy in a given year, or we can compare Germany to itself a few years earlier. If our theory is correct, we would expect a positive relationship between concentration and markups across time and space. In our work, Gutiérrez and I (2018a) find that this is indeed the case.

We can go even further using the data we have at the country, industry, and year levels. We can use relatively advanced statistical models with our panel data. We can ask if concentration explains markups controlling for broad changes at the country level or for changes in global technology at the industry level. In all cases, there is a strong positive correlation between changes in concentration and future changes in prices.

Finally, it is worth highlighting some interesting differences across European countries. The only country where we do not see a decrease in the markup is Italy. This is interesting because we know that the Italian economy has performed poorly over this period. This supports the idea that improving competition in the market for goods and services is important to macroeconomic performance.

Yes, US Prices Are Too High

Prices in the United States have increased 15 percent more than prices in Europe, but wages have increased only about 7 percent more than in Europe. Half of the relative price increase in the US comes from increasing markups. Moreover, we see that markups are systematically related, over time and across countries and industries, to the changes in concentration. The evidence strongly suggests that increasing concentration in the US is responsible for an excessive increase in prices by at least 8 percent over the past seventeen years.

That is a big deal. Workers who do not own stock are 8 percent poorer than they should be. And that is not the end of the story; there are indirect effects as well. Higher markups reduce investment and therefore reduce the capital stock. With less capital, the economy is less productive. When we simulate the path of the US economy since 1990 (Gutiérrez, Jones, and Philippon, 2019), we find that aggregate consumption would be significantly higher today if competition had remained at levels found in 2000.

What happened? Why have US policy makers let concentration increase so much?

In the next part of this book, we will show that the changes come from different policy choices in terms of regulations, barriers to entry, and antitrust. But first there is more we can learn from Europe. We need to discuss what is perhaps the most surprising result in this book: how did European markets become more competitive than American markets?

CHAPTER 8

How European Markets Became Free

> The problem was to break up excessive concentrations in the coal and
> steel industries of the Ruhr . . . The Americans had been the first to
> tackle the problem, many months earlier. Their economic and po-
> litical philosophy would not tolerate either the practice or the ap-
> paratus of domination, at home or abroad.
>
> JEAN MONNET, *MEMOIRS* (1978)

THE UNITED STATES invented modern antitrust laws in the late nineteenth century. It deregulated many of its industries in the early 1980s
and has been the champion of free markets ever since, to the great benefit of American consumers. The American free-market doctrine spread
globally and, by the 1990s, a broad international consensus had emerged
among policy makers in favor of US-style regulations for most markets.
This was particularly true in Europe. The US retained its head start, however, and it had a longer history of independent enforcement. Given
these initial conditions, one would have predicted that US markets would
remain more competitive than European markets.

But then something totally unexpected happened. Starting around
2000, profit rates and concentration ratios increased in the US but remained stable or decreased in Europe. Prices relative to wages increased
by 8 percent more in the US than in Europe despite similar productivity
growth. As US markets experienced a continuous decline in competition,
European markets did not. Today many European markets appear to be
more competitive than their American counterparts.

How did that happen? How did Europe, of all places, become the land
of free markets? Throughout its history, continental Europe often chose

state intervention over private competition. What has changed over the past twenty years to convince Europeans to embrace free markets?

The Freeing of European Markets

European policy makers seem to have heeded the warning of economists Alberto Alesina and Francesco Giavazzi in 2006: "If Europe is to arrest its decline . . . it needs to adopt something closer to the American free-market model." The European Union has streamlined its regulations to encourage entry and competition in many markets. Many indicators highlight these improvements, but let's first consider the ease of opening a business. Figure 8.1 shows that the number of days required to start a business in the EU has steadily decreased and converged toward the US number.

For example, it took fifteen procedures and fifty-three days to begin operating legally in France in 1999, versus three procedures and three days in New Zealand (Djankov et al., 2002). In 2016, it took only four days to start a business in France and one day in New Zealand. Over the same period, however, the entry delay in the US went up from four days to six days. In other words, opening a business used to be much faster in the US than in France, but it is now somewhat slower.

This is not an isolated indicator. The OECD compiles a measure of regulation called *product market regulation* (PMR) *indexes.** Figure 8.2 shows the various vintages of PMR indexes for EU countries and the US. In 1998, every EU country except the UK had more regulations than the US; in 2013, every EU country except Greece and Poland had *fewer* entry regulations than the US.

There is a deep irony to this story. The idea that free and competitive markets work best is supported by much empirical evidence, and

---

* PMR indicators are internationally comparable. They measure policies that promote or inhibit competition such as: state control of business enterprises; legal and administrative barriers to entrepreneurship; barriers to international trade and investment. The indicators are available for thirty-four OECD countries in (or around) 1998, 2003, 2008, and 2013, and in another twenty-two non-OECD countries in 2013.

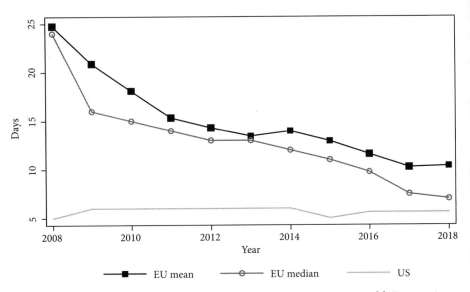

FIGURE 8.1 Number of days to start a business. *Data source:* World Economic Forum

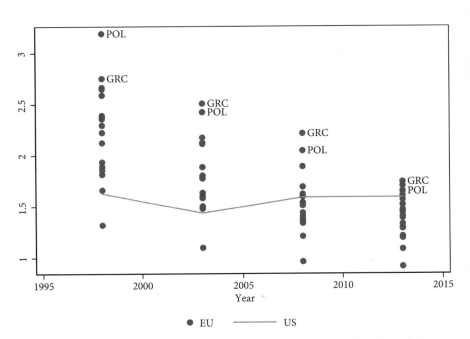

FIGURE 8.2 Product market regulation index. GRC = Greece; POL = Poland. *Data source*: OECD

economists spread the gospel of free markets in large part because it had proven so successful in America. In their highly influential paper, Simeon Djankov, Rafael La Porta, Florencio Lopez-de-Silanes, and Andrei Shleifer (2002) find that the regulation of entry is associated with higher levels of corruption, and that countries with more open and accountable political systems regulate entry less. Multilateral agencies such as the World Bank and the OECD provided similar advice around the world. In 1999, the OECD noted that the "United States has been a world leader in regulatory reform for a quarter century. Its reforms and their results helped launch a global reform movement that has brought benefits to many millions of people."

The irony is that Europe heeded this advice just as the US was starting to forget its own history of free markets. Note that I am referring to the markets for goods and services. I am not discussing labor market regulations, tax policy, or public spending. This is a deliberate choice. The theory I am going to present in this chapter explains why the EU project has an outsized influence on the market for goods and services, but has little effect on other markets. I am not arguing that the EU has become more competitive than the US in other areas. The US has better universities and a stronger ecosystem for innovation, from venture capital to technological expertise.

Despite these caveats, my view is very much at odds with the common caricature of the EU as an overreaching bureaucratic beast. This view is sometimes true, but more often than not, it is a reflection of ignorance and laziness on the part of commentators. If you have nothing interesting or relevant to say, you can always take a jab at European bureaucrats. It's the political equivalent of complaining about the weather: fundamentally useless, but substantive enough to hide an embarrassing void of interesting ideas.

What is true, of course, is that EU policy documents are a reader's nightmare. Policy makers in all countries have a terrible habit of coming up with pompous titles for everything they do, and the EU is no exception. In EU documents, the most basic idea is usually depicted as a grand, three-pronged strategy. It is annoying and painful to read, but it should not distract us from the fact that many of these initiatives are well-intentioned, and some are even successful. Technocratic jargon in Brussels might be unbearable, but one should not dismiss a child simply because her parents gave her an ugly name.

Let us try and understand how competitive markets came to be such an important feature of the European integration. We will discover that the fight against market dominance has been part of the DNA of the European project from the very beginning.

Churchill versus Monnet: A Brief History of the European Union

The history of the EU is fascinating but often misunderstood, especially in America. If you remember only one thing from this chapter, let it be this: the EU was founded on the ideas of a Frenchman who admired British and American institutions and who, above all, wanted to get things done.

The project of a unified Europe grew out of the ashes of World War II, and economics played an important role from the beginning. For deep historical reasons, the entire EU machine of economic regulations aimed to eliminate economic nationalism and excessive market dominance.

To understand the process of European integration, we first need to travel back to 1914 in order to understand the process of European *dis*integration. World War I was a European civil war, a tragedy of unprecedented scale. Europe had always been a continent of wars. French president François Mitterrand joked, when he gave his last address to the European Parliament in 1995, that throughout its long history, France had fought every single European country except Denmark.* But World War I was worse than any war the world had seen until then. Europeans sleepwalked into civilizational suicide.† The American Civil War had already demonstrated the destructive power of industrial-age weapons, but few understood just how terrible these weapons could be. World War I put

---

* This is the famous speech of January 1995 in which he said, "Le nationalisme, c'est la guerre." (Nationalism is war.) He would repeat the statement in his last speech as president four months later in Berlin.
† I am paraphrasing Christopher Clark's brilliant book, *The Sleepwalkers: How Europe Went to War in 1914* (London: Allen Lane, 2012).

them on full display for the first time. The scale of the destruction, the decimation of an entire generation of young men, and the massacre of civilian populations created a demand for lasting peace in Europe. French soldiers returning from World War I coined the phrase "La Der des Ders" (the last of the last), which expressed the hope of an end to wars in Europe.

It almost happened. US President Woodrow Wilson was the first to propose a League of Nations as part of his Fourteen Points plan for an equitable peace in Europe. The League of Nations came to be, but the US was never a member because many citizens and members of Congress wanted to keep America out of European affairs. Many German immigrants living in the US opposed the Treaty of Versailles, the acceptance of which was necessary for membership in the League.

Europeans tried to keep Wilson's idea alive despite the lack of American support. French foreign minister Aristide Briand proposed a unification of Europe in a speech at the League of Nations on September 5, 1929. His plan aimed at industrial cooperation and protection against the Soviet threat from the East. Unfortunately, German foreign minister Gustav Stresemann, the main supporter of the plan in Germany, died a month later, and the Great Depression soon plunged the world—and Germany in particular—into economic chaos.

Briand's plan had failed, and it would take another world war with an even greater death toll, including the highest death toll from genocide in history, before Europe could finally agree on a peaceful union.* The devastations of World War II, together with the increasing threat of encroachment by the Soviet Union, created powerful political pressures for unity in Europe. Shortly after World War II there were several visions of what a unified Europe might look like. At the risk of oversimplifying, let's call them the Churchill view and the Monnet view.

In September 1946, Sir Winston Churchill, twice prime minister of the UK, argued that Europeans "must build a kind of United States of Europe. In this way only will hundreds of millions of toilers be able to

---

* The estimated death toll for World War I is 10 million military and 8 million civilian deaths. For World War II, 22 million military and 50 million civilian deaths.

regain the simple joys and hopes which make life worth living."* Churchill
had a geopolitical perspective on the European project. Like most leaders
at the time, he was concerned with peace and security. He wanted a reconciliation between France and Germany. He always viewed the role of
the UK as outside of a unified Europe, not inside. In 1930 he explained, "We
see nothing but good and hope in a richer, freer, more contented European commonality. But we have our own dream and our own task. We
are with Europe, but not of it. We are linked but not compromised. We
are interested and associated but not absorbed." We can only wonder how
he would have analyzed the Brexit debate.

Churchill's vision was grand, but it had little to do with how the EU
was actually built. The spiritual father of the EU was a less well-known
and less charismatic figure, a Frenchman named Jean Monnet. Monnet's
vision focused on economic and industrial cooperation. Monnet was a
fascinating character and immensely influential as an adviser to the
French and other European governments, but he never ran for office. The
New York Times wrote in its obituary, "in many respects Mr. Monnet
could be readily identified as a Frenchman. Spruce, well-groomed and
with a neat, close-cropped mustache, he talked logically and precisely.
But in other ways he was un-French, for he admired (and practiced)
British and American pragmatism and scorned parochialism and po-
litical narrowness." Monnet did not oppose the political union that
Churchill alluded to, but he focused on more tractable economic issues.
He was convinced that "once a Common Market interest has been created, then political union will come naturally."†

Monnet's admiration for British and American institutions and prag-
matic attitude were reflected in his proposal for European integration,
which came to be known as the Schuman Plan. Robert Schuman was the
French foreign minister from 1948 to 1952. The Schuman Declaration of
1950 was a milestone in Franco-German cooperation and led to the creation of the European Coal and Steel Community, which later became
the Common Market.

---

* Speech at the University of Zurich, Switzerland, on September 19, 1946.
† "Jean Monnet, 90, architect of European unity, dies," *New York Times,* March 17,
1979. Monnet died on March 16.

Movement toward political unity soon followed. In 1963 Konrad Adenauer, the first chancellor of West Germany, and French president Charles de Gaulle signed a historic treaty of friendship between the two countries. Adenauer was committed to postwar reconciliation with France. Political visions matter, but to understand the EU, one must keep in mind that economic integration came first. It is not because economics is more important, but because economic solutions can be used to create incentives for peace and cooperation.

The Fight against Market Dominance

The US established the parameters for modern antitrust law with the Sherman Act of 1890, which was motivated by the growth of large-scale businesses during the Industrial Revolution, and the Clayton Act of 1914, which dealt with anticompetitive mergers and acquisitions.

The history of EU antitrust law is more recent and uncertain, but the fight against market dominance has been at the core of EU policies from the very beginning. In *Memoirs* (1978), Jean Monnet recalled that "In a note written for the Committee of National Liberation in Algiers on August 5, 1943, I had said: There will be no peace in Europe if States re-establish themselves on the basis of national sovereignty, with all that this implies by way of prestige policies and economic protectionism." In exile in Algeria in the middle of World War II, he knew that the postwar order should fight against "economic protectionism." He was thinking of "a system whereby the former Reich would be stripped of part of its industrial potential, so that the coal and steel resources of the Ruhr could be placed under a European authority and used for the benefit of all the nations involved, including a demilitarized Germany."

After the war, Jean Monnet made it clear that it was in France's interest to prevent excessive concentration of market power in the coal industry, especially among the large German *Konzerne* (trusts) of the Ruhr region. The way Monnet saw it,

> The problem was to break up excessive concentrations in the coal and steel industries of the Ruhr, where the *Konzerne* or trusts, which had underlain the military power of the former *Reich*, were

quite naturally being rebuilt. The Americans had been the first to tackle the problem, many months earlier. Their economic and political philosophy would not tolerate either the practice or the apparatus of domination, at home or abroad. They insisted that the German coal-selling organization . . . should lose its monopoly, and that the steel industries should no longer own the coalmines. (Monnet, 1978)

But how and why would Germany give up the ability to shape its industrial policy? In December 1949, Chancellor Adenauer agreed to an authority that supervised the mining and industrial areas of Germany, France, Belgium, and Luxembourg. The key point was that the International Ruhr Authority was *independent*. It would not be controlled by France or any other country. This was also the basis of the Treaty of Paris (1951) establishing the European Coal and Steel Community (ECSC). Monnet had an ambitious vision "of the High Authority's independence. It should, I argued, have its own revenue, drawn from a levy on coal and steel production, and not depend on government subsidies to finance its administration and its operational work."

It took several decades for Europe to create broad, independent, and powerful regulators. The Treaty of Rome laid the foundations of European competition policies in 1957 but did not specifically mention merger control. The need for merger control at the EU level was only recognized in the 1970s,* and the European Commission did not obtain merger control authority until 1989, as part of the Single Market.†

---

 * Around the same time, Germany amended its antitrust law to give merger control authority to its Bundeskartellamt (Federal Cartel Office), and the US Congress enacted the Hart–Scott–Rodino Act of 1976, which amended the Clayton Act and required premerger notification.

 † The Treaty of Rome built on the Treaty of Paris, which established the ECSC in 1951. Article 3(1)(g) of the Treaty of Rome envisions "a system ensuring that competition in the internal market is not distorted." Council Regulation 17 made the enforcement powers effective in 1962, and the EU Commission made its first decision in 1964. Article 101 (ex. 81) of the Treaty of Rome deals with horizontal conduct, vertical restraint, licensing, and joint ventures. Article 102 (ex. 82) deals with the anticompetitive effects of dominant position. Merger regulations were added in 1989.

The EU framework is similar to that of the US, with some important differences. The EU is more decentralized than the US, and member states have national competition authorities (NCAs) to deal with cases that have a mostly national impact. Which mergers are examined by the European Commission? If the annual turnover of the combined businesses exceeds specified thresholds in terms of global and European sales, the European Commission must be notified of the proposed merger. Below these thresholds, the national competition authorities in the EU member states may review the merger. These rules apply to all mergers, no matter where in the world the merging companies have their registered offices, headquarters, activities, or production facilities. The European Commissioner for Competition and the Directorate-General for Competition (DG Comp) enforce European competition law in cooperation with the NCAs. DG Comp prepares decisions in three broad areas: antitrust, mergers, and state aid. One significant difference between the two legal frameworks is that antitrust cases in the US are tried in courts. In the EU the DG Comp makes decisions first, which can then be appealed in courts. This effectively gives more power to DG Comp.

The similarities between the US and EU frameworks did not arise by chance: US ideas about regulation and antitrust played an important role in the construction of the EU's free-market doctrine.* By the late 1990s, the antitrust doctrines of the US and EU had largely converged. In 2004, amendments to the European Commission Merger Regulation (ECMR) made DG Comp more transparent and more accountable to the public (Foncel, Rabassa, and Ivaldi, 2007). It clarified the notion of unilateral effects in a way that resembles the US approach. At the same time, economic analysis became more prevalent, in particular with the creation of the position of Chief Competition Economist in 2003.

---

* The academic debate has evolved in three stages. At first, the common wisdom was that EU laws were direct descendants of US laws. Gerber (1998) challenged this view and showed that EU laws also had their own "indigenous" traditions. Since then, scholars have reached a more balanced view. Leucht and Marquis (2013) study the exchange of ideas between the US and Europe, and Leucht (2009) explores how the traditionally protectionist economies of Western Europe agreed on common competition rules.

The differences between the EU and the US come from the unique nature of the European Union. The EU is not one country in the way the US is. The EU is decentralized, and EU countries have broader powers relative to their federal institutions than US states have relative to US federal institutions.

Reciprocally, however, the few areas where decisions are truly made at the EU level become all the more important: trade policy, competition policy, and—for euro area countries—monetary policy. The president of the European Central Bank plays a key role in the EU. Similarly, the position of EU Commissioner for Competition is prestigious, attracts high-caliber politicians, and benefits from strong public recognition. Everyone remembers the tenure of Mario Monti (1999–2004), and within the EU, Margrethe Vestager has become a household name.

The Peculiar Case of State Aid Rules

Antitrust doctrines are largely comparable in the EU and the US, although there are important and growing differences in implementation, as we will discuss shortly. State aid, on the other hand, is a uniquely European concept.

After World War II, and following Monnet's idea, France and Germany agreed to set their production of coal and steel under a single international authority. This did not happen by chance. Monnet focused on the one area where economic nationalism was most prevalent and most dangerous: coal and steel. European nations, Germany and France in particular, had always intervened aggressively in these markets. From the very start, the EU project was therefore focused on limiting state interventions in important markets for goods and services.

State aid rules have no equivalent in American regulations, or anywhere outside Europe for that matter. As I have explained above, limiting arbitrary state aid was part of the DNA injected into the European project by Jean Monnet. These rules are at the core of the recent high-profile case forcing Apple to pay taxes to the Irish government that had originally been waived as part of a package of tax breaks. As a matter of principle, such rules require that illegal aid be repaid to remove the distortion of competition created by the aid. Commissioner Vestager, in charge of competition policy, argued that "Ireland has to recover up to 13 billion euros in illegal state aid from Apple."

Many of my American colleagues were perplexed by the whole story. It did not make much sense to them. Most of my European colleagues, however, found it rather straightforward. I am not taking a stand on the merits of this particular case, although the scale of tax evasion by large multinational corporations has become a severe problem, and internet companies are often among the worst offenders.* My broader point is that cases like this one should be expected given the foundational importance of state aid rules. Without such rules, corporations have incentive to shop around for subsidies, pitting one state against another and leading to inefficient outcomes. Amazon, for instance, selected New York City as one of two new campuses in November 2018 after securing almost $3 billion in tax breaks, which could have created an unfair advantage for Amazon over its competitors. The deal collapsed in early 2019, and the eventual result was a waste of time, effort, and legal fees. In Europe, wealthy regions cannot provide subsidies to lure large companies, with exceptions for smaller firms and poorer regions.

What is even more interesting in the example of Apple is the extension of state aid rules to fiscal issues as opposed to other forms of direct aid that the original state aid regulations were meant to cover. *"Natura abhorret vacuum,"* wrote François Rabelais. Like nature, politics abhors a vacuum. State aid rules were not designed to address fiscal issues, but once we agree that illegal aid is a problem, it is only logical to prosecute illegal tax subsidies as well.

Deregulation

In the late 1970s developed countries began to lift regulations in various markets. As in the case of antitrust enforcement, the US had a head start over Europe. The US government deregulated the air (1978), road (1980),

---

* Zucman, Tørsløv, and Wier (2018) find that 40 percent of multinational profits are shifted to tax havens, and the main winners are such countries as Ireland, Luxembourg, and Singapore. The main losers are EU countries (20 percent of profits shifted) and the US (15 percent of profits shifted).

and rail (1981) transportation industries, electric power (1978+), natural gas (1978), banking (1980), and telecommunications (1996). The deregulation effort was deemed a success. In 1999, the OECD noted that the "United States has been a world leader in regulatory reform."

In the US, the process was mostly led by the federal government and by federal agencies. Congress is the only body that can write federal laws, but more than sixty executive agencies can issue subordinate regulations. Indeed, these agencies issue thousands of new regulations each year, compiled in the Code of Federal Regulations.

Regulatory reform efforts in the EU are more recent. Some countries, such as the UK, pursued economic deregulation independently as early as 1979. But concerted, EU-wide reform efforts started in a limited way in 1985 with the Single Market Plan and accelerated in the 2000s with the Lisbon Strategy, which aimed at "removing obstacles to competition in Member States and creating a business environment more conducive to market entry and exit" (Zeitz, 2009).

EU institutions have only partial oversight over member states' regulatory environments.* So how does the EU influence reform efforts? *Name and shame* and *peer pressure.*

Take the implementation of the Lisbon Strategy, for example. The overall objectives were set jointly by the EU and member states. From then on, member states were in charge of implementation but were also required to submit progress reports to the European Commission.† Public EU reports and peer pressure were deliberately used to encourage reform. For countries in the process of accession (that is, countries applying for EU membership), stringent reform requirements were nego-

---

* The EU can directly prohibit certain domestic regulations, such as prohibition of golden shares and price controls in transportation industries. Otherwise, it can work with member countries to achieve mutual recognition of restrictions or can enact case law based on a treaty (for example, ongoing regulation of state aid by DG Comp). But beyond that, member states must implement reforms directly.

† The so-called Cardiff Reports from 2000 to 2004 were followed by national reform programs and implementation reports. The EU used those reports to continuously monitor and disclose progress. The EU created the microeconomic reform database (MICREF) to compile and track progress across all states.

tiated in advance, and new EU member states in Central and Eastern Europe made remarkable progress (Hölscher and Stephan, 2004). Finally, even for existing members, the commission can curtail the allocation of the EU Cohesion Funds to members that fail to implement reforms.

Although the Lisbon Strategy failed in some dimensions, substantial product market reforms were implemented. European economies have some of the lowest barriers to trade and foreign investment in the world.

Let us look at a few examples before we give a full account.

Airlines

The US began liberalizing air travel in 1978 when Congress passed the Airline Deregulation Act. By the 1990s, US skies were competitive. Figure 8.3 shows the evolution of concentration and profits in air transportation over the past two decades in the US and in Europe. Concentration was stable in the US during the 1990s and until 2008. Profits were highly cyclical and volatile. They were hit by the 2000 recession and even more by the 9 / 11 attack, but they returned to their 1990s level by 2007. But from 2008 onward both concentration and profits increased sharply. Concentration and profits per passenger are now much higher than they used to be. The rise in US concentration and profits closely aligns with a controversial merger wave that included Delta–Northwest (2008, noted by the vertical line), United–Continental (2010), Southwest–AirTran (2011), and American–US Airways (2014).

Europe began deregulating its airline industry a decade after the US. For most of the postwar period, European airlines were controlled, regulated, and protected by their states of origin. In fact, many were *owned* by the state. Competition was severely restricted. Less than 15 percent of the routes that existed in the European Community in the 1980s had more than two carriers. Air France and British Airways enjoyed a duopoly on the highly profitable London–Paris route and charged the highest fares on record at the time. This started to change in 1987 through the initiative of the EU Commission, and by 1997 European skies were formally deregulated. In theory, any European carrier could fly any intra-European route. I write "in theory" because in 1997, two-thirds of European routes still had only one carrier.

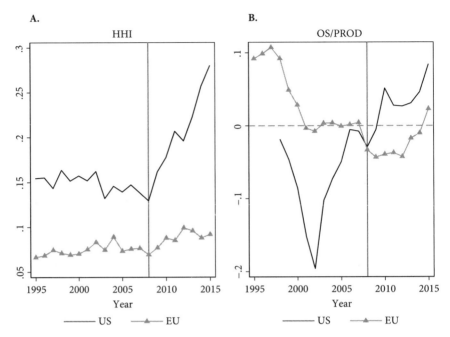

FIGURE 8.3 Air transportation concentration *(a)* and profits *(b)*, European Union versus United States. Chart compares concentration (HHI) and the evolution of net profit rates in the transportation–air industry (ISIC code 51) for the US and Europe. *Data sources*: Concentration based on Compustat, adjusted for database coverage using OECD STAN. Sales shares are defined as the ratio of firm sales to gross output from OECD STAN. Firms included only if data for the corresponding country are available in STAN. Profit rates are from OECD STAN.

As a result of the efforts of the commission, new airlines entered the market. Although the US pioneered the business model of low-cost airlines in the 1980s, they have mostly disappeared today. Even Southwest's cost structure resembles that of other major airlines. Europe pushed in the opposite direction. Europe has had two powerful low-cost airlines for more than twenty years: RyanAir and EasyJet. RyanAir has priced aggressively at the low end of the market, forcing other airlines to adjust.

You can see the impact of competition on profit margins of European airlines in Figure 8.3. Since 2000, concentration has remained stable in Europe. Meanwhile, concentration in the US airline industry has increased: today the top four firms control 80 percent of the market. In Europe, the top four control only about 40 percent of the market.

France provides a fascinating case study of the role of barriers to entry in the airline industry. For a long time, Air France had a near monopoly on domestic flights. Air France was also partly owned by the state. It had (and still has) a powerful pilots' union and high operating costs. By the mid-2000s, many government officials had given up hope that Air France would reform itself internally. In 2007, younger and reform-minded cabinet officials decided to bring in outside competition.* EasyJet was allowed to enter the French market in 2008, and its market share grew quickly. Low-cost airlines such as Transavia, Hop, and Vueling now provide more than a third of all domestic flights within France and about half of flights to other EU countries.

This is not to say that competition in French skies is completely free and fair today. Take-off and landing slots are heavily regulated. Paris has two airports. Charles de Gaulle is the larger one, with the most international connections. Orly is smaller and more conveniently located, especially for domestic flights. The rules for allocating slots are still severely biased toward incumbents. As a result, Air France continues to control half of the slots at Orly, which limits the expansion of EasyJet.

The situation is much worse in the US, however. The allocation of landing slots at major airports near New York, Washington, DC, and Chicago leads to an almost complete entrenchment of incumbent airlines. Moreover, the US forbids foreign airlines from flying domestic routes. In the late 1990s commentators lamented that the deregulation of European skies had not (yet) produced the same benefits for consumers as the ones achieved by the US.† Twenty years later, these commentators would

---

* For illuminating discussions, see Combe (2010).

† Richard Pinkham wrote, "The Brussels-mandated liberalization on Europe's airline sector plainly has made progress in its mission to promote enhanced competition and lower fares in the industry, as is evidenced by a net drop in fares and greatly increased levels of service. Nevertheless, the overall picture of Europe's commercial aviation sector is disappointingly unchanged, due to a continued combination of slot allocations inherited from the less liberalized era, anticompetitive behavior on the part of the Continent's incumbent carriers, and lingering national sentiment resulting in preferential treatment being accorded the flag carriers" (Pinkham 1999).

be pleased by the state of European skies and flabbergasted by what happened in the US.

The Entry of Free

The telecommunications industry provides another example of successful competition policy in Europe. National public monopolies had traditionally dominated the EU telecom markets, but starting in 1988, several legislative packages opened up competition.*

The combination of ex-ante market access regulation and ex-post enforcement has made EU telecom markets more competitive, providing consumers and businesses with increased choices, affordable prices, high quality, and innovative services. Figure 8.4 shows the price of communication in France relative to the US.

Once again, France provides a striking example. In the late 1990s, Free was an internet service provider and part of Iliad S.A., a telecom company founded by French entrepreneur Xavier Niel. Free offered internet access without a subscription or a surcharged phone number. A critical issue in the 2000s was unbundling, which forced the incumbent carrier France Telecom to lease the local loop (the pair of copper wires between the edge of the telecom network and the house or office of the subscriber, sometimes called the "last mile"). The unbundling process was supposed to start in 2000, but it was delayed until the end of 2002 by a long legal fight between France Telecom and the French regulation authority. Unbundling was a critical step for the expansion of fast internet access in France.

Today, Free Mobile is the wireless service provider of the Iliad group. When it obtained its 4G license in 2011, it became a significant competitor for the incumbents, making an immediate impact. Until 2011, French consumers paid between €45 and €65 per month for their smartphone plans, with limited data and a few hours of talk time. Free offered

---

* The process started in 1988 and culminated in 1998 with full liberalization. The current Telecoms Regulatory Framework for electronic communications was adopted in 2002 and updated in 2009; it has subsequently been supplemented by a number of additional legislative instruments.

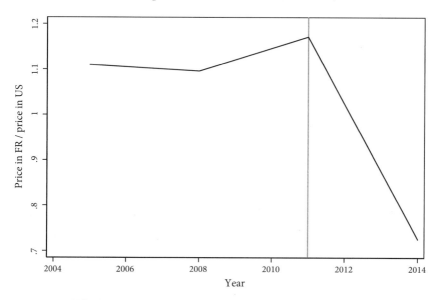

FIGURE 8.4 Telecom prices in France relative to the US. French prices are converted into dollars using the FOREX rate. The vertical line shows the entry of Free Mobile in the 4G market. *Data source:* ICP

unlimited talk, unlimited SMS and MMS messages, and unlimited data with a speed reduction after 3 GB for €20. The number of Free Mobile clients grew quickly, from about 2.6 million in 2012 Q1 to 8.6 million in 2014 Q1. Its current market share is around 20 percent, and it aims for 25 percent.

The benefits to consumers spread far and wide: incumbents Orange, SFR, and Bouygues launched their own discount brands, offering €20 contracts as well. In three years, France went from 15 percent more expensive than the US to 25 percent cheaper.

A Theory of Europe's Free Markets

Let us now return to our main puzzle: what happened in Europe, and why? Germán Gutiérrez and I have tried to understand how Europe became the land of free markets, and we have proposed an explanation in two parts.

We first argue that, although EU institutions look like American ones, there is a subtle but important difference: they are more independent. As we have explained, EU institutions resemble American ones in terms of goals, scope, and doctrine. They are, however, granted more political independence than their American counterparts. This is true of the two leading supranational institutions: the European Central Bank is not subject to the same level of parliamentary oversight as the Federal Reserve Board, and DG Comp is more independent than the DoJ or the FTC.

This is surprising because it appears to contradict the conventional wisdom about European and American preferences. Did Europeans make the European Central Bank fiercely independent because they studied Milton Friedman's writings more than Americans? Did they make DG Comp more independent because they trusted in free markets?

That does not seem plausible. Instead, we argue that bargaining among sovereign nations leads to supranational institutions that are more politically independent than what the average politician would choose. We build a formal economic model to show that this is exactly what game theory predicts. Imagine a world where politicians and civil servants design a regulator and can make it more or less independent from business and political influence. Our key result is that this degree of independence is strictly higher when two countries set up a common regulator than when each country has its own regulator.

The key insight is that politicians are more worried about the regulator being captured by the other country than they are attracted by the opportunity to capture the regulator themselves. French and German politicians might not like a strong and independent antitrust regulator at home, but they like even less the idea of the other nation exerting political influence over the institution. As a result, if they are to agree on any supranational institution, it will have a bias toward more independence. This is exactly how Monnet convinced Adenauer in 1950 to accept the Schuman Plan.*

Our theory makes three testable predictions:

1. EU countries agree to set up a regulator that is tougher and more independent than their old national regulators.

---

* One interesting historical precedent with some similar features is the Austro-Hungarian Empire. Austria and Hungary agreed to share a currency and a central bank but made the bank independent. See Flandreau (2001).

2. Countries with weaker ex-ante institutions benefit more from supranational regulation.

3. Returns to lobbying decrease in Europe, or at least increase less than in the US.

We test and confirm these predictions in our paper (2018a). I have already described in this chapter a long list of deregulation efforts spurred by the European Commission. These efforts were—and still are—critical to the success of the Single Market.

Product Market Reforms

Regarding product market regulations (PMR), data in Figures 8.1–8.4 indicate the efforts made by EU countries toward reform. We can conclude that they are catching up (at the very least) with the US. These reforms are the result of deliberate policy choices. Figure 8.5 plots the average number of product market reforms across EU countries. The creation of the Single Market was clearly accompanied by significant reform efforts.

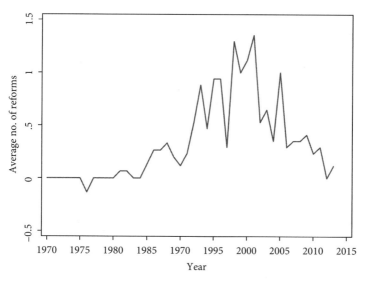

FIGURE 8.5 Product market reforms in Europe. *Data source*: Duval et al. (2018)

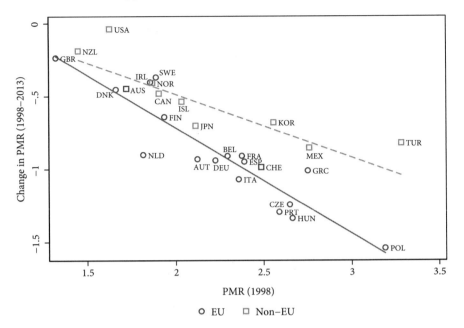

FIGURE 8.6 Global convergence of product market regulations. *Data source:* OECD

Detailed data on PMR convergence provide further support for our theory. Figure 8.6 plots the change in PMR from 1998 to 2013 against the starting value in 1998. The negative slope illustrates the process of convergence. Countries with initially high levels of regulation experience a stronger decrease in regulation. In other words, they are catching up with the US and the UK. The convergence toward less regulation is global, but the convergence is faster for EU countries than for non-EU countries. Portugal and the Czech Republic had approximately the same level of regulation as Mexico in 1998, and Poland had the same level as Turkey. Today these European markets are significantly freer than their foreign counterparts. The difference in the slopes of the two lines for EU and non-EU countries is statistically significant and consistent with our theory.

EU countries with initially weak institutions have experienced large improvements in antitrust and product market regulation. Moreover, the relative improvement is larger for EU countries than for non-EU countries with similar initial institutions. This shows the positive impact of EU-level enforcement and influence.

Antitrust

Antitrust activities play a significant role in market regulation, and their political impact is large and visible. To be clear, I don't think antitrust is necessarily the main channel through which Europe has freed its markets. The broad Single Market agenda goes beyond antitrust, and the lifting of entry restrictions has probably had more impact than merger reviews. Still, merger control is important.

Using indicators of competition law and policy from the OECD and from Hylton and Deng (2007), we find that DG Comp is more independent and more pro-competition than any of the national regulators. In fact, DG Comp is more independent than the DoJ and the FTC.

Figure 8.7 shows indicators of restrictions to antitrust enforcement from the OECD: the lower the bar, the tougher and more independent the regulator. DG Comp is represented by the dashed horizontal line. The US is represented on the far right of each bar graph. DG Comp attains

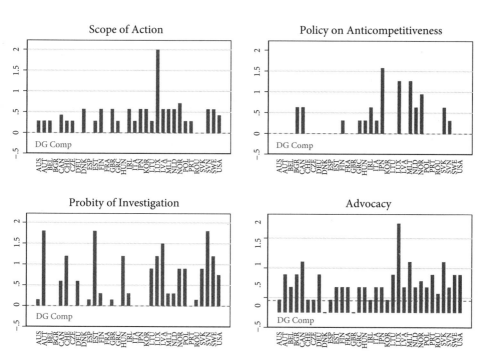

FIGURE 8.7 Restrictions on antitrust enforcement. *Data source:* OECD

the lowest possible index of restrictions in the three categories that directly map into our theory: scope of action, policy on anticompetitiveness, and probity of investigation. Probity of investigation measures the scope for government interference in antitrust policy. DG Comp is essentially free from interference by national governments, and its score is much lower than the average score of national authorities. The fourth dimension, advocacy (whether the regulator can advocate for a more competitive environment), is a bit less straightforward to map into our model. On that dimension, only the UK and Denmark offer more freedom than the EU.

Figure 8.7 depicts formal rules and policies. Perhaps these are all words and no action. Do tougher policies actually translate into tougher enforcement?

Let us start with merger enforcement because it is simpler to define and has been more extensively studied. We have already noted, following the work of John Kwoka, the decrease in antitrust enforcement in the US. We see no similar trend in Europe. We find that enforcement has remained stable (or even tightened) in Europe. For instance, DG Comp Abuse of Dominance enforcement has remained stable or increased since the 1970s, whereas the DoJ has brought only ten cases since 1990 and only one case since 2000.

Comparing antitrust enforcement across jurisdictions is difficult. In that respect the work of Mats Bergman and co-authors (2010) is particularly useful because they control for the specifics of each case. They ask the conceptually correct question: what would have been the outcome of the *same* case if it had been investigated by the *other* regulator? They study a detailed sample of EU and US merger investigations from 1993 to 2003 and find that the EU was tougher than the US for dominance mergers, in particular those involving moderate market shares. The differences are less stark following the 2004 EU Merger Reform, but the EU is still tougher on mergers involving moderate market shares, and it applies a more aggressive collusion policy than the US.

Cartel enforcement is one area where the US has historically been very tough and efficient. In recent years, DoJ has increased its focus on charging individuals as well as corporations—which has resulted in more individuals being incarcerated and for longer periods of time. In that domain, the EU has benefited and borrowed good ideas from the US. In addition, the EU commission appears to learn quickly over time, so enforcement has improved steadily (Duso, Gugler, and Yurtoglu, 2011).

Europe Means to Keep Its Markets Free

Comparing market regulation in the US and the EU is illuminating. If globalization or technology were responsible for declining enforcement in the US, we should observe similar trends on both sides of the Atlantic. However, this does not appear to be the case. European antitrust enforcement has remained active in recent years. Martin Carree, Andrea Günster, and Maarten Pieter Schinkel (2010) show that, on average, 264 cases of antitrust, 284 mergers, and 1,075 cases of state aid were investigated in Europe every year from 2000 to 2004. The commission made several controversial decisions, such as blocking the merger of General Electric and Honeywell that had been approved by US competition authorities. It also recently ruled against Google in a case that was dismissed by US authorities five years prior. Carree and co-authors find that the decisions are not biased against foreign firms, however. In fact, "firms from non-European countries have fewer infringements, lower fines, and also lower appeal rates." Moreover, there is virtually no discussion of weak antitrust enforcement in Europe—either in academia or the media—compared to a growing body of work in the US.

This is not to say that Europe is perfect. Far from it. France used to be very good at suppressing competition and designing bad policies. A fitting example is the regulation of supermarkets in France in the mid-1990s. Prime Minister Raffarin wanted to protect small retail stores and proposed legislation to block new supermarkets larger than 300 square meters (3,000 square feet) without special authorization. Construction of new supermarkets ground to a halt for ten years. Do you think large retail chains complained? Not really. The legislation prevented competition from discount stores and limited competition among the chains. Their stock prices went up.

It is also important to keep in mind some orders of magnitude: the vast majority of mergers are approved. From 1990 to January 2019, the European Commission reviewed 7,260 mergers. Out of these, 6,401 were approved, 152 withdrawn in phase 1, and 44 in phase 2. Others were referred to other jurisdictions (such as member states). At the end of the day, only 27 were outright prohibited.*

But Europe is also illuminating precisely because it is imperfect. It gives us a way to test a simple theory of free markets. The theory says that the EU set up fiercely independent institutions precisely because this was required to get all the countries on board. Each country wanted to be sure that other countries would not be able to influence the EU institutions to their advantage. As a result, the same politicians that might have been lukewarm supporters of free markets at home became supporters of free markets at the EU level. The direct predictions of the theory are strongly supported in the data: EU institutions are systematically more independent and more in favor of free markets than their domestic counterparts. As I was writing this book the case of Alstom and Siemens made the news and provided a good test of our theory. Germany's Siemens and France's Alstom had decided in 2017 to merge their rail activities. To be honest, I was worried because the EU Commission was under strong political pressures from its two largest and most influential member states, France and Germany. Paris and Berlin both wanted the merger approved. But Commissioner Vestager stood her ground. She and her team concluded that the merger "would have significantly reduced competition" in signaling equipment and high-speed trains, "depriving customers, including train operators and rail infrastructure managers of a choice of suppliers and products." The commission blocked the merger in February 2019.†

The last prediction of our theory is the most controversial: if we are right, we should observe more lobbying expenditures in the US than in Europe. Lobbying should also explain at least some of the differences that we observe across time, regions, and industries. In our next chapters, we will dig into lobbying and campaign finance. For now, I simply note that US firms do spend substantially more on lobbying and campaign con-

---

* Data at http://ec.europa.eu/competition/mergers/statistics.pdf. I am grateful to Tomaso Duso for helping me understand these facts.

† EU Commission, "Mergers: Commission prohibits Siemens' proposed acquisition of Alstom," press release, February 6, 2019.

tributions and are far more likely to achieve their lobbying goals than European firms and lobbyists.

Before we turn to lobbying, however, I must address the elephant in the room: Brexit. Needless to say, I am saddened by the UK's decision to leave the EU. Looking back, it is clear that the EU made progress toward free markets in part because the UK was an active participant in designing the rules of the Single Market. The market was very much a joint effort that would not have succeeded without the UK. It is then a striking paradox that the UK would choose to leave the EU after having worked hard—and succeeded—in creating the free-market environment it always wanted.

[THREE]

POLITICAL ECONOMY

Let us summarize what we have found so far. Most US domestic markets have become less competitive, and US firms charge excessive prices to US consumers. Excess profits are used to pay out dividends and to buy back shares, not to hire and invest. At the same time, barriers to entry have increased, and antitrust enforcement has weakened. These trends in the US were not exported to Europe, and, in a stunning reversal of history, many European markets (airlines, cell phones, and internet providers, among others) are now more competitive and cheaper than their American counterparts.

My interpretation of the European experience is that it is mostly a consequence of the push for the Single Market and the necessary institutional change that entailed. The US served as a role model in the process, and many of the beneficial ideas that are now being applied in continental Europe came from the US and the UK. Europe adopted these ideas and saw competition flourish. Chapter 8 explains why Europe took a different path. It makes specific predictions about the design of regulatory institutions and about antitrust enforcement and the removal of barriers to entry. It makes specific predictions about which groups of industries and countries are most affected. All the predictions that I have been able to test have been verified. This gives me some confidence in the theory. With this in mind, I now want to come back to the US and see if the same theory can help us understand why competition declined in American markets.

What We Can Learn by Comparing the United States and Europe

I will argue that political contributions and lobbying expenditures are responsible for some of the weakness in enforcement and the rise of regulatory barriers to competition within the US. My focus will be on lobbying and campaign finance in the US, but I will use Europe again as a control group to highlight some peculiarities of the US system. Is this a valid comparison? In Part Two of the book, I compared the US and the EU in terms of economic outcomes. I argued that this was warranted by the broad similarity of the two economies. But is this true of the two political systems? Are they similar enough or are political differences so large as to render the comparison misleading?

I see two main differences between Europe and the US in that respect. The first, and by far the most important, is that the US is a military superpower while Europe is not, nor does it aspire to be one, much to the chagrin of French diplomats. The political and technological implications of military dominance are immense and reach far beyond the scope of this book. The second difference, which follows from the first, is that the US dollar plays an outsized role in the global economic and financial system. The US dollar is the main reserve and invoicing currency. The US trade deficit reflects in part the desire by many other countries to park their wealth in US dollars.

These differences matter. American lobbying and politics might be different if the US did not have to maintain the largest military in the world. But this state of affairs is not new. It cannot by itself account for the *changes* that have happened in the US over the past twenty years. By the same token, I think there is much to learn from a joint analysis of lobbying and campaign finance on the two sides of the Atlantic.

CHAPTER 9

Lobbying

Careful investment in a Washington lobbyist can yield enormous returns in the form of taxes avoided or regulations curbed—an odd
negative sort of calculation, but one that forms the basis of the economics of lobbying.

JEFFREY BIRNBAUM, *THE LOBBYISTS*

BIG BIRD, the giant yellow Muppet beloved by generations of children
on *Sesame Street,* may seem like an odd figure to mention at the outset
of a chapter on political lobbying. But in the mid-1990s, Big Bird played
a key role in a very public lobbying campaign that forced the most
powerful politician in the US into an embarrassing retreat.

After Republicans, led by Newt Gingrich, the firebrand Speaker of
the House of Representatives, took over Congress in 1995, they targeted
the Public Broadcasting Service for budget cuts. PBS produces, among
other programs, *Sesame Street.* Gingrich and his fellow Republicans believed that the federal government had no business funding a media
outlet, and suspected that PBS was indoctrinating people with a liberal
worldview.

The plan was to slash federal funding for PBS in the upcoming
budget bill. But that was before a grassroots lobbying campaign was
launched by PBS supporters, who were clever enough to cast the debate
as a battle between Gingrich and Big Bird. With some careful nudging
from PBS—which was technically barred from lobbying Congress itself—PBS viewers across the country practically buried their representatives in Washington with letters of support for Big Bird and, by
extension, PBS.

"It was a wonderful lesson in democracy," an executive with one local station told the *New York Times*. "Here was 'evil Newt' trying to kill Big Bird. There was a public outcry and we were inundated with calls from viewers. We told them that if they cared about the issue, they should let their elected representatives know."

In the end, Gingrich was forced to back down. (In a mock ceremony before the second session of the 104th Congress, he even publicly swore not to "kill" Big Bird.) In the budget bill for fiscal 1997, Congress appropriated $300 million for PBS as far out as 2000, a 20 percent increase over the previous year's funding.

Normally, of course, lobbying efforts in Washington are rarely as easy to spot as the campaign to save Big Bird, and their results can be even more obscure. This makes large-scale data hard to collect, and research tricky.

We've spent a lot of time analyzing data in previous chapters of this book—but at least it was good data. Aggregate economic quantities are complex to measure, but at least the numbers are relatively transparent. We can measure investment, employment, and incomes. We can relatively easily measure sales at the firm level. The study of prices across countries is more difficult, but it's still a walk in the park compared to the study of lobbying and political influence over time, across industries, and between countries.

To analyze the impact of lobbying on political outcomes is to enter the realm of bad data and wild guesses. When it comes to lobbying and campaign contributions—expenses to influence the political and regulatory process—we can really only measure the tip of the proverbial iceberg. An especially pernicious effect of lobbying and campaign contributions is that the lack of pristine data creates a tendency to let the data available dictate the questions we ask. In the normal course of research, you first choose a question that you deem interesting and important, and then you look for ways to answer it. This, however, can sometimes be terribly slow and frustrating, especially when there is no available data. It is also risky because you might never get the data you need to obtain a convincing answer. There is a natural tendency, then, to reverse the logic. You might decide to work with the data you already have, knowing full well it will not let you answer the more interesting question. At least it will let you answer something. This is the research equivalent of looking for your keys under the streetlight.*

Fortunately, political economy is a field where we will encounter some of the most creative and pugnacious researchers in economics. Thanks to their work, we will be able to draw some striking conclusions about the role of lobbying and money in American politics.

There is nothing inherently bad in lobbying. In fact, hiring a lobbyist is a right protected by the US Constitution. The First Amendment of the US Constitution protects free speech and guarantees the right "to petition the Government for a redress of grievances." Political scientists John de Figueiredo and Brian Richter (2014) explain that

> One of the central tenets of representative democracy is the right of individuals, by themselves or in groups, to petition elected officials and the government. These petitions are designed to influence the opinions, policies, and votes of legislators and other government officials. One outgrowth of this right has been the creation and evolution of organized interest groups comprised of individuals, companies, and other organizations. These organized interests employ a variety of methods to influence government policies including campaign contributions, endorsements, grassroots campaigns, media campaigns, and lobbying.

In a democracy, citizens have the right to petition their government, and we all agree that it is a good thing. But it also opens the door to lobbying by large corporate interests. As with most things in life, then, it is a matter of balance. Let us find out how this balance has changed over the past twenty years.

---

* This is a reference to an old joke: A police officer sees a drunk man searching for something under a streetlight and asks what the man has lost. He says, "I've lost my keys," and they look under the streetlight together. After a few minutes the policeman asks, "Are you sure you lost them here?" The man replies, "No, I lost them in the park." The policeman asks why he is searching here, and the drunk man replies, "This is where the light is."

Why Measuring the Impact of Lobbying Is an Uphill Battle

Before discussing lobbying and campaign contributions, I should explain at the outset why it is difficult to measure the outcome of these contributions. Small legislative or regulatory changes—often buried in larger documents running to hundreds of pages—can be worth millions of dollars to a particular industry or interest group. But they can be virtually impossible for a nonexpert to identify and to understand. Harder still is detecting what things an effective lobbying effort persuades legislators to leave out of a bill entirely. And even when such changes can be uncovered, it is often impossible to definitively link them to specific lobbying efforts or campaign contributions.

This explains the lack of consensus in the literature on the real effects of lobbying. It has led some commentators to doubt that lobbying matters at all. This strikes me as implausible, for at least four reasons.

First, at a theoretical level, you would need to hold a rather strange view of the world to think that lobbying does not matter. As Marianne Bertrand and her co-authors (2018) explain: "At the intersection between the political and the economic spheres lies the lobbying industry. Trillions of dollars of public policy intervention, government procurement, and budgetary items are constantly thoroughly scrutinized, advocated, or opposed by representatives of special interests." In order to deny the influence of lobbying, you would have to explain why businesses voluntarily spend substantial human and financial resources on something useless. The fact that lobbying has always taken place (and, if anything, seems to be increasing) is enough, under conditions of minimal rationality, to argue that it must matter. Put another way, if we hold the view that firms spend money on lobbying but it is useless, then we must recognize that this view is inconsistent with most of what we know about economics and human nature. It's not strictly impossible, but I am not going to take this idea very seriously.

Second, rent seeking is a zero-sum game, and zero-sum games are difficult to identify in the data. For instance, suppose firm A spends $100 to lobby for a regulatory change that would give it an advantage over firm B. Firm B then spends $200 to fight this change. Firm B prevails. What do we see? We see that they collectively spent $300 and that *nothing* has changed:

the relative market shares, growth rates, and productivity of the two firms are the same as before. Any naive model would conclude that lobbying does not matter, even though it obviously does. This is not just a theoretical possibility. Frank R. Baumgartner, Jeffrey M. Berry, Marie Hojnacki, David C. Kimball, and Beth L. Leech (2009) conducted a long-term study of the lobbying efforts of 2,200 lobbyists. They found that both sides of the issues that they analyzed were able to muster roughly similar resources.

Third, rent seeking, even when it is legal, is not something that the parties involved want to advertise: neither the firms at the contributing end, nor the regulators and politicians at the receiving end. We should therefore expect the outcomes to be hidden. This creates a particularly difficult problem for researchers. Difficult does not mean impossible, however. Carnegie Mellon economist Karam Kang (2016) used a sophisticated model to estimate the returns from lobbying in the energy industry. She built a data set containing all federal energy legislation and lobbying activities by the energy sector during the 110th Congress. She then computed a game-theoretic model of lobbying. This means that she described a game between lobbyists and policy makers using mathematical equations. This allowed her to estimate the returns from lobbying expenditures. The average return is above 130 percent.

Fourth, and finally, contributions are choices, not random inputs. In the language of econometrics, contributions are endogenous variables and the research is plagued by endogeneity and omitted-variable bias. Human beings have an unfortunate tendency to think ahead, at least some of the time. This makes my life as a researcher rather difficult.

People Do Stuff for a Reason

Endogeneity bias is a pervasive issue in economics and in social sciences more generally, so it's worth taking a moment to explain what it is. In fact, once you think about it, you'll see that is one of the two main differences between the natural sciences and social sciences, the other difference being the ease or difficulty of running controlled experiments. Let me illustrate with a few examples of endogeneity bias.

Suppose you want to answer the following question: is seeing a doctor good for your health? We know the answer is yes, at least on average. (I am not talking about bloodletting in medieval medicine.) But how would you test this simple idea? Suppose I gave you data on doctors' visits paired with data on health outcomes six months later. What would you find? Well, you would find that people who visit doctors are more likely to be sick or even dead six months later. Why? Because sick people are the ones who go to the doctor in the first place. Healthy individuals do not. Technically, we say that the decision to visit (or call) the doctor is an *endogenous* decision. This means that people make this decision for a reason. Therefore, you cannot treat the doctor's visit as a random event as you would in an experiment in the natural sciences. How can you answer the question? You need to find changes in access to doctors that are independent of health status, such as the random opening or closing of a medical facility in the neighborhood. Even then, you need to be confident that the opening or closing is not itself driven by the average health of the population in the neighborhood.

Another example involves the law of supply and demand. Suppose you want to know by how much people decrease their consumption of milk when the price of milk goes up. The two major factors in question are the price—how much does the grocery store charge for milk—and the level of demand—how much do milk consumers want? The problem is that in the real world, both of these factors are being determined simultaneously. The store owner adjusts prices according to demand, and consumer demand fluctuates with prices. Suppose the store owner can predict when the demand for milk will go up. On days when she expects the demand to be high, she might want to increase the price a little bit to increase her profit margin. What would you see in the data? You would see that people consume more milk when the price goes up, and you would be puzzled because that certainly does not look like a demand curve. The issue in that example is that price setting is endogenous and depends on expected demand.*

---

* The ideal experiment would involve a random change in prices not linked to demand, such as a supply chain problem that randomly increased the stock of milk in the store. Then the owner would lower the price to decrease the stock, and you would be able to estimate the response of consumers (their demand elasticity).

Endogeneity is less of a problem in the physical sciences. Subatomic particles do not behave like human beings. Particles are not forward looking. They do not change their behavior because they expect something to happen. Humans do, fortunately for them, unfortunately for researchers. We will come back to these points, but for now it's enough to say that these are tricky issues and that real ingenuity is needed to deal with them.

How does this translate to lobbying and campaign finance? Let's look at lobbying. Which firms or industries have an incentive to lobby? Well, precisely the ones that feel potentially threatened by new rules and regulations, or the ones that have something to hide, or the ones that have rents to protect. In later chapters we will study the giants of the internet economy, the GAFAMs (Google, Apple, Facebook, Amazon, and Microsoft). They have recently increased their lobbying expenditures. Do you think this is by accident, or do you think this is because they feel the risk of a regulatory backlash? Yes, this is a rhetorical question.

In other words, firms that have an incentive to lobby are the ones that are most likely to be targeted. Just like with doctor's visits or the price of milk, the endogeneity of the lobbying decision renders the simple correlation uninformative. The correlation between lobbying today and enforcement actions tomorrow might be zero or positive, and a naive model would conclude that lobbying does not work, or even that it backfires, just like a naive model would conclude that doctors' visits are bad for health or that people drink more milk when its price goes up. We will discuss specific examples in the chapters on finance, health care, and internet firms. We will see how banks, asset managers, and internet giants all beef up their lobbying efforts precisely when they feel that some new regulations or new competitors might come their way.

To deal with endogeneity, economists have learned to turn the twists of history into quasi-natural experiments. For instance, to understand the causal influence of political preferences on antitrust enforcement, Richard Baker, Carola Frydman, and Eric Hilt (2018) use the sudden accession of Theodore Roosevelt to the presidency after the assassination of President William McKinley. McKinley presided over the largest merger wave in American history. He had no interest in antitrust and no intention of putting limits on mergers. Teddy Roosevelt had very different opinions. Firms with greater vulnerability to antitrust enforcement lost more after the assassination. The researchers conclude that "the transition from McKinley to Roosevelt caused one of the most significant changes in antitrust enforcement of the Gilded Age—not from new legislation, but from a change in the approach taken to the enforcement of existing law."

Why Lobbying Creates Inefficiencies

As we have noted, lobbying is not necessarily bad. There are basically two views of lobbying, one benign or even beneficial, and one negative. The benign view of lobbying is that it allows the sharing of relevant information between businesses, regulators, and politicians. Technology and tastes are always changing, and it is difficult for policy makers to keep up. It is difficult to know when "laissez-faire" is appropriate or when regulations are preferable. It is difficult to figure out what is important and what does not matter. In this context, lobbies can be beneficial. They have a strong incentive to provide relevant—even if biased—information. At the very least, they show that some people and businesses care about a particular issue.

The alternative perspective holds that lobbying is essentially rent-seeking. That is the view articulated by economists Gene M. Grossman and Elhanan Helpman (1994, 2001). Simply put, businesses lobby to protect their rents. This explains, for instance, the steel and aluminum tariffs imposed by the Trump administration in 2018. Lobbying spending by large American steel companies increased by about 20 percent between 2017 and 2018. They successfully pushed the Trump administration to impose tariffs, which led to higher prices and higher profits. In the case of aluminum, a midsize company with fewer than 2,000 workers, Century Aluminum, was at the center of the lobbying effort. As *Business Week* reported on September 27, 2018, "what wasn't mentioned was that Century's biggest shareholder is Glencore Plc, the Swiss trading company that is the biggest buyer and seller of commodities in the world . . . While Century was lobbying the Trump administration, Glencore, along with a handful of other commodity trading companies, was stockpiling record amounts of foreign aluminum in the U.S.—the idea being, if tariffs were announced, prices would rise, and all that cheap foreign metal would suddenly become more valuable. And that's what happened."

Rent-seeking causes loss of wealth in two ways. First, the direct expenditures that interest groups spend on lobbying could be used for productive work, rather than zero sum games. The second loss is the policies themselves. The policies advocated by lobbyists are rarely efficient. They do not take the form of simple transfers or lump-sum taxes. Consider, for instance, the regulation of entry. Imagine a world where entrants pay a lump-sum tax to compensate for the disruption and harm they inflict on incumbents. In that world, there would be no indirect loss through inefficiency. New firms would still enter and bring benefits in terms of price competition and innovation. The entrant would have to write a check to the incumbent, but that would be a transfer, not a deadweight loss. Some criminal enterprises follow these rules because they understand that it's efficient to let other businesses operate and "tax" them. It is also the policy advocated by many economists when entrants destroy the value of existing assets, such as Uber with respect to taxi medallions.

Yet we rarely observe this kind of outcome in our economies because incumbent rents are usually not legitimate. The transfer would be too transparent and would cause an outcry. It would also not be enforceable ex post. The entrant could simply refuse to pay after it enters. As a result, incumbents typically resort to inefficient ways to protect their rents. Oftentimes it means blocking entry altogether. That creates a large inefficiency.

What You Know or Whom You Know?

It is difficult to assess how much of the lobbying that we observe reflects the useful sharing of information, and how much is rent seeking. We can, however, answer a related question that sheds light on the issue. We can ask whether lobbyists provide *specific information* to members of Congress or whether they provide special interests with *privileged access* to politicians. This later view is consistent with what insiders believe, as Conor McGrath (2006) reports: "there are three important things to know about lobbying: contacts, contacts, contacts."

Some evidence clearly suggests that *whom you know* matters. Jordi Blanes i Vidal, Mirko Draca, and Christian Fons-Rosen (2012), for example, show that lobbyists who used to work as senatorial aides experience a significant drop in revenue when their senators leave office. Also consistent with this interpretation is the fact that the big lobbying firms, such as Squire Patton Boggs or Cassidy and Associates, are not exactly famous for their technical expertise.

Thomas Hale Boggs Jr., whose name is associated with the Patton Boggs firm (now Squire Patton Boggs), is a prime example of connections being the key to success in the lobbying business. His parents both served in Congress. As the *Washington Post* wrote in his obituary (September 15, 2014), "Young 'Tommy' Boggs's first job in Washington was operating the private elevator for then-House Speaker Sam Rayburn, the Texas Democrat." Able to get virtually anyone in Washington on the phone on demand, Boggs held court at the famed Palm restaurant in DC and used his vast web of connections to lobby for clients of all descriptions. He helped the American Bankers Association in its effort to overturn the onerous regulations of the Glass-Steagall Act, was instrumental in rewriting a massive telecommunications bill in 1996, and helped a string of foreign politicians, some of them rather unsavory, secure the assistance of the US government. To be clear, Boggs was no expert in banking, telecommunications, or foreign relations. But he always knew the right people to call, the effective place to apply political pressure, and the value of a well-placed contribution.

It's pretty clear that whom you know is important, but that does not rule out that *what you know* might also be important.

Until recently we did not know much about the relative importance of these two effects. Thanks to the brilliant work of Marianne Bertrand, Matilde Bombardini, and Francesco Trebbi, however, we now have a sharper picture. They show that both channels (what you know and whom you know) matter, but that whom you know matters more. They show that lobbyists follow politicians to whom they were initially connected when those politicians receive new committee assignments. For instance, "a lobbyist who is connected to a legislator whose committee assignment includes health care in one Congress is more likely to cover defense-related issues in the next Congress if the legislator he or she is connected to is reassigned to defense in the next Congress."

They also find some support for the expertise view. They show that there is a group of experts whom even politicians of opposite political affiliations listen to. Politicians often maintain relationships with lobbyists of the same political orientation, but they are more likely to cross the aisle when talking to experts, as one would expect if they are trying to obtain accurate information.

Bertrand and her colleagues are thus able to document both effects. On balance, however, they find a significantly larger monetary premium for connections than for expertise. And the expertise that seems to matter the most is knowledge of a politician's constituency. Knowledge of specific policy issues appears less important.

Lobbying for Fiscal Privilege

Finally, a lot of lobbying directly targets government purchases, transfers, and taxes. Beth L. Leech, Frank R. Baumgartner, Timothy M. La Pira, and Nicholas A. Semanko (2005) show that more lobbying resources are spent on issues and agencies with larger budgets. Trade associations often lobby for lower taxes. Lobbying for lower taxes is fundamentally inefficient because tax breaks create distortions in the allocations of economic resources, and because someone else must then pay these taxes. The economists Tanida Arayavechkit, Felipe E. Saffie, and Minchul Shin (2014) show that when firms lobby for capital-based tax benefits they become too large. They use lobbying and firm-level data from the US to document that firms that lobby are larger, more capital intensive, and enjoy lower effective tax rates. Their marginal product of capital is lower than that of firms that do not lobby. They argue that lobbying firms overaccumulate capital by 5.5 percent on average.

You might think that lower taxes can have beneficial incentive effects. That is true, but that is almost never the outcome of lobbying. When economists advocate for lower taxes, we mean lower marginal tax rates on as broad a base as possible. The tax breaks obtained by lobbyists take the form of loopholes and rarely improve investment and hiring decisions.

Lobbying Both Sides of the Atlantic

We have explained why lobbying is likely to be inefficient, and why it is difficult to measure. Let us now come back to our comparison of the US and Europe. The theory presented in Chapter 8 predicts higher lobbying expenditures in the US than in the EU. Is that true?

Figure 9.1 shows total lobbying expenditures directed at the US federal government and at EU institutions. Lobbying expenditures in the US appear to be more than twice as large as in Europe. Moreover, the share of lobbying done by business, lawyers, and lobbyists is higher in the US (87 percent) than in Europe (70 percent). Several caveats are warranted with these data but the differences are so large that even if we are 20 percent off, it would not change our main conclusions. The most important caveat is that many lobbying expenditures go unreported, and it is difficult to know which way the bias goes. In the US, nonprofit entities play an active role in the lobbying process. Financial ties between firms and nonprofit entities are legal and tax exempt, but difficult to trace. Marianne Bertrand and co-authors (2018) find that corporations strategically deploy charitable grants to induce nonprofit grantees to make comments that favor their benefactors. In Europe, there is a long tradition of dark lobbying. It is common wisdom among Italian political scientists and economists that there is an entire lobbying industry in Italy that goes completely unreported, with wealthy individuals operating networks of connections while never being mentioned in the press. This bias might be smaller at the EU level, but it's impossible to know for sure.

Figure 9.1 is consistent with the literature on lobbying. In their survey, John M. de Figueiredo and Brian K. Richter (2014) document four main empirical regularities about lobbying. The first regularity is that lobbying is pervasive in the US and in other developed countries. Lobbying expenditures at the federal level in the US are several times larger than campaign contributions by political action committees (PACs). "In 2012, organized interest groups spent $3.5 billion annually to lobby the federal government, whereas interest groups' PACs, super PACs, and 527 organizations spent approximately $1.55 billion over the two-year 2011 to 2012 election cycle (or approximately $750 million annually) on campaign contributions." If you do not know exactly what PACs and super PACs

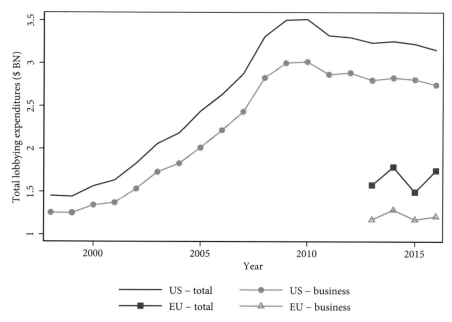

FIGURE 9.1 Lobbying expenditures in US and EU. See caveats for EU lobbying totals in the text. US business sector includes agribusiness, electronics, construction, defense, energy, finance, insurance, real estate, health, lawyers and lobbyists, misc. business, and transportation. EU business sector includes professional consultancies / law firms / self-employed consultants, and in-house lobbyists and trade / business / professional associations. *Data sources*: US, Center for Responsive Politics and Federal Lobbying Disclosure Act Database; EU, LobbyFacts.eu and the EU Transparency Register

are, hold on until Chapter 10, which will tell you everything you need to know about campaign finance.

The second regularity is that "Corporations and trade associations comprise the vast majority of lobbying expenditures by interest groups." Indeed, we can see that fact in Figure 9.1. In contrast, issue-ideology membership groups represent 2 percent and 7 percent of lobbying expenditures at the federal and state levels, respectively.

The third regularity is that "large corporations . . . are more likely to lobby independently than are smaller groups," while "small interest groups are more likely to lobby using only trade associations." This, of course, is exactly what the theory of collective action would predict. Mathilde Bombardini and Francesco Trebbi (2011) consider the role of trade associations. These associations appear to be more effective than individual firms at influencing policies.

The fourth empirical regularity is that lobbying increases when the stakes are higher and the issues more salient. This is precisely what makes the empirical research challenging: it means that lobbying is endogenous and therefore that we cannot hope to estimate the impact of lobbying with naive statistical models and correlations.

How Skewed Are You?

Figure 9.2 looks at the lobbying and campaign finance activities of firms that belong to the S&P 1500 (roughly, the 1,500 largest firms in the US). We see that the fraction of firms that make positive campaign finance contributions or have positive lobbying expenses has grown over time. The fraction of S&P 1500 firms that engage in lobbying has increased from about 33 percent to about 42 percent.

Political activism by US firms is thus becoming more pervasive. At the same time, the distribution of campaign finance contributions and

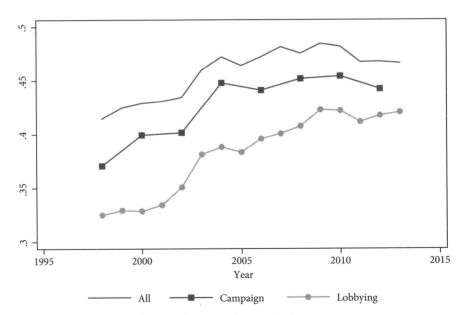

FIGURE 9.2 Fraction of politically active firms in S&P 1500

lobbying expenses has been and remains very skewed. *Skewness* is an interesting word that means different things to different people. When we say that an argument is skewed, we mean that it is biased, unfair, or misleading.

In statistics, we talk about a skewed distribution to describe an asymmetry around the mean. Symmetric data have a skewness of approximately zero. The normal distribution (the nicely bell-shaped curve) has a skewness of exactly zero. A distribution is skewed to the right when there is a long right tail of large outcomes.

Table 9.1 describes the distributions of firms' sales, campaign finance contributions, and lobbying expenses. The distribution of the logarithm of sales across firms is (positively) skewed. Its skewness coefficient is 0.23. This is a well-known fact; the firm-size distribution has a fat right tail. This means that large firms play an outsized role in the economy. Table 9.1 also shows the elasticity of campaign finance contributions and lobbying expenses relative to sales. For campaign contributions, the elasticity is 0.63. This means that, on average, when the revenues of a firm increase by 10 percent, its campaign contributions increase by 6.3 percent. For lobbying, the elasticity is 0.67.

Given that the distribution of firms' revenues is skewed and that contributions increase with revenues, we expect a high concentration of lobbying expenses and campaign contributions. Table 9.1 shows that this is indeed the case by looking at concentration ratios. Even if we only look

TABLE 9.1

Skewness of Lobbying and Campaign Finance Contributions by Firm Size

(logarithm of)	Among S&P 1500 firms			All firms
	Skewness & elasticities	CR50	Industry CR4	Industry CR4
Sales	0.23 (skew.)	42%	52%	15%
Campaign finance	0.63 (elas.)	49%	65%	35%
Lobbying	0.67 (elas.)	54%	68%	45%

The elasticities of campaign and lobbying expenses to sales are computed by regressing log(expenses) on log(sales) for expenses above $10,000 and controlling for year fixed effects.
Source: Compustat and OpenSecrets.com

within the S&P 1500, so only within large firms, we see that the top fifty firms account for 42 percent of sales but 49 percent of campaign finance and 54 percent of lobbying. If we group them by industries, and we look at the CR4 by industry, it is 52 percent versus 65 percent and 68 percent. Among the very large firms, the super-large therefore play an outsized role. But these comparisons among very large firms understate the actual skewness. If we consider all the firms in the economy, small and large, the average industry CR4 for sales is 15 percent. On average, the top four firms control 15 percent of the revenues in their industries. But they account for 35 percent of campaign finance contributions and 45 percent of lobbying expenditures. In other words, lobbying expenditures are three times more concentrated than revenues, which are themselves already fairly concentrated. This means that large firms play an even more outsized role in the political system than they do in the economy itself.

Gutiérrez and I show that this fact is true in essentially all industries. The CR4 for lobbying is almost always much larger than the CR4 for sales. Our data show that, in nearly all industries, the role of large firms in politics and lobbying is even larger than would be suggested by their economic size alone.

Let us go back to the comparison with Europe. How confident are we that lobbying is indeed a larger factor in the US? EU lobbying might be underestimated; joining the European Commission's Transparency Register is not mandatory. However, we have seen that lobbying expenditures are extremely skewed, so what really matters is to capture lobbying by large firms. For these firms, as far as we can tell, the data seem reliable.*

---

* Greenwood and Dreger (2013) estimated that 75 percent of businesses and 60 percent of NGOs active in engaging EU political institutions were in the register, and the number of registrants has increased by more than 50 percent since 2013. On the other hand, lobbying may be overestimated due to double counting: the data contain the corporations that employ lobbying intermediaries as well as the lobbying intermediaries themselves. There are also some measurement issues with small firms, and we follow LobbyFacts.eu in applying restrictions based on the number of European Parliament passes and European Commission meetings to mitigate these issues. In particular, we drop observations in the top 5 percent of lobbying expenditures by year for firms that have

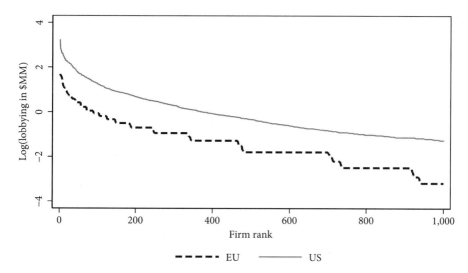

FIGURE 9.3 Distribution of large lobbying firms in the EU and in the US. Only firms are included—no trade associations or nonbusinesses. EU bunching is a result of how these data were processed (reporting in bins). *Data sources*: US, Center for Responsive Politics; EU, LobbyFacts.eu

One may also worry that our measures of lobbying toward EU institutions is lower because firms must lobby their individual countries as well. But this is also true in the US. In fact, according to FollowTheMoney.org, a website of the Campaign Finance Institute, total lobbying expenditures for only twenty states in the US (which account for 58 percent of US GDP) totaled $1.43 billion in 2016—nearly as much as total lobbying to the EU.

We can perform a more precise comparison using firm-level data. Figure 9.3 considers the top 1,000 lobbying firms in the EU and in the US. The shapes of the curves are similar for both entities, suggesting that qualitatively similar economic forces are at play. The US curve, however,

---

no European Parliament passes and no European Commission meetings. We also replace lobbying expenditures for "University College Dublin–National University of Ireland, Dublin" in 2015 with the prior year's quantity because it is an extreme outlier. The totals after applying these restrictions roughly match those reported in media outlets such as the *Guardian* (May 8, 2014). Note also that most firms report ranges of lobbying expenditures rather than specific amounts. We take the midpoint of all ranges in our estimates. Annual totals for the EU are based on the complete register available through LobbyFacts.eu as of year end 2012, 2013, 2014, and 2015.

is higher, which indicates that the propensity to spend on lobbying is materially higher in the US. The same results hold if we control for sector fixed effects. Konstantinos Dellis and David Sondermann (2017) estimate an elasticity of lobbying expenditures to log-sales of 0.15 in the EU. Using a sample of US firms from Compustat, we obtain an elasticity more than four times larger (0.620) in the US. The punch line is clear. Large firms in the US spend a lot more on lobbying than large firms in the EU, and this explains the large differences that we observe in the aggregate.

Do Lobbyists Succeed?

Our final question is also the most difficult to answer for the reasons explained earlier: the decision to lobby is highly endogenous. The big tech companies beefed up their lobbying efforts precisely when they started to hear complaints about their size and behavior, which meant they were more likely to be investigated precisely when they began to lobby more.

Most of the existing research on lobbying has focused on legislative outcomes: either votes or the composition of committees. The study of regulations and the influence on regulators is more recent. Regulators are often appointed and reappointed by legislators, and their budgets are usually determined by the votes of legislators. Firms want to influence regulators to increase their profits, and regulators might want to please legislators to increase their chance of reappointment and the size of their budgets.

Rui J. P. de Figueiredo Jr. and Geoff Edwards (2007) analyze lobbying by telecom firms toward state public utility commissions. They find that firms with larger contributions receive favorable regulatory decisions. Guy Holburn and Richard Vanden Bergh (2014) study mergers and acquisitions in the electrical utility industry. They find that firms contribute significantly more in the twelve-month period before the relevant regulatory decision than in other periods. This shows that firms attempt to strategically contribute, but we do not know if they actually succeed in influencing the decisions of regulators.

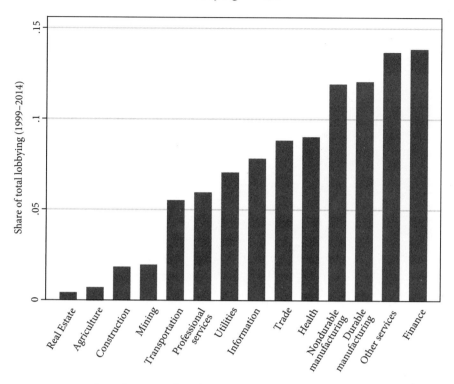

FIGURE 9.4 Contribution of industries to aggregate lobbying expenditures, 1999–2014

Figure 9.4 breaks out the aggregate expenditures on lobbying among industries. The finance industry is among the largest overall contributors, followed closely by durable and nondurable manufacturing and other services. Lobbying *intensity* also varies a lot across industries. Some industries (for example, finance) spend a much larger fraction of their gross income on lobbying than other industries (such as trade).

At the same time, some industries are targeted with a high number of antitrust cases, whereas some only receive a few. We focus here on non-merger cases because the literature has already studied mergers in detail. Figure 9.5 shows the distribution of nonmerger cases among industries. The number of cases varies a lot and, as one would expect, industries with more cases (for example, durable and nondurable manufacturing) lobby more. This highlights the reverse causality issue.

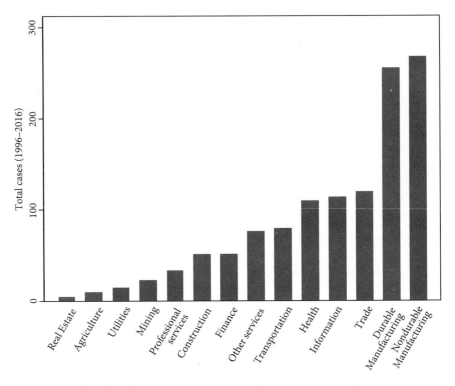

FIGURE 9.5 Number of cases brought against industries, 1996–2016

The first thing we can do to get around the reverse causality issue is to look at changes in lobbying over time. We can ask whether *increases* in lobbying lead to *decreases* in the number of cases. We find that the answer is yes, but the significance is weak. This naive estimate suggests that a doubling of lobbying expenditures to the DoJ and FTC reduces the number of cases in a given industry by about 4 percent. On the other hand, we know that this estimate is biased downward by endogeneity. We just don't know by how much.

We can do more if we use Europe to shed light on the US. Gutiérrez and I look at nonmerger antitrust cases and lobbying across industries (Gutiérrez and Philippon, 2018a). We find that there are more nonmerger cases in industries that are profitable and concentrated, as expected. Working with European data, however, gave us another idea. We can use EU cases as a measure of the unobserved "danger" that the industry faces, such as the threat of regulatory scrutiny. Let us assume for now that (1) lobbying in the US does not affect EU regulators, and (2) EU and US regulators have the same information about industry dynamics (technology, consumer taste, potential for bad behavior by large players, and so on).

If we accept these two assumptions, then cases in the EU can be used to proxy for "potential" regulatory scrutiny that is unaffected by US lobbying, and these cases should be positively correlated with excess lobbying in the US. We do show this to be true, and the link is significant. Whenever we observe more cases against one industry in the EU, we find more lobbying by that same industry in the US. We can then use EU cases to estimate the size of the reverse causality bias in the US—that is, the increase in lobbying in response to potential scrutiny. We find that the bias is substantial. One extra case in Europe increases US lobbying expenditures by 6 to 10 percent. This is a large effect since the standard deviation of lobbying expenditures (after accounting for industry and time effects) is only 38 percent.

Finally, now that we have an estimate of the magnitude of the reverse causality, we can de-bias the estimate of the impact of lobbying in the US. We find that the estimated effect more than doubles. The de-biased estimate implies that a doubling of lobbying expenditures to the DoJ and FTC reduces the number of cases in a given industry by 9 percent. This is a sizable effect, considering that such lobbying nearly tripled from 1998 to 2008. If our estimates are correct, increases in lobbying can thus account for most of the decrease in enforcement in the US.

Our model also predicts that lobbyists are more likely to succeed in the US than in the EU. Christine Mahoney (2008) finds that this is indeed the case. She performs a large-scale comparative study of the two systems, researching the work of 150 lobbyists fighting over forty-seven different policy issues, half in the US and half in the EU. She concludes that "In the US, 89% of corporations and 53% of trade associations succeed, while the majority of those fighting for the broader good—60% of citizen groups and 63% of foundations—fail in their lobbying goals . . . In the EU, we see that industry often wins as well (the success rates are 57% for trade associations and 61% for lobbying firms) but citizen groups and foundations fighting for the public good win at equal rates (56% and 67%)." She argues that these differences exist because legislators in the US depend on wealthy interests for campaign contributions.

The Impact of Lobbying

While there may be much that we don't know about the precise impact of lobbying, the data we've been able to assemble tell us two key things for our purposes here.

First of all, lobbying efforts work. Whether it's a grassroots movement to save a beloved television show or an under-the-radar push to scuttle a new regulation before it ever becomes public, lobbying has a very real impact on public policy.

Second, lobbying expenditures are growing rapidly in the US, and the vast majority are undertaken by the business community, either directly or through trade associations. These groups' primary aims seem to be to protect (or create) economic rents.

In its January 19, 2019, edition, the *Wall Street Journal* reported the illuminating example of the fight to outlaw online gambling. Gambling in America is mostly regulated by the states, and until 2011 the view of the Justice Department was that online gambling was prohibited by the federal Wire Act. In 2011, the DoJ changed its mind and decided that the prohibition applied to online sports betting but not to other forms of gambling. Casino magnate and top Republican donor Sheldon Adelson was displeased. In April 2017, his lobbyists drafted a memo arguing that the DoJ's 2011 decision was wrong. In January 2019, the DoJ made an unusual move: it reversed its opinion. The *Wall Street Journal* noticed that the statement by the DoJ contained the same legal language and arguments as the 2017 memo written by Adelson's lobbyists.

The comparison with lobbying in Europe is interesting. There are many similar cases in which lobbyists' language has made its way into regulations in Europe as well. In fact, in the case of technically complex regulations, this is exactly what one would expect, and it is consistent with the expertise and information-sharing view of lobbying. On balance, however, it seems that lobbying is less prevalent in Europe. This suggests that lobbying may be one potential driver of the decline in competitive pressures in US markets compared to EU markets. An important factor is that legislators in the US depend on wealthy interests for campaign contributions.

This not the end of the story, then. Our next task is to understand how political campaigns are financed.

CHAPTER 10

Money and Politics

Politics has got so expensive that it takes lots of money to even get
beat with nowadays.

WILL ROGERS

HOW SUCCESSFUL would a candidate running for a seat in the US House
of Representatives be if, during every campaign event, she said that she
would take a part-time job that would claim thirty hours of every work
week if she were elected? She'd likely be laughed right out of the race,
right?

The problem is, she would have accurately described the amount of
time that actual members of Congress spend on fundraising every week,
year in and year out, as long as they remain in office.

Politics has become so expensive that new members of Congress are
told in no uncertain terms that their first and highest priority in Washington is to raise the money they need to ensure their re-election. In 2016,
Representative David Jolly, a Republican from Florida, told the news program *60 Minutes* what his first days in Washington were like. He had
arrived after winning a special election, which meant that he would face
voters again only six months later.

"We sat behind closed doors at one of the party headquarters back
rooms in front of a white board where the equation was drawn out," he
said. "You have six months until the election. Break that down to having
to raise $2 million in the next six months. And your job, new member of
Congress, is to raise $18,000 a day. Your first responsibility is to make
sure you hit $18,000 a day."

And it never stops. Democrats and Republicans alike are given quotas
to meet every year, depending on their seniority and placement on

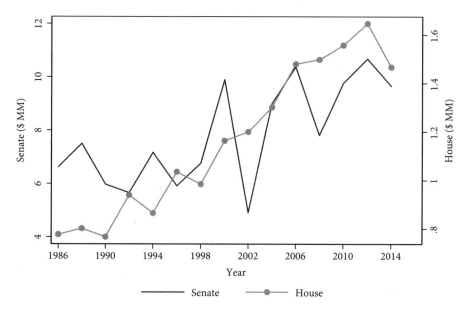

FIGURE 10.1 Average direct spending by winning candidates. All spending is in 2014 dollars to neutralize the effect of inflation. *Data source:* Center for Responsive Politics

different committees. A Democratic memo prepared for new House members in 2013 advised them to set aside at least four hours every day to call potential donors—"dialing for dollars," it's called. The same memo suggested they set aside only two hours for activity on the House floor or in committee meetings.

Will Rogers, quoted in the epigraph to this chapter, noted the presence of too much money in electoral politics in 1931. The problem isn't a new one. But the kind of money politicians are now expected to raise is orders of magnitude larger than it was back then.

Figure 10.1 shows the average direct campaign spending of winning candidates for the Senate and for the House. The cost of winning a Senate race was around $4 million in 1986 (adjusting for inflation). In 2014 it cost $12 million. Winning a seat in the House is cheaper, but the cost has still doubled over the past thirty years, from $800,000 to $1.6 million.

Moreover, Figure 10.1 does not tell the full story. It shows only the direct spending by the candidates' campaigns. Political action committees (PACs), super PACs, and political nonprofits, which we will dissect in this chapter, have become increasingly important since 2010.

TABLE 10.1

Five Most Expensive Senate Races of 2014

	Total spending	Campaign	Outside groups
North Carolina Senate	$113,479,706	$32,390,468	$81,089,238
Colorado Senate	$97,285,589	$27,887,734	$69,397,855
Iowa Senate	$85,364,286	$23,452,451	$61,911,835
Kentucky Senate	$78,231,062	$44,838,119	$33,392,943
Georgia Senate	$66,136,490	$39,579,101	$26,557,389

Data source: Center for Responsive Politics

Table 10.1 shows the expenditure of the top five Senate races in 2014. The most expensive race was the one pitting an incumbent Democratic senator, Kay Hagan, against a Republican challenger, Thom Tillis, for the North Carolina Senate. What is interesting is that the two candidates spent just $32 million of the total $113 million spent in the election. Most of the spending came from outside groups.

Naturally, campaign contributions and election costs go hand in hand. Figure 10.2a shows the contributions by various groups. Total contributions have increased by about $6 billion. By far the largest donors are business lobbies. It is also the group that has increased its contributions the most, from $2 to $6 billion, thus accounting for two-thirds of the overall increase. The other big increase comes from very wealthy individuals, the top 1 percent.

Figure 10.2b shows the concentration of donors, pooling all groups together, and breaking them down by largest contributors. The top 1 percent of donors contribute about three-quarters of the total. As we discussed in the previous chapter, political contributions, just like lobbying expenses, are extremely skewed. It's really only the big donors that matter.

Among individual contributions, the skewness is even more impressive. Consider the top 0.01 percent. One way of thinking about this is that a person in the top 0.01 percent is the richest among 10,000. This segment has increased its share of national income, and today earns about 5 percent of total income, as we know from the famous work of Thomas Piketty and Emanuel Saez. That is a very skewed distribution. But it's

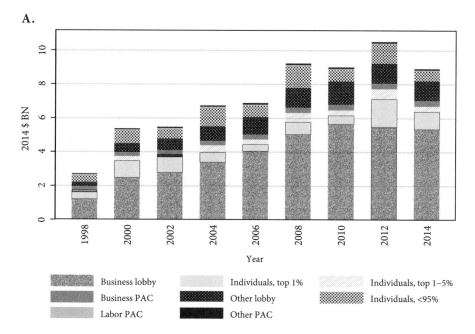

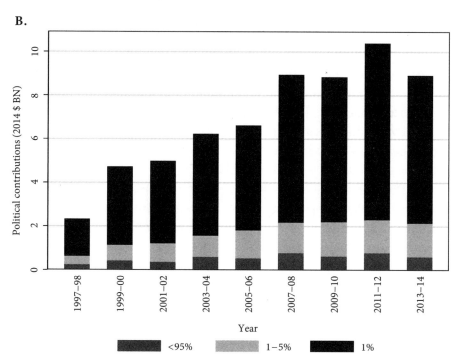

FIGURE 10.2 (*a*) Political expenditures by groups; (*b*) The concentration of contributions (both in 2014 dollars). *Data source:* Center for Responsive Politics

TABLE 10.2

2016 Election Donations ($MM)

	Hillary Clinton	Donald Trump
Raised by candidate	$973	$564
Raised by super PACs	$217	$82
Total	$1,190	$646

nothing compared to the distribution of campaign contributions. The top 0.01 percent of donors contribute an astounding 40 percent of all contributions.

This does not mean that the biggest spender always wins. Donald Trump won the presidential election in November 2016 despite raising and spending much less than Hillary Clinton (see Table 10.2). A few months earlier, he beat better-funded candidates in the Republican primaries. In fact, Donald Trump raised less outside money than any major party presidential nominee since John McCain in 2008. Yet he dominated the airwaves and won the election.

On average, however, the largest spender usually wins. For instance, analysis of the 2014 elections by the Center for Responsive Politics shows the candidate who spent the most prevailed 94.2 percent of the time in House races and 81.8 percent of the time in Senate races. But that does not mean that money is the reason that they win. The fundamental problem of endogeneity that we have discussed in Chapter 9 is back with a vengeance in the case of political campaigns. We observe a correlation, but we do not know which way the causality runs.

Perhaps incumbents would win even if they did not outspend their opponents. Perhaps people simply like to give money to the winning team: this is called *reverse causality*. Or perhaps it the same underlying qualities that make some people better candidates and better fundraisers at the same time: this is called an *omitted variable bias*.

Our task in this chapter is to understand how money and politics interact and to tease out the causal effects of one on the other. Like lobbying, this is difficult because spending decisions are strategic choices, not random decisions. The curse of endogeneity is still with us. Businesses might strategically bid on winners, but that does not mean that money is necessary to win. On the other hand, it does suggest that businesses expect some returns and that politicians value their contributions.

Campaign Finance Laws

Campaign finance controversies are as old as the Republic, and their history is full of irony, misleading laws, and half-baked solutions. Theodore Roosevelt received more than $2 million in corporate contributions for his 1904 campaign. After his election, the donations created a controversy, and Roosevelt himself called for the prohibition of corporate contributions. In his annual address to Congress in 1905, he said: "All contributions by corporations to any political committee or for any political purpose should be forbidden by law; directors should not be permitted to use stockholders' money for such purposes; and, moreover, a prohibition of this kind would be, as far as it went, an effective method of stopping the evils aimed at in corrupt practices acts."

Roosevelt signed the Tillman Act in 1907. It was the first legislation prohibiting monetary corporate contributions to national political campaigns. But the act did not include an effective enforcement mechanism. It included penalties, but nobody to apply them. There was no Federal Election Commission and no disclosure requirements for candidates. In addition, the act did not apply to primary elections. In many places (much of the Democratic South, for instance), the general elections were not really contested, so the primary election was the most important one. And finally, a corporation could ask its officers or directors to make personal contributions to a candidate and reimburse them later with bonuses or other perks.

Disclosure requirements and extensions to primary elections came in 1910 and 1911. There were also some spending limitations, but these were later struck down by the US Supreme Court.* Political action committees wouldn't appear for a few more decades, and the way they did is

---

* Henry Ford lost the US Senate race in Michigan to Truman Newberry. Ford alleged Newberry exceeded the $100,000 limit during his campaign. Newberry was convicted in 1921 and appealed his conviction to the US Supreme Court, which sided with Newberry and struck down the spending limits.

quite illuminating. Congress tried to ban labor union contributions to candidates through the Smith–Connally and Taft–Hartley Acts of the mid-1940s. The Smith–Connally Act forbade unions from contributing to federal candidates. In response, the Congress of Industrial Organizations (CIO) formed the first PAC in 1944 to raise money for the re-election of President Franklin D. Roosevelt. The PAC's money came from voluntary contributions from union members rather than union treasuries, so it did not violate the Smith–Connally Act. PACs were unfettered by the political advertising and spending laws that applied to the candidates, so they could spend as much as they wanted to independently promote specific candidates and issues among their membership and to the general public.

As Thomas Stratmann (2019) explains, "the modern era of campaign finance laws at the national level began in the 1970s, and these laws have changed a few times since in subsequent legislation and court rulings." The Federal Election Campaign Act (FECA) of 1971 initially proposed spending caps but not the resources to enforce them. FECA was refined in 1974 to create the bipartisan Federal Election Commission (FEC)—the body that enforces campaign finance law to this day. In 1976, Sen. James Buckley, a Republican from New York, argued in front of the Supreme Court that FECA limits on campaign spending violated free speech rights. The Supreme Court agreed, and its ruling in *Buckley v. Valeo* was ultimately interpreted as allowing unlimited spending by political candidates.

In 2002, the Bipartisan Campaign Reform Act—also called the McCain–Feingold Act—attempted to limit spending and ban political ads within thirty days of the election. The law was quickly challenged, and the Supreme Court struck down several of its provisions.

Follow the Money . . . If You Can

As we have explained in the previous chapter, measuring the impact of lobbying and campaign finance is fundamentally difficult.

Figure 10.3 shows the flow of money and influence from firms and wealthy individuals to government agencies, political parties, and elected officials. The complexity of the chart is immediately apparent. The figure

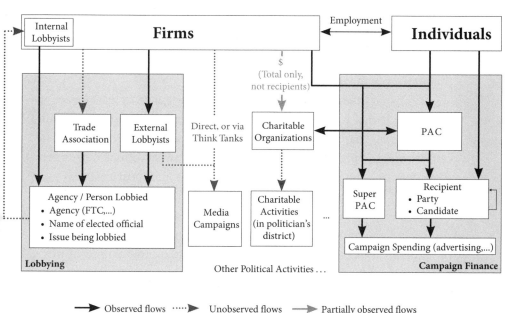

FIGURE 10.3 What we see, and what we don't

highlights the flows that we observe, the flows that we observe partially, and the flows that we do not observe.

An important distinction must be made between "hard" money and "soft" money. Hard money consists of direct donations to campaigns, political parties, and traditional PACs, and is typically restricted. Soft money consists of donations to the nonfederal accounts of a political party. Soft money is typically spent on television and radio ads. These ads focus on issues and do not expressly endorse candidates, but they are clearly aimed at affecting votes in federal elections.

There is a corollary in the world of lobbying. Firms can hire internal or external lobbyists. Internal lobbyists are employees of the firm and lobby on its behalf. We can observe which agency or which politician they meet, and the issue that they discuss. The same is more or less true with external lobbyists, who must report the name of the firm that hired them.

But much lobbying happens via trade associations. Trade associations create an opaque filter between the firms and their targets. When lobbyists from a trade association meet with a government official, we observe it, and we know the issue being lobbied. However, we do not observe the contributions of firms to the trade association, so we cannot link the lobbying to a particular firm. This means that we cannot compute the total lobbying effort of a particular firm.

Campaign finance is relatively more transparent, or at least it used to be. Most of what we know comes from the Center for Responsive Politics, a nonpartisan research group tracking money in US politics. The center's website provides most of the data and observations in this section regarding the direct contributions of firms and individuals, as well as those of PACs and super PACs.

Political action committees are used to raise and spend money to help some candidates and defeat others. Most PACs represent business, labor, or ideological interests. PACs can give $5,000 to a candidate committee per election (primary, general, or special). They can also give up to $15,000 annually to any national party committee, and $5,000 annually to any other PAC. PACs may receive up to $5,000 from any one individual, PAC, or party committee per calendar year.* Table 10.3 lists the top PACs of the 2015–2016 election cycle. You can see that most of the contributors are typically large (AT&T), heavily influenced by regulations (banks and credit unions), or reliant on government contracts (Lockheed Martin, Northrop Grumman).

Many politicians also form leadership PACs as a way of raising money to help fund other candidates' campaigns.† During the 2016 election cycle, leadership PACs raised $49 million. The Democrats received $19 million (38 percent) and the Republicans received $30 million (63 percent). The top five leadership PACs of 2016 are listed in Table 10.4.

---

* A PAC must register with the FEC within ten days of its formation, providing the name and address of the PAC, its treasurer, and any connected organizations. Affiliated PACs are treated as one donor for the purpose of contribution limits. Although commonly called PACs, federal election law refers to these accounts as "separate segregated funds" because money contributed to a PAC is kept in a bank account separate from the general corporate or union treasury.

† Since June 2008, leadership PACs reporting electronically must list the candidate sponsoring the PAC, as per the Honest Leadership and Open Government Act of 2007. Leadership PACs are often indicative of a politician's aspirations for leadership positions in Congress or for higher office.

TABLE 10.3

Top Sixteen PACs of the 2016 Election Cycle

PAC name	Total	Democrats	Republicans
National Association of Realtors	$3,973,350	42%	58%
National Beer Wholesalers Association	$3,322,700	43%	57%
AT&T Inc.	$2,953,750	38%	62%
Honeywell International	$2,861,364	40%	60%
National Auto Dealers Association	$2,659,250	28%	72%
Lockheed Martin	$2,612,750	38%	62%
Blue Cross / Blue Shield	$2,573,398	36%	64%
International Brotherhood of Electrical Workers	$2,570,650	96%	4%
American Bankers Association	$2,444,007	21%	79%
Credit Union National Association	$2,380,350	47%	53%
Operating Engineers Union	$2,250,300	74%	26%
Comcast Corp.	$2,242,300	36%	64%
National Association of Home Builders	$2,185,625	17%	83%
Boeing Co.	$2,163,135	43%	57%
Northrop Grumman	$2,135,500	39%	61%
Nat. Assn. of Insurance & Financial Advisors	$2,091,950	33%	67%
Total	$41,420,379	42%	58%

Data source: Center for Responsive Politics calculations using data released by the FEC on November 27, 2017

Super PACs are a new form of PAC created after a court decision, *SpeechNow.org v. FEC*, in 2010 that has reshaped the campaign finance landscape. In February 2008, SpeechNow.org—an organization that pools individual contributions—filed suit against the Federal Election Commission in the US District Court of the District of Columbia, challenging the federal contribution limits and disclosure requirements for political committees that make independent expenditures in elections. The district court denied the request, and SpeechNow.org appealed the decision to the US Court of Appeals for the DC Circuit.* The Court of Appeals

---

* Applying intermediate scrutiny, the district court held that limits on contributions to committees making solely independent expenditures serve important

TABLE 10.4

Top Leadership PACs in 2016

PAC name	Affiliate	Total	Democrats	Republicans
Majority Committee PAC	Kevin McCarthy (R-Calif)	$2,086,513	$0	$2,086,513
Prosperity Action	Paul Ryan (R-Wis)	$1,326,238	$0	$1,326,238
AmeriPAC	Steny H. Hoyer (D-Md)	$1,019,499	$1,019,499	$0
Eye of the Tiger PAC	Steve Scalise (R-La)	$942,485	$0	$942,485
More Conservatives PAC	Patrick McHenry (R-NC)	$697,000	$0	$697,000

decided to stay the case to await a decision by the Supreme Court in a related and highly controversial case.

Citizens United v. FEC

While SpeechNow.org was appealing its denial, the US Supreme Court was considering the case of *Citizens United v. FEC*. The conservative nonprofit organization Citizens United wanted to air a film critical of Hillary Clinton shortly before the 2008 Democratic primary, but federal law—based on the McCain–Feingold Act of 2002—prohibited any corporation (or labor union) from doing so within thirty days of a primary or sixty days of an election. In addition, corporations could not spend money to advocate for the election or defeat of a candidate. The court found that these provisions of the law conflicted with the US Constitution. On January 21, 2010, the Supreme Court held that the free speech clause of the First Amendment prohibits the government from restricting independent expenditures for communications by non-

government interests by preventing actual and apparent corruption. Looking to the past behavior of so-called "527 groups" that did not register with the commission, yet had close ties with the major political parties and made millions of dollars of expenditures influencing the federal elections of 2004, the court found that such "nominally independent" organizations are "uniquely positioned to serve as conduits for corruption both in terms of the sale of access and the circumvention of the soft money ban."

profit corporations, for-profit corporations, labor unions, and other associations.

This landmark decision would affect constitutional law, campaign finance, and corporate law. It was a divisive and controversial decision with a 5–4 majority. Justice Kennedy's majority opinion—with Justices Scalia, Alito, Thomas, and Chief Justice Roberts joining—found, "If the First Amendment has any force, it prohibits Congress from fining or jailing citizens, or associations of citizens, for simply engaging in political speech." A dissenting opinion by Justice Stevens—joined by Justices Ginsburg, Breyer, and Sotomayor—argued that the majority decision "threatens to undermine the integrity of elected institutions across the Nation. The path it has taken to reach its outcome will, I fear, do damage to this institution . . . A democracy cannot function effectively when its constituent members believe laws are being bought and sold." The Citizens United ruling is one of the most controversial in the history of the court. For its proponents, it was a defense of the First Amendment. For its critics, it basically legalized corruption.

Let us now go back to SpeechNow.org. Based on the Supreme Court decision, the Court of Appeals for the DC Circuit struck down the federal contribution limits of independent expenditure committees in March 2010. The basic motivation was that "the government has no anticorruption interest in limiting contributions to an independent expenditure group." These independent expenditure committees are known today as super PACs.

The decisions did not affect disclosure requirements. The Citizens United case also did not affect the federal ban on *direct* corporate contributions to candidates or political parties. The Court of Appeals upheld the political committee disclosure requirements.

In sum, the difference between PACs and super PACs is that super PACs can raise as much money as they want from corporations, unions, associations, and individuals, then spend unlimited sums to overtly advocate for or against political candidates. However, unlike traditional PACs, super PACs cannot donate money directly to political candidates, and their spending must not be coordinated with that of the candidates they benefit. Super PACs make no contributions to candidates or parties, but they make independent expenditures in federal races to advocate the election or defeat of a specific candidate—running ads, sending mail, and so on. These committees file regular financial reports with the FEC that include their donors along with their expenditures.

TABLE 10.5

Super PACs with Over $3 Million in Independent Expenditures in 2018

Super PACS	Supports/opposes	Independent expenditures	Viewpoint	Total raised
Congressional Leadership Fund		$70,579,180	Conservative	$100,999,974
Senate Majority PAC		$46,632,153	Liberal	$95,693,285
Senate Leadership Fund		$40,977,919	Conservative	$61,962,292
House Majority PAC		$16,366,917	Liberal	$51,456,232
Women Vote!		$13,572,937	Liberal	$19,134,659
New Republican PAC	supports Scott	$12,129,362	Conservative	$10,864,801
DefendArizona	supports McSally	$11,057,869	Conservative	$1,375,200
Club for Growth Action		$9,831,861	Conservative	$13,266,020
National Association of Realtors		$8,071,191		$11,050,215
With Honor Fund		$7,026,669		$17,683,994
America First Action		$6,879,805	Conservative	$18,129,004
Patients for Affordable Drugs Action		$6,402,502		$3,117,279
Restoration PAC		$6,334,807	Conservative	$7,252,065
Americas PAC		$5,807,485	Conservative	$5,657,500
Highway 31	supports Jones	$4,232,558	Liberal	$4,367,528
Wisconsin Next PAC	supports Vukmir	$4,110,362	Conservative	$2,940,050
Change Now PAC		$3,897,079	Liberal	$1,782,491
Integrity New Jersey	opposes Menendez	$3,462,048	Conservative	$2,125,000
Total		$277,372,704		$428,857,589

As of October 6, 2018, 2,153 groups organized as super PACs had reported total receipts of $792 million and total independent expenditures of $350 million in the 2018 cycle. Table 10.5 lists the super PACs with more than $3 million in independent expenditures. Conservative super PACs have raised $225 million and liberal ones have raised $172 million.

What's in It for Politicians and Businesses?

It's always been difficult for researchers to draw a straight line from campaign contributions to lawmakers and specific effects, so it's especially helpful when former lawmakers pull back the curtain for us.

In a speech in April 2018, Mick Mulvaney, a former representative from South Carolina who left Congress to serve in various positions in the Trump administration, told a group of banking industry executives exactly how things worked during his time in the House.

"We had a hierarchy in my office in Congress," he said. "If you're a lobbyist who never gave us money, I didn't talk to you. If you're a lobbyist who gave us money, I might talk to you." He encouraged his listeners to continue sending lobbyists to engage with Congress, presumably after having opened the door with a contribution, calling the process one of the "fundamental underpinnings of our representative democracy" and adding, "You have to continue to do it."

Research supports this perspective. For instance, Stephen Ansolabehere, John M. de Figueiredo, and James M. Snyder Jr. (2003) show that campaign contributions and lobbying are positively correlated, suggesting that campaign contributions are a way for interest groups to buy access to politicians. Once they gain access, lobbyists have a chance to voice the interests of their clients.

So what's in it for politicians and business groups? The short answer is: re-election and influence.

However, straight-up admissions that money buys access, like Mulvaney's, are very much the exception to the rule. In general, it is extremely difficult to collect evidence demonstrating what feels like a pretty straightforward insight. On the one hand, it should be obvious. Campaign finance and lobbying allow businesses to gain access and influence regulators. As Thomas Stratmann (2019) explains: "It may be that contributions influence the positions of a candidate, the roll call votes a candidate casts, or even the amount of access time contributors receive from a candidate. These conjectures all derive from the assumption the firms are profit-maximizing and don't make contributions for reasons that do not benefit their bottom line. They contribute with the expectation of receiving something in return for their contribution."

Reciprocally, campaign finance should help win elections. However, as Stratmann notes: "from the beginning of the empirical literature up to the present day a consensus has not developed about the role of campaign expenditures for winning elections."

It is important to keep in mind that money is not the only source of influence. The first thing lobbyists do when they want to move legislation on behalf of a firm is to study the distribution of that firm's employment across districts. That is a good way to locate one's allies. Matilde Bombardini and Francesco Trebbi (2012) show that when an industry carries a lot of employment locally, the member of Congress from that district tends to vote as the industry wants. As a result, the industry does not need to spend much in the form of direct campaign contributions.

It is pretty clear that the goal of campaign contributions is to influence not only the outcome of elections, but also the behavior of the politicians after the election. W. P. Welch (1980) shows that most donations go to incumbents who are likely to win and not to those in a close race. Similarly, Stratmann (1998) finds that the timing of donations follows the timing of legislative debates at least as much as the timing of the expenditures of the election cycle.

What is it exactly that firms get in exchange? It's hard to know. Measurement of outcomes is difficult because the parties have an incentive to hide any quid pro quo. Researchers are forced to work with whatever data are available. For instance, the research on the impact of campaign finance has traditionally focused on roll-call votes because roll-call data are most easily accessible. But do we expect influence to show up in roll-call votes? A quid pro quo exchange of contribution for a roll-call vote would be rather obvious. It might well be noticed and bring in a suspicion of corruption. Interest groups prefer to follow a long-term influence strategy rather than to seek short-term influence on a particular vote (Snyder, 1992). Randall S. Kroszner and Stratmann (2005) argue that the nature of committees actually facilitates long-term influence via repeated interactions. But this makes it much harder to measure.

When we look at election outcomes, we encounter the same endogeneity issue as with lobbying. A classic paper by MIT political economist James Snyder shows that the allocation of campaign resources is deliberate and strategic (Snyder, 1989). Think about it: who would like to spend a lot of money on a campaign: someone who is sure to win or someone who is unsure about winning? Probably the second one. On the other hand, incumbents have an easier time raising funds, and they are also more likely to win because they have already won once. Simply looking at the probability of winning an election and the amount spent on the campaign trail cannot tell us how much money matters and why incumbents have an advantage.

Alexander Fouirnaies and Andrew B. Hall (2014) get around the issue in a smart way. They estimate the incumbency advantage by comparing, at the district level, the campaign contributions to the party that barely lost versus the party that barely won the *previous* election. They can then tease out the causal impact of campaign contributions on the likelihood of winning the next election. They find that campaign contributions explain a large part of the incumbency advantage, and that interest groups motivated by access to the politician account for two-thirds of the financial advantage of the incumbent.

How much do political connections matter for businesses? To document the link between money and politics, you need really smart and creative researchers. Seema Jayachandran (2006) documented a clear "Jeffords effect" on US firms. In May 2001, Senator James Jeffords left the Republican Party and tipped control of the US Senate to the Democrats. Jayachandran focuses on the consequences of this switch. Firms more closely aligned with the Republican Party lost, and firms aligned with the Democratic Party gained. She measures alignment using a firm's soft-money donations to the national parties. She uses stock market prices to assess how valuable politicians are to a firm. She estimates that an additional $100,000 donated to the Republican Party in the previous election

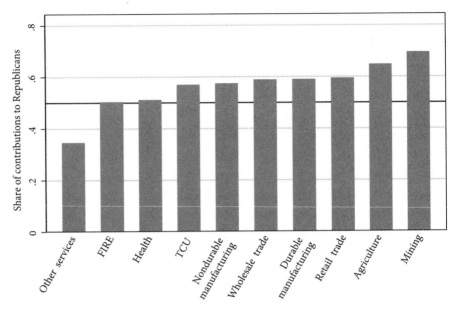

FIGURE 10.4 Contributions by industry sector to the Republican Party. FIRE = finance, insurance, and real estate; TCU = transportation, communications, and utilities

cycle is associated with a .33 percent lower stock return during the event window—that is, the week of Jeffords's switch.

Political connections are therefore clearly valuable to firms. But politics is notoriously risky. In this context, we would expect firms to hedge their bets. And they do. Figure 10.4 shows that industries give to both parties, though most of them give a somewhat higher fraction to Republicans.

A Less Prominent Role in Europe

Money seeks to influence politics in every country. In France, despite fairly strong campaign finance laws, Yasmine Bekkouche and Julia Cagé (2018) find that campaign donations do influence election results. They collected data on 40,000 candidates from four municipal and five parliamentary elections. The level and evolution of spending is quite different from what we have discussed in the US. Following changes in campaign finance laws in the 1990s—lower spending limits and prohibition of corporate contributions—there was a decrease in parliamentary election spending from around €22,000 per candidate in 1993 to €10,000 in 2007.

Within an election cycle, however, there is still a tight connection between spending and votes, which brings us to the endogeneity issue. Perhaps candidates who are likely to win are also better at fundraising. Perhaps people like to give to winners. We cannot conclude that money buys votes simply by looking at the correlation. That is where research ingenuity really kicks in. Bekkouche and Cagé note that, between 1993 and 1997, France enacted a law prohibiting contributions from legal entities, such as corporations and unions. The law was applied for the first time in the 1997 legislative elections. The law affected mostly those candidates who previously relied on private donations from legal entities. Bekkouche and Cagé estimate that an additional euro received from legal entities in 1993 is associated with a 0.46 euro decrease in total revenues between 1993 and 1997. In other words, these candidates could replace only about half of the lost revenues.

Here is the really cool part. We agree that we cannot use the actual spending pattern to show that money can buy votes, because of reverse causality and omitted variable bias. But we can use the predicted change in revenues triggered by the change in legislation. That predicted change in revenue is not caused by the ability of the candidate or by the expectation of winning. The predicted loss in revenues can be used to tease out the causal role of money in winning elections. They find a significant causal effect of spending on vote shares in the 1997 election. The price of a vote is about €10 for the legislative elections.

This discussion could be expanded to most other European countries. Money influences politics everywhere. What sets the US apart is therefore not that money seeks to influence politics; it is rather the scale of the money involved that is exceptional. If differences in lobbying expenditures between the US and the EU are large (a factor of two, or three for corporate lobbying, as we saw in Chapter 9), differences in campaign contributions are staggering. Figure 10.5 shows total campaign contributions for federal elections in the US and total campaign expenditures for several European countries, normalized by GDP. The sample of European countries is primarily based on EU Parliament in 2015 and was chosen to be representative of the European economy.

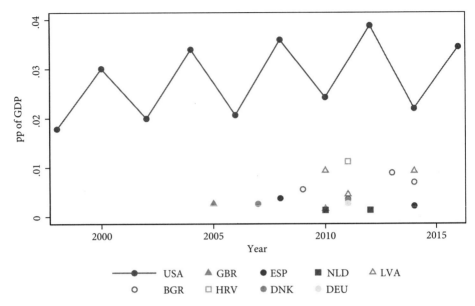

FIGURE 10.5 Total campaign expenditures divided by GDP. *Data sources*: US, Center for Responsive Politics; EU, EU Parliament (2015). For Germany, see Bundestags-Drucksache (2013).

Campaign contributions in the US are fifty times larger than those in most European countries.

The evidence is once again consistent with the model developed in Chapter 8. Europe has so far avoided the outsized role of money in politics that we observe in the US. Money in politics spills over to regulatory agencies. Federal Trade Commission and Department of Justice officials are likely to be influenced by elected politicians, or at the very least, elected politicians will attempt to influence the process. For instance, upon initiating its investigation of Google, the FTC received a number of letters from members of the US Congress, including at least one encouraging that agency to desist, noting the ability of Congress to limit the FTC's power. Members of the European Parliament would be unlikely to write such letters, and even if they did, their efforts would not be very influential. The European Commission's Directorate-General for Competition (DG Comp) is entirely independent from actions taken by the European Parliament.

State Politics in the United States

Let us now turn to state politics in the US. This research is particularly useful because there are many more elections to consider, and they do not all happen at the same time, thereby giving us a chance to rule out confounding factors.

State regulators play an important role in the US economy. State attorneys general are in charge of competition policy. The attorney general serves as the chief legal adviser and chief law enforcement officer for the state government and is empowered to prosecute violations of state law. The National Association of Attorneys General (NAAG) facilitates interaction among attorneys general and collects data that we will use below.

Campaign finance is also regulated at the state level. Robert J. Huckshorn (1985) identifies five primary types of regulation across states: restriction of the source of campaign contributions; restriction of the size of contributions; restriction of the size of political expenditures; disclosure laws; and public campaign financing laws.

There is evidence that unlimited contributions help mostly incumbents. Thomas Stratmann and Francisco J. Aparicio-Castillo (2007) use changes in campaign finance regulations across states to show that races are more competitive in states with stricter limits on campaign contributions. Specifically, they find that limits on contributions reduce the advantage of incumbents. Keith E. Hamm and Robert E. Hogan (2008) find that contribution limits tend to reduce incumbency advantage and make electoral races more competitive. Timothy Besley and Anne Case (2003) focus on limits to corporate contributions and find that states with tighter restrictions have higher voter turnout and a higher fraction of women and Democrats holding positions in the legislature. Robert Feinberg and Kara Reynolds (2010) study the determinants of state-level antitrust activity. They find that states with larger economies and larger government expenditures file more antitrust cases and that antitrust activity increases during periods of high unemployment. They also find that state attorneys general who are appointed to their position file fewer antitrust actions than attorneys general who are elected.

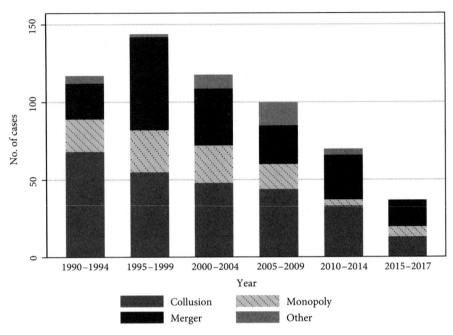

FIGURE 10.6 The type and number of enforcement cases with state attorneys general as plaintiffs. *Data source*: National Association of Attorneys General (NAAG) State Antitrust Litigation Database

German Gutiérrez and I have tested the effects of political expenditures on enforcement at the state level. We gather a list of antitrust enforcement cases initiated by state attorneys general from the Antitrust Multistate Litigation Database. We obtain campaign contributions for state elections from the Campaign Finance Institute. Case data is available since 1990, but contributions are available only after 2000. Figure 10.6 shows that state-level enforcement has decreased since the 1990s, just like federal enforcement. The decrease is particularly pronounced for nonmerger cases involving monopolization or collusion.

Figure 10.7 plots nonmerger antitrust enforcement cases at the state level against total campaign contributions, which have nearly doubled since 2003. We use the four-year moving average because contributions exhibit substantial seasonality—increasing in years with gubernatorial elections.

We then ask if these two trends are related. To do so, we check to see if state campaign contributions predict the number of enforcement cases

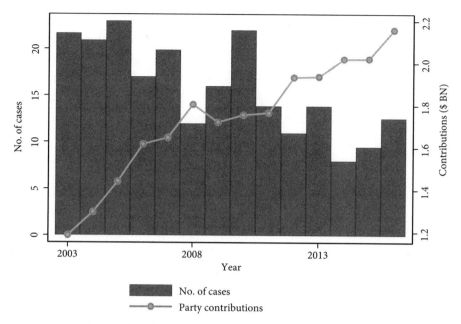

FIGURE 10.7 State political contributions and nonmerger antitrust cases. Four-year moving average contributions control for the seasonality of election cycles. *Data sources*: Case data, NAAG State Antitrust Litigation Database; state campaign contributions, Campaign Finance Institute

for each state election cycle. The nice feature of state-level panel data is that we can net out the effects of election cycles and persistent state heterogeneity (we include state and election-cycle fixed effects). We can also control for a state's economic conditions (growth and unemployment).

We find that high contributions in a state's election cycle predict significantly fewer nonmerger enforcement cases in the following years. Broadly speaking, then, we find that companies strategically use campaign finance contributions across states to shield themselves from future enforcement cases.

Dark Money, Charitable Foundations, TV Commercials, and Revolving Doors

There are significant gaps in our ability to track political expenditures. We do not know the source of the money for a growing fraction of political spending. Political nonprofits do not have to disclose their donors. They can if they wish, but if they do not, no one knows where the money comes from. In theory, super PACs are supposed to disclose their donors. The problem is that they can accept donations from political nonprofits that have no obligation for disclosure. Spending without disclosure of donors has increased dramatically since 2008, and since 2012, has been more than $100 million per election cycle.

The nonpartisan, nonprofit advocacy organization Issue One has traced most of the increase in "dark money" to spending by only fifteen groups.* These groups include labor unions, corporations, megadonors, and other special interest groups. As the report explains, "dark money comes into politics in many forms—from opaque limited liability companies (LLCs) to secretive social welfare organizations and trade associations." Issue One provides a few striking examples. In Utah in 2011 "an innocuously named group called Freedom Path began airing ads" promoting Sen. Orrin Hatch, the incumbent, and opposing his primary challenger, state senator Dan Liljenquist. It was only in November 2012—months after the primary election and weeks after Hatch had won the general election—that a public document revealed that "a trade association called Pharmaceutical Research and Manufacturers of America (PhRMA), the nation's pharmaceutical drug lobby, had provided nearly 90 percent of Freedom Path's initial funding in 2011." And, as one might have guessed, Senator Hatch enjoyed a friendly relationship with PhRMA. Voters in Utah did not have access to this information because, following the Supreme Court's Citizens United decision discussed earlier, Freedom Path was formed as a nonprofit "social welfare" organization under Section 501(c)(4) of the US tax code—allowing its donors to remain hidden. In a more recent case, "one month before the 2017 special election to fill the Senate seat vacated by incumbent Republican Sen. Jeff Sessions . . . a super PAC called Highway 31 popped up in Alabama and began spending more than $4 million to boost Democratic Senate candidate Doug Jones." A legal loophole allowed Highway

---

* See Issue One, "Dark money illuminated," https://www.issueone.org/wp-content/uploads/2018/09/Dark-Money-Illuminated-Report.pdf.

31 to avoid disclosing that it was controlled by groups aligned with the Democratic Party until a month after the election.

Dark money is both prevalent and difficult to trace. But it's when the task gets harder that great researchers stand out. Marianne Bertrand, Matilde Bombardini, Raymond Fisman, and Francesco Trebbi have managed to shed light on some of the dark money flows in a 2018 study. They show how firms use their philanthropic foundations to influence politicians. Bertrand and her co-authors find that these foundations give larger grants to charitable organizations located in congressional districts with a representative seated on a committee that matters for the firm. The pattern looks strikingly similar to that of publicly disclosed political action committee (PAC) spending. Furthermore, they show that a member of Congress leaving office leads to a short-term decline in charitable giving to his district, as well as in PAC spending. Charities directly linked to politicians exhibit similar patterns of political dependence. Bertrand and her co-authors show that firms deploy their charitable foundations as a form of tax-exempt influence seeking. Based on a straightforward model of political influence, they estimate that at least 7.2 percent of total US corporate charitable giving is politically motivated. This is almost three times larger than annual PAC contributions, and this is a conservative estimate. Charitable giving is not subject to formal disclosure requirements. It is therefore a form of political influence that goes mostly undetected by voters and shareholders, and which is directly subsidized by taxpayers.

Firms are always looking for ways to influence politicians, and not only in the United States. Italian firms appear to be quite creative. In a fascinating paper, Stefano DellaVigna, Ruben Durante, Brian Knight, and Eliana La Ferrara (2014) show that Italian firms shifted their advertisement spending to benefit Silvio Berlusconi while he was in power. Berlusconi was in office three times between 1993 and 2009, and he maintained control of Italy's major private television network, Mediaset, throughout. They find a significant pro-Mediaset bias in the allocation of advertising during Berlusconi's political tenure, especially for companies in more regulated sectors. They estimate that Mediaset profits increased by one billion euros during this period and that regulated firms anticipated sizable returns on their political investment.

Finally, there is the revolving door issue. Thomas Boggs, the famed lobbyist whom we encountered in Chapter 9, "helped pioneer the 're-volving door' culture of hiring former members of Congress and others with enough prestige to get the right people on the phone, fast," noted the *Washington Post* in Boggs's 2014 obituary. Just like lobbying, revolving doors can be good or bad. When you hear people complain about "pro-fessional politicians" or the lack of understanding of private sector chal-lenges among civil servants, you are effectively hearing people asking for *more* revolving doors. Revolving doors are useful when they allow a better sharing of expertise and information. They are bad when they distort the incentives of regulators or lead to regulatory capture. In Washington, DC, there's no shortage of examples of regulators leaving their government jobs to join a company that lobbies the very agency they worked for, or powerful executives of major firms taking jobs as top regulators of their former companies, often after receiving a generous payout on the way out the door.

One of the most egregious revolving doors over the years has been at the Federal Communications Commission, which regulates, among other things, telephone, internet, and television services. Michael Powell, FCC chairman from 2001 to 2005, would go on to become CEO of the National Cable and Telecommunications Association (NCTA) in 2011. Jonathan Adelstein, an FCC commissioner from 2002 to 2009, left to take over PICA, a trade group representing wireless telecommunica-tions firms. In 2011, FCC commissioner Meredith Baker left her job after serving only two years of a four-year term and jumped over to a top lobbying position at Comcast. In 2013, Barack Obama appointed Tom Wheeler, a former president of the NCTA and a former CEO of the Cellular Communications & Internet Association, to be FCC chair. When Wheeler resigned, Donald Trump appointed Ajit Pai, a former Verizon employee and communications industry lawyer, to replace him.

The movement of executives between regulatory agencies and the businesses they regulate is well documented in multiple industries. David Lucca, Amit Seru, and Francesco Trebbi (2014) study workers' flows be-tween US banking regulators (both federal and state) and the private sector. Workers' flows within the private sector are large. Workers are constantly moving from job to job, losing a job and finding a new one.

Between one-third and one-half of all new hires are workers moving from one firm to another. There are also significant flows between financial regulators and private firms. On average, each year, about 5 percent of regulators leave their job for the private sector and about the same number travel the other way. These total gross flows are thus around 10 percent annually. Total gross flows within the private sector are typically around 20 percent to 25 percent annually (for instance, in the Current Population Survey). The regulator-to-private-industry flows are thus between a third and a half of the private-industry-to-private-industry flows, but they have increased over time. Regulatory agencies face a retention challenge, especially for their most talented employees.

The trouble with revolving doors is that they can lead to regulatory capture. Capture can be direct (quid pro quo) or intellectual (ideological). Haris Tabakovic and Thomas Wollmann (2018) find evidence of direct capture in the regulation of patents. Using detailed data from the US Patent and Trademark Office, they find that patent examiners grant more patents to the firms that later hire them or are likely to hire them. These firms also enjoy better intellectual property protection. This might be consistent with some form of information sharing, but Tabakovic and Wollmann also find that the extra patents granted are of lower quality, based on the observation that they are less frequently cited in subsequent patent applications.

Revolving doors also exist in Europe. José Manuel Barroso, former president of the European Commission, was criticized when he moved to Goldman Sachs in 2016, just two months after the end of his mandated cooling-off period. Four of the five former officials who headed the European Commission directorate responsible for financial regulation between 2008 and 2017 have gone on to work for financial industry companies or lobbying firms that represent them (Vassalos, 2017).*

However, European *competition* authorities do not seem to be subject to the same revolving-door effect. A look at the data for revolving doors over the past ten years turns up eighteen cases involving finance and only four cases involving DG Comp. The same is true with the

---

* See also Corporate Europe Observatory, "Revolving door watch," https://corporate europe.org/en/revolvingdoorwatch.

national competition authorities in Europe. They appear for the most part to be made of committed regulators. Consistent with our theory, antitrust lobbying plays a smaller role in the EU (at least so far), and revolving doors are less common.

Will Europe Remain Insulated?

US campaign finance has changed dramatically over the past twenty years. In their 2003 survey, Stephen Ansolabehere, John M. de Figueiredo, and James M. Snyder Jr. asked why there was so little money in politics.

> Much of the academic research and public discussion of campaign contributions appears to be starting from some misguided assumptions. Campaign spending, measured as a share of GDP, does not appear to be increasing. Most of the campaign money does not come from interest group PACs, but rather from individual donors . . . It doesn't seem accurate to view campaign contributions as a way of investing in political outcomes . . . Because politicians can readily raise campaign funds from individuals, rent-seeking donors lack the leverage to extract large private benefits from legislation.

It is tempting to compare this statement to the "permanently high plateau" prediction for US stocks that Irving Fisher made in October 1929. To be fair, however, they did not claim to make a prediction about the future, as Fisher did. They were instead reflecting on the common wisdom at the time and, based on their reading of the evidence, they suggested a reorientation of research away from its focus on rent-seeking donors.

Much has changed since then, and Luigi Zingales, an economist at the University of Chicago, worries in a 2017 article about a diabolic loop between economic power and political power. Firms can use their economic power to acquire political power, and then they can use their political power to prevent entry and competition. Zingales argues that we have seen that movie before. The Medici dynasty of Florence, Italy, used their lending relationships with the Roman Catholic Church in the fifteenth century to gain political influence in Europe. Is the United States going to look more like late medieval Florence or more like an open society?

One of the most surprising facts that I have uncovered while doing this research is that most EU markets are freer that their American counterparts. As Mario Monti, the former EU commissioner, explains, "In competition policy, for example, the E.U. embraces not just antitrust but also controls how much aid a state can provide a business and provides other forms of oversight for how national governments intervene in economic and financial markets."

One reason for the weakness of competition policy in the US is that its framework is outdated. There are two federal agencies with overlapping competencies and conflicting objectives and fifty state attorneys general. Europe, on the other hand, modernized its competition architecture in 2004. National cases are decentralized to national competition authorities under effective oversight by the European Commission.

The other reason for weak competition policy is that US enforcement agencies are directly influenced by the electoral cycle. The administrative system of European enforcement is better shielded from political pressures.

As we have seen, one of the main goals of those who donate to politicians in the US is to change the rules that regulate state aid to companies and government intervention in the markets. One question for Europe is whether its relative insulation from the influence of money in politics will continue. There are two views on this issue.

The pessimistic view is that it simply takes time for institutions to become corrupt, but eventually they do. Europe, then, is headed the US way, only with a ten-year lag. DG Comp is still new and strong, but this will not last.

The optimistic view is that Europeans were lucky when they set up their institutions, that they made them more independent than anyone would have imagined, and that this quality will persist. Much of the research on institutions shows that they have long-lasting effects and a life of their own, so I tend to be in the second, more optimistic camp, but this is in no way an assured outcome, and there is no room for complacency.

[FOUR]

AN IN-DEPTH LOOK AT
SOME INDUSTRIES

The first three parts of this book propose a broad analysis of the evolution of economics and politics in the United States over the past twenty years. I can summarize my thesis in three points. First, US markets have become less competitive: concentration is high in many industries, leaders are entrenched, and their profit rates are excessive. Second, this lack of competition has hurt US consumers and workers: it has led to higher prices, lower investment, and lower productivity growth. Third, and contrary to common wisdom, the main explanation is political, not technological: I have traced the decrease in competition to increasing barriers to entry and weak antitrust enforcement, sustained by heavy lobbying and campaign contributions.

I have also tried to give you, the reader, an understanding of how economists think about free markets, regulation, and political economy. I have shown you some of the tools that we use to analyze economic developments. You understand the fundamental law of investment, the dynamics of entry, merger reviews, and the impact of wealth on the price of domestic goods and services (remember, haircuts versus Ferraris).

Let's use these tools to think about a few controversial industries: finance, health care, and the internet giants. In all these cases, we will see the same economic forces at play: lack of competition, barriers to entry, and lobbying. But the details vary, and this is what makes these industries interesting. Finance will teach us that efficiency and complexity are not the same thing and that deregulation is easier said than done. Health care will teach us how oligopolies can spread from one side of an industry to another. Finally, the internet giants are particularly relevant because they are often presented as examples of efficient concentration driven by "network" effects. While there is some truth to this argument, it is widely overrated. The data will also teach us that the stars of today may be no match for the stars of yesterday. This sounds like fun, at least to me . . . but then again, I *am* an economist.

CHAPTER 11

Why Are Bankers Paid So Much?

I would rather see Finance less proud and Industry more content.

WINSTON CHURCHILL, 1925

FINANCE IS THE one industry that (almost) everyone loves to hate. And it would be somewhat peculiar to write a book about rent-seeking oligopolies and political capture without dedicating at least one chapter to banks. For better or for worse, however, no country has ever become prosperous without a well-developed financial system. So, we might as well try to understand what these bankers are doing.

Economists have disagreed about the proper role of finance for as long as capitalism has been around. British economist Joan Robinson (1952) viewed finance as a sideshow. She argued that "where enterprise leads, finance follows." Financial economist and Nobel Prize winner Merton Miller (1998), on the other hand, wrote that the idea "that financial markets contribute to economic growth is a proposition almost too obvious for serious discussion."

These statements seem to support Winston Churchill's dim view of economists. Churchill famously quipped that "If you put two economists in a room, you get two different opinions, unless one of them is Lord Keynes, in which case you get three opinions."

As you can see, the debate is not new. But I would argue that we have made progress and that the range of disagreement has narrowed substantially. My generation of economists is less interested in ideology, and we have a lot more data. That is not a sufficient condition for success, but it's a better starting point, in my opinion.

The history of finance is replete with financial crises, followed by changes in regulations, followed by periods of relative calm, followed by new crises. From the outside, finance seems to always be changing. More-over, one would think that, with the advent of computers, financial services would have become a lot more efficient and a lot cheaper. I am going to show you that this did not happen and that, in fact, little has changed over the past 100 years, at least until very recently.

What Does Finance Actually Do?

Financial intermediation arises from the need for expertise in channeling capital from savers to borrowers. In the absence of financial intermediaries, households with savings would have to interact directly with borrowers. That would not be easy.

Borrowers typically need long-term, committed capital. Prime examples are mortgages and corporate loans. If you finance the purchase of a home or a factory, you want to spread the repayments over many years. In addition, these loans are fundamentally risky: good borrowers can be unlucky and lose their jobs or their customers, and bad borrowers can pretend to be good.

Savers, on the other hand, want less risk and more liquidity. They don't want to buy rotten eggs, they don't want to put all their eggs in the same basket, and they want to be able to sell their eggs if they need to. These issues have names in economics: rotten eggs are *moral hazard* and *adverse selection*; placing one's eggs in different baskets is called *diversification*; eggs that can be sold are called *liquid assets*.

The trouble—and the opportunity for financiers—is that borrowers and savers have conflicting demands. This creates the need for financial intermediaries. Without intermediaries, information costs would make it difficult for households to screen and monitor corporations and for corporations to pool household funds to raise sufficient capital. These costs would also make it difficult for households to diversify their investments and obtain liquidity when they need it. Financial intermediaries specialize in these tasks and in turn are compensated for acting as brokers between savers and borrowers, for providing means of payment, record keeping, insurance, and liquidity.

Here is how Finance 101 works. Figure 11.1a shows a simplified banking system with $100 in deposits and $100 in loans. The banks offer 5 percent returns on deposits and charge 7 percent on the loans that they make. At the prevailing borrowing rate of 7 percent, borrowers (firms or households) want to borrow $100. At the prevailing savings rate of 5 percent, savers are happy to save $100. The money flowing back and forth between savers and borrowers goes through the banking system. The income of the banks is the difference between the interest revenues from their loans and the interest expenses on their deposits. This income is called *net interest income.*

Where is that money going? Banks, like all firms, have labor and capital expenditures. They need to maintain their branches, ATMs, and IT systems, and they need to pay their employees. The banks therefore retain $2 to pay their wage bills and capital expenditures. When we look at the banking system in Figure 11.1a, we would say that the quantity of intermediation is $100, the intermediation cost is $2, and the unit cost is 2 / 100 = 2 percent.

Modern finance has evolved beyond the simplicity of the traditional banking model. Figure 11.1b presents a different, yet fundamentally equivalent way of organizing financial intermediation. In traditional banking, intermediation occurs under one roof: the bank makes a loan, keeps it on its books, and earns a net interest income. This income compensates for the costs, including screening and monitoring the borrower, managing the duration and credit risk of the loan, and collecting payments.

The originate-and-distribute model, in contrast, involves a daisy chain of intermediation. Many transactions occur inside a black box. There is no simple measure of net interest income as in the traditional model: there are origination fees, asset management fees, trading profits, and the like.

Here is the tricky question: how can you measure financial intermediation over time when it is a changing mix of the two models?

The answer is to focus on what goes into the box, what comes out of the box, and how much the box costs. There is a sense in which the latter, more complex model and the traditional model are the same. The sum of wages and profits for all intermediaries is still $2, and the quantity of assets intermediated seen from *outside* the black box is still $100. And the unit cost of intermediation is still 2 percent.

At some fundamental level, finance deals with information. One would therefore assume that the advent of computers and information

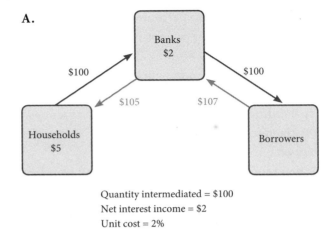

Quantity intermediated = $100
Net interest income = $2
Unit cost = 2%

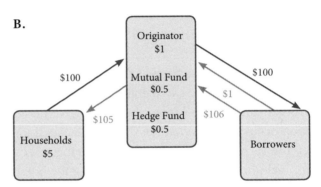

A new division of labor:
• Monitoring and screening fee = $1
• Asset management fee = $0.5
• Credit risk hedging cost = $0.5

FIGURE 11.1 (*a, b*) Two equivalent financial systems

technologies would make finance cheaper and more efficient. Surprisingly, this did not happen.

Finance Still Costs 200 Basis Points

As we have just explained, the sum of all profits and wages paid to financial intermediaries represents the cost of financial intermediation. In Philippon (2015), I measure this cost from 1870 to 2010, as a share of GDP. As you can see in Figure 11.2, the total cost of intermediation varies a lot over time.

The cost of intermediation grows from 2 percent to 6 percent of GDP from 1880 to 1930. It shrinks to less than 4 percent in 1950, grows slowly to 5 percent in 1980, and then increases rapidly to almost 8 percent in 2010.

Why are we spending more on financial intermediation today than 100 years ago? To answer that question, let us construct the amount of intermediation. For the corporate sector, we need to look at stocks and bonds, and for stocks, we want to distinguish between seasoned offerings and IPOs. We also need to look at the liquidity benefits of deposits and money market funds. The principle is to measure the instruments on the balance sheets of nonfinancial users, households, and nonfinancial firms. This is the correct way to do the accounting, rather than looking at the balance sheet of financial intermediaries. After aggregating the various types of credit, equity issuances, and liquid assets into one measure, I obtain the quantity of financial assets intermediated by the financial sector for the nonfinancial sector, displayed as the shaded line in Figure 11.2.

The solid line with circles in Figure 11.2 is the share of GDP that we spend on financial intermediation in the US. It is literally the equivalent

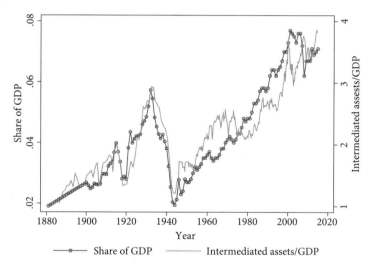

FIGURE 11.2 Income of the finance industry and intermediated assets. Both series are expressed as a share of GDP. Finance income is the domestic income of the finance and insurance industries, that is, aggregate income minus net exports. Intermediated assets include debt and equity issued by nonfinancial firms, household debt, and various assets providing liquidity services. The data range for intermediated assets is 1886–2012.

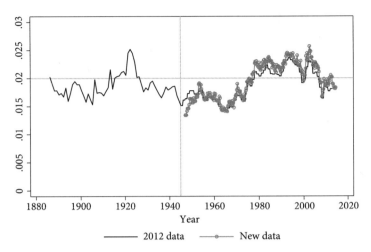

FIGURE 11.3 Raw unit costs of financial intermediation. The raw measure is the ratio of finance income to intermediated assets, as shown in Figure 11.2. The 2012 data are from Philippon (2015), while the new data were accessed May 2016. The data range is 1886–2015. *Source:* Philippon (2015) with updated data

of the $2 paid to intermediaries in Figure 11.1. The shaded-line series is built by adding the series of debt, equity, and liquidity services with the proper theory-based weights. It is the equivalent of the $100 in Figure 11.1.

Notice that the underlying data sources for both series are entirely different. The fact that the two series track each other very closely is not a coincidence! We are now ready to compute the price of finance by dividing how much we pay (solid line) by how much we get (shaded line).

Figure 11.3 shows that this unit cost is around 200 basis points, just like in our example in Figure 11.1, and relatively stable over time. In other words, I estimate that it costs two cents per year to create and maintain one dollar of intermediated financial assets. Equivalently, the annual rate of return of savers is on average two percentage points below the funding cost of borrowers. The updated series are similar to the ones in the original paper. The raw measure of Figure 11.3 does not take into account changes in the characteristics of borrowers. In the Appendix I discuss the issue of quality adjustment in financial services, and elsewhere I show that the same patterns hold when finance is measured as a share of services, and when net financial exports are excluded (Philippon, 2015).

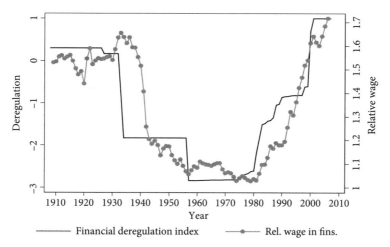

FIGURE 11.4 Wages and regulation in finance. *Data source*: Philippon and Reshef (2012)

Financial intermediation costs around 200 basis points today—about the same as a century ago. The more you think about it, the more puzzling it becomes. Despite all its fast computers and credit derivatives, the current financial system does not seem more efficient at transferring funds from savers to borrowers than the financial system of 1910.

Prices in finance have not come down, but wages have certainly gone up. Philippon and Reshef (2012) compute the wages of employees in finance relative to employees in the rest of the private sector. We also construct a measure of financial deregulation. The industry was mostly deregulated until 1930. Regulations were put in place in the wake of the Great Depression. These were progressively lifted in the 1980s and 1990s. Over the same period, the historical data reveal a U-shaped pattern for education, wages, and the complexity of tasks performed in the finance industry relative to the nonfarm private sector (Figure 11.4).

From 1909 to 1933 finance was a high-education, high-wage industry. The share of skilled workers was 17 percentage points higher than in the private sector. These workers were paid over 50 percent more than those in the rest of the private sector, on average. A dramatic shift occurred after the mid-1930s. By 1980, the relative wage in the financial sector was approximately equal to the wage in the nonfarm private sector. From 1980 onward, the financial sector became a high-skill and high-wage industry again, and relative wages and skill intensities returned almost exactly to their 1930s levels. There was some wage moderation following the 2007–2009 crisis, but it was relatively limited.

Technological development of the past forty years should have disproportionately increased efficiency in the finance industry. How is it possible for today's finance industry not to be significantly more efficient than the finance industry of John Pierpont Morgan?

Information technologies (IT) must have lowered the transaction costs of buying and holding financial assets. An apt analogy is with retail and wholesale trade. After all, retail banking and retail trade both provide intermediation services. As we discussed in Chapter 2, the retail and wholesale industries invested in IT. They became more productive, and their prices went down. The contrast is striking with finance. Finance invested in IT, but prices did not decrease.

What Is the Matter with Finance?

The previous figures are puzzling. Finance is expensive, and computers have not made it cheaper. While most of the existing work has focused on the United States, Philippon and Reshef (2013) and Bazot (2013) provide similar evidence for other countries. Finance has obviously benefited from the IT revolution, and this has certainly lowered the cost of retail finance. Yet the cost per dollar of intermediation has remained constant, and the share of GDP spent on financial services has increased. So why is the nonfinancial sector transferring so much income to the financial sector?

When an industry is deregulated, wages and prices usually fall. In finance, they seem to rise. In most industries, innovation is good for growth, but financial innovations do not seem to improve capital allocation very much.

What, then, is the matter with finance? Why does it appear to behave differently from other industries? I am going to highlight three main issues: a high prevalence of zero-sum games, entrenched market power, and heavy and sometimes misguided regulations.

Harvard economists Robin Greenwood and David Scharfstein (2013) study what goes on inside the black box and provide an illuminating picture of the growth of modern finance. They show that growth of finance since 1980 comes mostly from asset management (in the securities industry) and the provision of household credit (in the credit intermediation industry). The credit intermediation industry grew from 2.6 percent of GDP in 1980 to 3.4 percent of GDP in 2007. Traditional banking income has remained roughly constant, while fee-based transactional services, including loan origination and cash management, have grown. In other words, they document a shift from Figure 11.1a to 11.1b. Securitization and short-term funding also grew, giving rise to what is now commonly referred to as the shadow banking system.

The securities industry grew from 0.4 percent of GDP in 1980 to 1.7 percent of GDP in 2007. Within this industry, the traditional sources of income (trading fees and profits, underwriting fees) have declined. At the same time, asset management fees and profits from derivative contracts have increased. Regarding asset management, they uncover an important stylized fact: individual fees have typically declined, but the allocation of assets has shifted toward high-fee managers in such a way that the average fee per dollar of assets under management has remained roughly constant.

The wealth management industry also contributes to tax evasion, which is a negative sum game. The creativity of financial thieves is unbounded. For instance, the so-called CumEx network defrauded EU treasuries from billions of euros of revenues. Traders would lend each other shares in large companies to confuse tax authorities and make them think that each share had several owners. One side would falsely claim that taxes on dividends had been paid, and the other side would be able to claim a tax refund.

The point is not that finance does not innovate. It does. The point is that these innovations do not seem to improve the overall efficiency of the system. For every useful innovation in online banking, there are several mostly useless or even harmful ones. The race for ever-faster access to market information is an obvious example. If you observe the information flow and you manage to trade on this information just a microsecond before everyone else, you can make a lot of money. Yet that activity does not contribute to the overall efficiency of the system.

It does not matter whether information gets embedded in the price every microsecond or every second or even every minute. There is a large difference between foreknowledge and discovery as far as social welfare is concerned, even though the two activities can generate the same private returns, as economist Jack Hirshleifer explained in 1971. This tension between private and social returns exists in most industries, but economists tend to think that entry and competition limit the severity of the resulting inefficiencies.

Lack of entry, however, has been an endemic problem in finance in recent decades. Allen Berger, Rebecca S. Demsetz, and Philip E. Strahan (1999) review the evidence on consolidation during the 1990s. The number of US banks and banking organizations fell by almost 30 percent between 1988 and 1997, and the share of total nationwide assets held by the largest eight banking organizations rose from 22.3 percent to 35.5 percent. Several hundred mergers and acquisitions occurred each year, including mega-mergers between institutions with assets over $1 billion. The main motivations for consolidation were market power and diversification. Berger and colleagues find little evidence of cost efficiency improvement, which is consistent with Figure 11.3. Robert De Young, Douglas Evanoff, and Philip Molyneux (2009) show that consolidation continued during the 2000s. They argue that there is growing evidence that consolidation is partly motivated by the desire to obtain too-big-to-fail status, and that mergers and acquisitions have a negative impact on certain types of borrowers, depositors, and other external stakeholders.

Entry in finance is also limited by heavy—and sometimes biased—regulations. A good example of the benefits of entry, one that brings us back to Chapter 2, is Walmart. Why did we get the bloated finance industry of today instead of the lean and efficient Walmart? As it turns out, Walmart applied for a banking license in 2005, but it was denied under—who would have guessed—heavy lobbying by bankers. That's an important lesson: where retail store owners largely failed to prevent Walmart's expansion, the bankers prevailed. Of course, this lobbying always takes place in the name of the separation of banking and commerce and for protecting community banks, as if debit cards and savings accounts were magical products that a retail firm could not possibly provide.

What Technology Could Offer Finance

Finance could and should be much cheaper. Finance has benefited more than other industries from improvements in information technologies. But unlike in retail trade, for instance, these improvements have not been passed on as lower costs to the end users of financial services. Asset management services are still expensive. Banks generate large spreads on deposits (Drechsler, Savov, and Schnabl, 2017).

This might be changing, however, thanks to the entry of financial technology (fintech) players. Fintech includes digital innovations that can disrupt financial services. As usual, innovation is a double-edged sword. Innovations can provide new gateways for entrepreneurship and democratize access to financial services, but they also create significant privacy, regulatory, and law-enforcement challenges. Examples of innovations that are central to fintech today include mobile payment systems, crowdfunding, robo-advisors, blockchains, and various applications of artificial intelligence and machine learning. All the large financial firms have jumped on the tech wagon. JPMorgan Chase & Co. recently announced that it will require its asset management analysts to learn to use Python, a powerful and flexible coding language.

This is not to say that all fintech ideas are great. There is a lot of hype and buzzword use. "Big" data is just data. "Machine learning" often simply means running a large number of nonlinear regressions on large data sets. Most of the transactions in Bitcoins involve drugs, pornography, and weapons.

But there are also some genuinely useful ideas. A clear winner is the market for remittances. Remittances are the transfers of money by a foreign worker back to their home country. Poor households have been ripped off for decades by a highly concentrated banking industry. Thanks to entrants such as Transferwise, remittances have become cheaper. For instance, the cost of sending $200 in the World Bank sample of forty-eight sending countries has fallen from 9.8 percent to 7.1 percent over the past decade. Of course, 7.1 percent is still expensive. But at least the trend is in the right direction.

For fintech to really succeed, however, regulations must be adapted. As in other industries, fintech startups propose disruptive innovations for the provision of specific services. The key advantages of incumbents are their customer base, their ability to forecast the evolution of the industry, and their knowledge of existing regulations. The key advantage of startups is that they are not held back by existing systems and are willing to make risky choices. In banking, for instance, successive mergers have left many large banks with layers of legacy technologies that are, at best, partly integrated (Kumar, 2016). Fintech startups, by contrast, have a chance to build the right systems from the get-go. Moreover, they share a culture of efficient operational design that many incumbents lack.

How to Better Regulate Finance

Competition is biased between entrants and incumbents in the finance industry. Ensuring a level playing field is a traditional goal of regulation. Serge Darolles (2016) discusses this idea in the context of fintech and argues, from a microeconomic perspective, that regulators should indeed ensure a level playing field. This line of argument, however, cannot be readily applied to many of the distortions that plague the finance industry. For instance, what does a level playing field mean when incumbents are too big to fail? Or when they rely excessively on short-term leverage? The level-playing-field principle applies when entrants are supposed to do the same things as incumbents, only better and cheaper. But if the goal is to change some structural features of the industry, then a strict application of this principle could be a hindrance.

History proves that regulations are likely to be more effective if they are put in place early, when the industry is young. Let's imagine a simple, counterfactual history of the money market mutual fund industry. Suppose that regulators had decided in the 1970s that, as a matter of principle, all mutual funds should use and report floating net asset values (floating NAVs) instead of fixed NAVs. A fixed NAV is like a deposit: you put $1 in and you can always withdraw $1; no questions asked and no matter what happens. But that's a trick. The only ways to guarantee that your $1 is completely safe is either to invest it entirely in short-term government bills or insure it. That's why bank deposits are insured, and that's why banks pay insurance premia to the Federal Deposit Insurance Corporation (FDIC). The money market fund industry wanted to attract savings away from the banks—which is totally fair, that's just competition—and they knew that people loved the idea of fixed, safe, dollar-for-dollar deposits. They then decided to report fixed NAVs, pricing their shares at $1 at all times, to make it look like they were offering deposits. But they were not investing in safe, short-term government bills. In September 2008, the Reserve Primary Money Market Fund (a large money market fund) "broke the buck" (that is, admitted that the value of its shares was less than $1) because it had invested in Lehman Brothers commercial paper. Lehman declared bankruptcy and the Reserve Fund posted a loss, triggering a run as investors pulled their money out to avoid further losses. The fund was forced to freeze redemptions and the US Treasury Department had to create a temporary guarantee program for the entire money market fund industry! So much for a safe investment . . . After the crisis, regulators proposed a set of reforms to force funds to float the NAV of their portfolios and avoid the illusion of safety. It did not go well. The industry fought back, and it took years to arrive at a mediocre compromise. My point here is that implementing these regulations would have been a relatively straightforward process when the industry was small, and they would have guided market evolution and encouraged innovations consistent with sound principles of finance. It is significantly more difficult to change the regulations when the industry has several trillion dollars under management.

Thus the challenge for regulators is to look ahead when dealing with fintech. Effective regulation requires them to identify some basic features they would like fintech to have and mandate them as early as possible. I think that is a key lesson for the regulation of fintech. I recall a fascinating exchange at a recent conference about blockchains and privacy. There is a tension between the principles of blockchains (such as their permanence) and the right of individuals to request that their personal data be erased. To my surprise, however, the blockchain specialists said this would not be a big challenge, provided they knew what the regulator wanted. In other words, it is possible to implement a blockchain in which private data can be erased under some conditions. But it must be conceived as such from the beginning. It would be much more difficult to let it grow and then, ten years later, ask for new features to protect privacy.

Fintech is also likely to create new issues of consumer protection. Think of the example of robo-advisors for portfolio management. Robo-advising will certainly create new legal and operational issues, and it is likely to be a headache for consumer protection agencies, as discussed in Baker and Dellaert (2018). Yet if the goal is to protect consumers, robo-advising does not need to be perfect: it only needs to be better than the current system. One must keep in mind just how bad the track record of human advisers has been. Investment advisers have a powerful and aggressive lobby. They have managed until recently to keep their fees high by hiding them from their clients. Most people simply do not know what they pay. Conflicts of interest are pervasive in the industry. For instance, Daniel Bergstresser, John M. R. Chalmers, and Peter Tufano (2009) find that broker-sold mutual funds deliver lower risk-adjusted returns, even before subtracting distribution costs. John Chalmers and Jonathan Reuter (2012) show that brokers' client portfolios earn significantly lower risk-adjusted returns than matched portfolios based on target-date funds. Broker clients allocate more dollars to higher-fee funds. In fact, investors tend to perform *better* when they do not have access to brokers. Sendhil Mullainathan, Markus Noeth, and Antoinette Schoar (2012) document that advisers fail to de-bias their clients and often reinforce their biases. Advisers encourage returns-chasing behavior and push for actively managed funds with higher fees, even if a client starts with a well-diversified, low-fee portfolio. Mark Egan, Gregor Matvos, and Amit Seru (2016) show that, in the US, financial adviser misconduct is concentrated in firms with retail customers and in counties with low education and elderly populations. They also document small labor market penalties for misconduct.

Watch for the Lobbyists

One can make the case that finance is (slowly) moving toward providing cheaper and more reliable financial services. But the road will be bumpy. Let me highlight three pitfalls.

The first pitfall is that financial incumbents still earn large rents, and they are going to fight to protect them. To take but one example, private equity firms are heavily subsidized by taxpayers. They benefit from unjustifiable tax advantages for carried interests. Carried interest is the portion of an investment fund's returns eligible for a capital gains tax rate of 23.8 percent instead of the ordinary income tax rate of up to 37 percent. President Trump promised to close the loophole during his presidential campaign, but Congress caved in to the lobbying of private equity firms and did not close the loophole. Instead of an outright repeal, Congress required that a fund's general partners hold the relevant investments for three years instead of one. Moreover, private fund managers discovered a way to keep the carried interest advantage in the tax law's exemption for corporations. They set up corporate structures for executives entitled to receive carried interest.

The second pitfall is that the US lacks a framework for data protection and data ownership. US banks want to keep control of their clients' information to stave off competition. The same debate occurred in Europe, and, as you might expect, European banks lobbied hard against the idea of sharing their data. Unlike in the US, however, where legislators caved in immediately, the EU pressed ahead. Their fortitude was a consequence of the General Data Protection Regulation (GDPR), which essentially states that people own their data. According to the GDPR, since you own the information in your bank account, you should be able to decide who has access to it and who does not. This stands in sharp contrast to what happened in the US. In effect, US banks' customers do not own their data, and US legislators have let it happen.

I grew up in a country, France, where large banks traditionally had more influence over policy than in America. I did not imagine that one day this fact would be turned on its head. There is a growing gap between open banking in Europe and in the US, and it is not happening by chance. It is consistent with the theory of European regulation that we developed in Chapter 8. Europeans are probably less naturally inclined toward free markets than Americans are, but when they agree to regulate a market at the EU level, they opt for tough, independent regulators. I have shown why this is the equilibrium of the political game. As it turns out, following the crisis of 2010–2012, Europeans decided to move banking supervision and regulation at the EU level. Since then, banking regulators have become tougher and more independent, and banks' lobbyists have lost some of their influence. This was clear during the GDPR debate and during the revision of the Payment System Directive (PSD2). We will return to the GDPR and the issue of privacy more broadly when we discuss Facebook and Google in Chapters 13 and 14.

The third pitfall is that asset management can become too concentrated. Index funds and exchange-traded funds (ETFs) are great inventions. They are cheap, they are simple, and they are certainly better for 95 percent of investors than actively managed funds. They have also expanded rapidly. The share of listed equity value owned by institutional investors has increased since 2000—primarily driven by the growth of quasi-indexer institutions. These trends are encouraging, but they imply significant concentration in the management of equity portfolios. One issue is that large money managers seem to have a marked preference for share buybacks over capital expenditures. In Gutiérrez and Philippon (2017), we show that buybacks have increased faster for firms with high quasi-indexer ownership. Large investors are looking for firms protected by barriers to entry because they understand the value of market power. Investors such as Warren Buffett have been amazingly successful in part by doing just that. This is, of course, a perfectly legitimate investment strategy. However, directly or indirectly, the growth of large money managers might reinforce the trends toward high markups and low investment in the US economy.

To conclude, there are new things in finance, and there are valuable things in finance. All too often, however, what is valuable is not new, and what is new is not valuable. There are some reasons to think that this might be changing, in large part thanks to fintech firms. But fintech innovations will not automatically enhance stability or democratize access to financial services. If we want to reap the benefits from better technology in finance, we need financial regulators who can stand up to the lobbies.

CHAPTER 12

American Health Care
A Self-Made Disaster

People in middle age now have a fair chance of getting to Longevity Escape Velocity.

AUBREY DE GREY

Those in midlife now are likely to do worse in old age than the current elderly.

ANNE CASE AND ANGUS DEATON

NOTHING BETTER HIGHLIGHTS the clash between economists and techno-optimists than the topic of health. It is a sad irony that precisely at the time when scientists are beginning to argue that it is technologically plausible to prolong human life indefinitely, the US is experiencing the first peacetime decline of life expectancy of any democratic nation since the Industrial Revolution.

Techno-optimists view the world through the lens of what is technologically feasible. But sadly, we've long known that what is technologically feasible can be rendered practically impossible by bad public policy. Nobel Prize–winning economist Amartya Sen demonstrated nearly forty years ago that cases of mass starvation are, above all, political issues: "Starvation is the characteristic of some people not having enough food to eat. It is not the characteristic of there being not enough food to eat. While the latter can be a cause of the former, it is but one of many possible causes. Whether and how starvation relates to food supply is a matter for factual investigation" (Sen, 1982). The problem, Sen argues, is rarely that there isn't enough food, but that those in power lack the will or desire to make it available to the hungry. In other words, starvation is usually a manmade policy disaster.

The same seems to be true with health care in the US. The gap between what we could do and what we actually do is much greater than the rate of technological change over at least several decades. The US has the best hospitals and the best technologies, and yet it has mediocre health outcomes. An inefficient, oligopolistic, and sometimes corrupt health-care system is not the only reason, but it is a major contributor.

The US is the largest economy in the world and one of the richest on a per-capita basis. Yet, compared to other rich countries, a higher percentage of its population lives in poverty, infant mortality is higher, and life expectancy is shorter.*

Figure 12.1 shows the evolution of life expectancy at birth in the US, France, the UK, and Costa Rica. I chose Costa Rica to broaden the comparison and to emphasize the difference between income and health. In 2000, the life expectancy of French newborns was 79.2 years. In the US it was two and a half years lower, at 76.7. By 2016, the gap had increased to 4.2 years, as life expectancy reached 82.8 years in France versus only 78.6 in the US. The US has lower life expectancy than other rich countries, certainly, but US life expectancy is lower than less wealthy countries, too: a Costa Rican newborn's life expectancy in 2016 was 1.2 years longer than that of a child born in the US, and the gap has been increasing in recent years.

Figure 12.2 shows the evolution of infant mortality. It has been decreasing around the world. In the US infant mortality stopped decreasing after 2010 and settled at a higher level than in other rich countries, such as the UK and France. Data from 2014–2016 indicate 5.9 deaths per 1,000

---

* In 2016, 40.6 million people, or 12.7 percent of the US population, were "poor," as defined by the official poverty measure, which is 6 million fewer people than at the peak of 46.7 million in 2014. The official poverty measure is determined by a household's pre-tax income; for example, in 2016, a family of four earning less than $24,339 would be considered poor. Poverty measures are complicated because they often do not properly account for social transfers. Bruce Meyer and James Sullivan explain that "the debate over inequality relies almost exclusively on income data that indicate that inequality has increased sharply in recent decades. It turns out that these data paint an incomplete and at times distorted view of how inequality in economic wellbeing has changed in the US." See Meyer and Sullivan (2018). I focus on life expectancy and child mortality because they are easier to compare across countries.

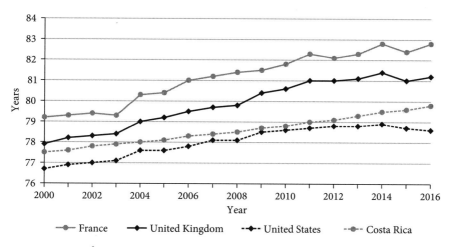

FIGURE 12.1 Life expectancy. *Data source*: OECD

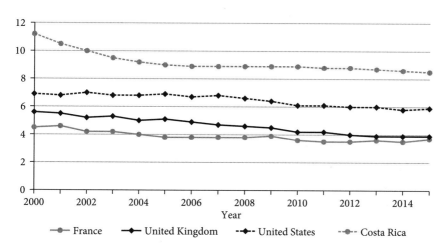

FIGURE 12.2 Infant mortality rates. Deaths per 1,000 live births. *Data source*: OECD

live births in the US versus 3.7 in France and 3.9 in the UK. Costa Rica's rate was significantly higher, around 8.

Health-Care Costs in the United States

In addition to dispiriting outcomes, health-care costs are much higher in the US than in similar countries. The average cost of employer health coverage is close to $20,000 for a family plan in 2018. You need to be a

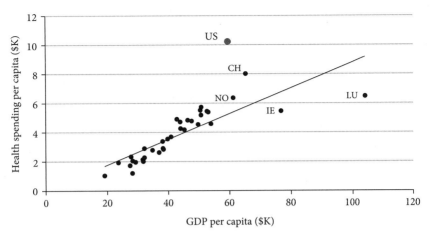

FIGURE 12.3 Health-care cost versus GDP per capita in select countries. US = United States; CH = Switzerland; NO = Norway; IE = Ireland; LU = Luxembourg. *Data source*: Kaiser Family Foundation analysis of OECD data

bit careful with this number, because the US is a rich country and, as we have discussed in Chapter 7, the Balassa-Samuelson theory tells us to expect that nontraded goods and services will be systemically more expensive in rich countries. Health care, then, should also be more expensive in rich countries.

Figure 12.3 shows the Balassa-Samuelson effect for health care. You can see that per-capita health-care costs increase systematically with income per capita. However, Figure 12.3 also shows that US health-care costs are completely off the chart (or off the regression line, to be precise). Health-care costs per capita are much higher in the US than in Norway or Switzerland, both of which have similar levels of GDP per capita. (GDP per capita in Luxembourg and Ireland is biased by the activities of large multinationals.)

Figure 12.4 shows the shares of GDP spent on health care for the US and for the average of comparable OECD countries. Two facts stand out. First, health-care costs are rising everywhere. Second, the increase is much larger in the US. The US has always spent more than other rich countries on health care, but the gap has increased dramatically since the 1980s.

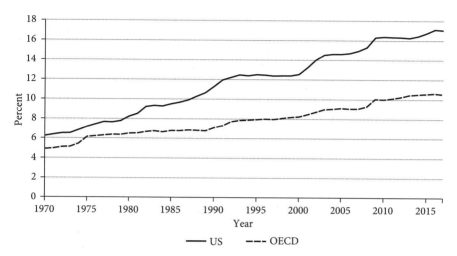

FIGURE 12.4 Health-care spending, share of GDP. US versus OECD, averages. *Data source*: Kaiser Family Foundation analysis of OECD data

In 2018, the US spent about 18 percent of GDP, or $3.3 trillion, on health care. Where do these costs come from? Hospital care is the largest single component of health-care spending in the US. It accounts for more than $1 trillion per year. The second largest category is physician and clinical services, many of which are now provided by hospital systems as well. The third largest category is prescription drugs, at about $330 billion.

The allocation of public versus private spending on health care is also informative. Public spending in the US is almost exactly the same as in other countries. Private spending, on the other hand, is three times higher than the OECD average. The US has several health systems within the public and the private spheres. The public sector consists of Medicare, Medicaid, the Indian Health Service, and the Veterans Administration, all of which are separate systems. Moreover, the different states are also quite different when it comes to how they organize their health systems. Similarly, the private health-care system is not just one system but many subsystems. This complexity certainly explains part of the excess costs.

The US might soon spend 20 percent of its GDP on health care, almost double what other countries are spending. How do we understand this fact?

Price versus Quantity

The reason Americans spend so much on health care is because prices are higher, not because they consume measurably more care. The Health Care Cost Institute finds that the growth in insurer claims from employer-sponsored coverage from 2012 to 2016 "was almost entirely due to price increases" for emergency-room visits, surgical hospital admissions, and administered drugs. The real quantity of health care, on the other hand, "remained unchanged or declined."

"The marketplace is just not working," Gerard Anderson, a health-care economist at Johns Hopkins University, told the *Wall Street Journal* in 2018. Insurers that must negotiate reimbursement with health-care providers for plans offered by employers pay on average 50 percent more than Medicare, and those rising costs are "the main culprit for why the U.S. spends so much on health care" (Mathews, 2018).

Researchers have also compared the costs of specific health-care items across countries to find out why the US is so expensive.* Neither the number of doctor visits nor the length or frequency of hospital stays can account for the extra cost. These are similar to the average in other rich countries. Once again: it's the prices that explain the difference. Annual costs for drugs were $1,443 per person in the US, compared with an average of $749 per person in Europe.

Another significant driver of high prices in the US is the large layer of "administrative" costs, which include costs related to planning, regulating, and managing health systems and services. These administrative costs appear to be high in the US, at around 8 percent of total health-care spending. That's more than double the average of 3 percent in other countries. Other studies consider broader definitions of administrative cost—taking into account indirect costs such as time spent on administrative tasks—and put the figure as high as 25 percent of total costs (Tseng et al., 2018).

---

* See Papanicolas, Woskie, and Jha (2018). They use international data over 2013–2016 for eleven high-income countries: the US, the UK, Canada, Germany, Australia, Japan, Sweden, France, Denmark, the Netherlands, and Switzerland.

I put "administrative" in quotation marks because these are really rents extracted by dozens of layers of health intermediaries and providers, from insurance companies to hospitals. We know from much research in economics that lax competition leads to high "administrative" costs.

Labor costs also explain part of the difference. The salaries of physicians and nurses are higher in the US than in other countries. For example, generalist physicians earn around $220,000 in the US, compared to $120,000 on average in other rich countries. That is a lot more than the average difference in GDP per capita and is not accounted for by the Balassa-Samuelson effect. A caveat, however, is that other countries have nearly free medical education. In the US, medical students graduate with over $200,000 in educational debt.

US Health-Care Productivity Is Low

One way to summarize these results, then, is that the US does not seem to be very efficient at keeping its citizens in good health: it spends more than any nation, and its citizens live shorter and less healthy lives on average.

Of course, the health-care system is not the only culprit here. Other factors—such as genetics, behavior, social circumstances, environmental and physical influences—also contribute to life expectancy. Most studies find that medical care accounts for less than 20 percent of the observed variations in morbidity and mortality.* Tobacco, poor diet, and lack of physical activity have a large impact. In pathbreaking research Anne Case and Angus Deaton (2017) document increases in mortality and morbidity among white non-Hispanic Americans in midlife since the turn of the century. Among white non-Hispanic people without a college degree (high school or less), mortality is rising in all age groups. Mortality rates among blacks, by contrast, fell across all age groups. They find striking increases in suicides, overdoses, and alcohol-related liver diseases among those with a high-school degree or less. "Mortality declines from the two biggest killers in middle age—cancer and heart disease—were off-set by

---

* In the language of public health professionals, morbidity and mortality are two separate conditions. Morbidity is the condition of being ill. Mortality is the condition of being dead.

TABLE 12.1

Top-Scoring Countries for Health-Care Access and Quality

HAQ index	Countries
97	Iceland, Norway
96	Netherlands, Luxembourg, Australia, Finland, Switzerland
95	Sweden, Italy, Andorra, Ireland
94	Japan, Austria, Canada
93	Belgium
92	New Zealand, Denmark, Germany, Spain, France
91	Slovenia, Singapore
90	UK, Greece, South Korea, Cyprus, Malta
89	Czech Republic, US

marked increases in drug overdoses, suicides, and alcohol-related liver mortality in this period."

A better metric to compare health-care systems around the world would then be to use mortality amenable to health care. A recent large-scale study uses data on diseases, injuries, and risk factors to build the Healthcare Access and Quality Index (HAQ) for 195 countries (GBD 2016 Healthcare Access and Quality Collaborators, 2018). They track thirty-two diseases and injuries that are not supposed to kill you if you have access to effective care and see how many people actually survive. If everyone survives these theoretically preventable deaths, that's a perfect score. Table 12.1 shows the first nine scores.

The top scores are found in European countries, plus Canada, Australia, and New Zealand. The US ranking does not reflect its wealth or level of spending on health care. Two other features distinguish the US in this study. It has the lowest absolute improvement in the index between 2000 and 2016 among rich and middle-income countries, and there is relatively high inequality in HAQ indexes within its borders. Mississippi has the lowest score (81.5), while a subset of northeastern states, Minnesota, and Washington state have European-style scores.

This study is not perfect. It still suffers from attribution problems. Any outcome measure has its own difficulties, but if we look at a broad range of studies, it is clear that the US does quite well on acute care outcomes and really badly on population health outcomes.

It is fair to say, then, that the US health-care industry suffers from low productivity. If we dig deeper, however, we also find that the US health-care system offers prime examples of several economic illnesses, such as oligopolistic industries, conflict of interest, regulatory capture, and political capture. Unfortunately, these lead to high costs and poor results.

Concentration

Hospitals have increased their market power by mergers. There have been almost seventy mergers per year since 2010. Today, close to 80 percent of Americans living in metro areas are in highly concentrated hospital areas. Recently, for example, two large hospitals based in Texas, Baylor Scott & White Health in Dallas and Memorial Hermann Health System in Houston, have announced their plan to merge. This would create a massive sixty-eight-hospital system, among the largest in the US. Although these hospitals are nominally classified as nonprofit organizations, their combined revenue is more than $14 billion.

Managers always justify mergers by claiming they will increase efficiency, lower costs, and improve care. They carefully avoid the issue of market power. And if history is any guide, the efficiency gains are unlikely to happen, but price increases are very likely.

Amazingly enough, the hospital sector seems to view the airline industry as a role model. "Scale done right is vital," said John Starcher, Jr., chief executive officer of Bon Secours Mercy Health, in an interview with the *Wall Street Journal*. "It's no secret to anybody . . . how far behind the consolidation curve the hospital sector is compared with others, such as airlines."

Yes, you have read it correctly. Airlines as the example that hospitals plan to follow? Yikes!

In reality, an important reason that hospitals merge is the opportunity to acquire more bargaining power for negotiations with health insurers. Insurance company executives (who, ironically, also enjoy virtual monopolies in many US states) are quick to offer an opinion when hospitals try to merge. When there is a dominant provider in town, all insurers have to include them in their plans. When a hospital system is the only provider of in-patient services in a region, an insurer serving people in that area has no option but to include them. As a monopoly, the hospital is practically free to charge whatever it wants.

Of course, concentration on one side of the market gives ammunition to the other side to do the same. The CVS pharmacy chain, which recently bought health insurer Aetna for $70 billion, plans to continue buying physician practices.

Restricted Contracts

Anticompetitive behavior is ubiquitous in the health-care industry and is often embedded in contracts between health-care providers and insurance companies. Let's review a few examples of contracts used to decrease competition.

Forced Inclusion

Hospitals often have contracts that force insurers to include them in any plan that the insurers might offer. This can prevent insurers from offering cheaper contracts. For instance, the insurance company Cigna and the health provider Northwell wanted to develop an insurance plan for low-cost coverage by excluding certain health providers. It was blocked because of a separate contract between Cigna and New York Presbyterian, which is a rival of Northwell. The existing contract prevents Cigna from offering a plan that does not include New York Presbyterian.

In Charlotte, NC, the Justice Department is suing Atrium Health, a system with huge market share in the area, arguing that the hospital operator "uses its market power to impede insurers from negotiating lower prices with its competitors and offering lower-premium plans." The California attorney general is suing Sutter Health, a twenty-four-hospital operator in Northern California, citing anticompetitive practices.

Antisteering

Another competition-reducing element of health-insurance contracts is a provision that prevents insurers from steering patients to less expensive or higher quality health-care providers. Forced inclusion prevents insurers from keeping high-cost providers out of the system. In tandem, antisteering provisions block insurers from creating incentives for patients to use less expensive or higher quality health-care providers.

In September 2018, the *Wall Street Journal* reported that Walmart sought permission from the insurers that provide coverage to its employees to remove the worst-performing 5 percent of providers from their networks. The three insurers—Aetna, Arkansas Blue Cross & Blue Shield, and United Healthcare—informed the company that their contracts with provider networks would not allow it.

Opacity

In the finance industry, investment advisers have always fought hard to keep their fees hidden. So do health-care providers. Another provision in many contracts allows providers to restrict access to information about pricing.

When insurers offer online price-comparison tools to their customers, in other words, this means that they must allow some providers to opt out of making that information available. The contract literally prevents the patients from seeing the prices they will be charged. As of this writing, the US administration is considering issuing an executive order that would require insurers and hospitals to disclose their prices. Let us hope that they follow through with this idea.

Regulatory Capture

If you've read the section above and thought, "Why haven't regulators done something about this?" then you're on to another aspect of the problem: regulatory capture.

In the US, insurance is regulated at the state level, meaning that across the country there are state insurance commissioners charged with overseeing the industry. These posts are extremely influential even though the actions of regulators fly below the radar of most news media. But if the general public pays little attention to insurance commissioners, insurance companies more than make up the difference.

In a report issued in 2016, the Center for Public Integrity found evidence of intensive campaigns by insurance firms, usually including lavish entertainment, trips, and other benefits, to influence insurance commissioners (Mishak, 2016). In one example uncovered by CPI, Arkansas insurance commissioner Julie Benafield Bowman met multiple times with United Healthcare lobbyists for drinks, meals, and more while adjudicating a hospital billing dispute involving the company. "I had a blast with you Monday night," she emailed one United Healthcare attorney. "Thank you so much for entertaining us." It may come as no surprise that she ruled in the insurance firm's favor—a decision that held up for two years before the courts intervened, overturning the ruling because of the "appearance of impropriety." By that time, though, Bowman had left her position to take a job at—you guessed it—United Healthcare.

The Opioid Epidemic

Regulatory capture can have more sinister consequences. Some of the worst have manifested during the opioid epidemic, which has been spreading rapidly through the US since the early 2000s. The opioid epidemic is the worst overdose epidemic in US history. Overdose deaths from prescription opioid pain relievers nearly quadrupled between 1999 and 2010, exceeding the death rate during the crack epidemic of the 1980s. Mortality due to crack was two per hundred thousand. Mortality due to opioids is ten per hundred thousand and has reached forty per hundred thousand in West Virginia.

The opioid epidemic has a demand side and a supply side. The demand side has been attributed to social and economic conditions in the US and thus cannot be blamed on deficiencies in the health-care system. But the supply side has been strengthened by failures within the health-care system. The evidence suggests that incentives and regulatory capture were aligned to foster overprescription. Both supply and demand matter. The "deaths of despair," to quote Case and Deaton, existed long before OxyContin, but overprescription certainly made them worse.

Even in the midst of the opioid crisis, drug makers were busy lobbying against prescription limits. For instance, the Pain Care Forum spent about $740 million over a decade lobbying federal and state legislatures against limits to opioid prescriptions (Perrone and Wieder, 2016). Julianna Goldman and Laura Strickler reported for *CBS News* in January 2018 that "donations from drug companies to political associations for state attorneys general have risen in the past three years, totaling almost $700,000 to Democrats and $1.7 million to Republicans." Today the manufacturers of opioids are lobbying for protections from being sued over their role in the epidemic. Goldman and Strickler add, "The contributions are legal, but they allow companies to gain access to the attorneys general at exclusive meetings, golf outings and high-end dinners." Tom Marino, who was President Trump's nominee to become the US drug czar, was forced to withdraw his candidacy after a report by the *Washington Post* and CBS's *60 Minutes* highlighted his role in forging legislation that hinders the US Drug Enforcement Administration's ability to move against drug distributors or pharmacies dispensing opioid painkillers. "The drug industry, the manufacturers, wholesalers, distributors and chain drugstores, have an influence over Congress that has never been seen before," Joseph T. Rannazzisi, head of the DEA's drug regulation division until 2015, noted in the *Wall Street Journal*. "I mean, to get Congress to pass a bill to protect their interests in the height of an opioid epidemic just shows me how much influence they have" (Higham and Bernstein, 2017).

And once the spread of opioids was underway, it was difficult to reverse. US authorities tried to limit access, but abuse had become so pervasive that restrictions led to widespread substitution of other drugs, such as heroin. An attempt was made to limit the misuse of opioids by introducing an abuse-deterrent version of OxyContin in 2010. Several groups of researchers have found that the new abuse-deterrent formulation led many consumers to substitute heroin, however.* Today more than half a

---

* Abby Alpert, David Powell, and Rosalie Liccardo Pacula attribute a substantial share of the dramatic increase in heroin deaths since 2010 to the reformulation

million Americans are addicted to heroin, and 80 percent of these abused opioids beforehand.

A Failure of Public Policy

The dynamics of concentration in the US health-care industry are worrisome. If the players had to appear in a dramatic reading, their script might be:

HOSPITALS: We want to consolidate so that, like the banks, we are also too big to fail. Then we can treat our patients like the airlines treat their customers.

INSURERS: We need to consolidate. Then we can negotiate better with hospitals and big Pharma.

BIG PHARMA: We are already concentrated, but why not continue? Especially if these hospitals and insurers start merging.

Delivering health care efficiently is a global fight. All countries struggle with this issue, not just the US. In emerging countries underfunding, lack of infrastructure, and lack of qualified personnel lead to poor quality of care and frequent misdiagnosis. Rich countries struggle with excessive costs, overmedication, and overuse of expensive procedures. Even in this diverse landscape, however, the US is an outlier. It has by far the highest cost of health care, but its results are below average. One would think that American policy makers would be busy trying to fix what looks like

---

of OxyContin. They find that states with higher pre-2010 rates of OxyContin misuse experienced larger reductions in OxyContin misuse, but also larger increases in heroin deaths immediately after reformulation (Alpert, Powell, and Pacula, 2018). William N. Evans, Ethan Lieber, and Patrick Power (2019) also attribute much of the quadrupling of heroin death rates to the reformulation of OxyContin: "Opioid consumption stops rising in August, 2010, heroin deaths begin climbing the following month, and growth in heroin deaths was greater in areas with greater pre-reformulation access to heroin and opioids." The reformulation did not generate a reduction in combined heroin and opioid mortality—each prevented opioid death was replaced with a heroin death.

a massive failure of public policy. Unfortunately, it seems almost impossible to have a rational debate about health care in the US.

All countries have their irrational sides. France believes its social model is the envy of the world. The UK believes it has a special relationship with the US. When a country is stuck in this mindset, rational debate is nearly impossible.* No matter how much evidence one brings to bear, nothing changes. In the US, one of these issues is health care and the other is gun control. Gun control is not the topic of my book, and I was definitely planning to avoid the issue, but an article recently published in a medical journal forced my hand (Schuur, Decker, and Baker, 2019). It turns out that PACs affiliated with physicians' organizations donate more money to political candidates who oppose gun safety legislations—such as background checks—than to candidates who support these legislations. This appears to contradict the public stance of several groups of physicians who have publicly called for stronger gun safety laws in the US. It seems plausible that these PACs support candidates who oppose health-care reform, and that these candidates also happen to oppose gun safety laws. When you mix economic rents and politics, the results never fail to surprise.

When I hear some of the arguments used in the American health-care debate, I have to admit that my head spins a bit. Let me highlight two of them. One argument I hear often is that the US is a country of free markets where people do not want the government to run their health system. Let's talk about it. First of all, the government is already involved in health care: it's called Medicare. Second, you don't have to look very far to find another major market where the government is deeply involved, even though it should not be: housing. The US government insures trillions of dollars of mortgages via inefficient and badly run companies (Fannie Mae, Freddie Mac).

---

* In France, it is nearly impossible to have a rational debate about two economic issues: state-imposed reductions in hours worked and productivity in the public sector. Many people think that forcing people to work fewer hours can solve the unemployment problem. Many people (often the same ones) also refuse to see that it is often possible to cut costs and jobs in the public sector without destroying the entire social model.

Now ask yourself: which market is more likely to experience market failures that justify government involvement? Health care or mortgages? Yes, this is almost a rhetorical question because the answer is obvious. The health-care market is "Exhibit A" for externalities, adverse selection, and market failures. This should be obvious to everyone. In fact, it *is* obvious to everyone outside the US, and that is why all governments around the world are involved in some way in health care.

On the other hand, most countries have a private mortgage market. Denmark has a liquid, efficient private mortgage market, and a state-run, efficient health-care system, not the other way around. In France, when you buy a house, you get a private loan from a private bank. Poor households get subsidies—often inefficient, by the way—but the loan market is private. The US has an inefficient semi-private, semi-public health-care system and a distorted mortgage market subsidized by taxpayers. The idea that Americans are fundamentally against government intervention in markets does not withstand scrutiny.

A second argument I often hear is that US companies are responsible for a large share of global research and development of health-related products, which is why prices are so high. US households, by paying high prices, are willingly subsidizing worldwide research on new drugs, which in turn benefits everyone on earth. Beyond being suspiciously self-serving, this argument defies credibility. Why would American citizens subsidize people who enjoy a longer life expectancy? To accept this argument, you have to believe that US politicians and regulators are somehow willing to hurt their citizens to subsidize the rest of the world. It is true that the National Institutes of Health is the largest funder of basic medical science, but that does not justify high drug prices in the US.

Early in this book we discussed the need to reassess our prior assumptions when confronted with evidence disproving them. Nowhere is that more necessary than in the US health-care debate. True, one size does not necessarily fit all. Countries are different and make different choices. But a rational decision maker can see that virtually all other advanced countries have adopted systems of health-care delivery that are different from the US model and that these countries produce better outcomes at a lower cost.

And keep in mind that this does not require a single-payer system. The goal should be universal coverage, that is, a system that provides quality medical care to all citizens. The way to achieve this goal, however, should be open for debate. Many countries reach universal coverage without a single-payer system. In most of Europe, for instance, there are regulated private insurance markets where residents must select a basic package from private insurers. Many of these countries also have private for-profit hospitals, and they accept patients with public insurance.

If the goal is to avoid increasing the footprint of the government in the economy, a rational deal could involve the closing of Fannie Mae and Freddie Mac against some combination of Medicaid, Medicare, and regulated private insurance that achieves universal coverage. That would keep the government out of a market where it does not belong and improve the efficiency of a market that badly needs to be fixed.

CHAPTER 13

Looking at the Stars
Are the Top Firms Really Different?

> I thought what was good for the country was good for General Motors and vice versa.
>
> CHARLES WILSON

LET US TALK about the stars of the internet economy: Google, Amazon, Facebook, Apple, and Microsoft, or the GAFAMs for short. I need to say a word about acronyms here. In Europe, these firms are calls GAFAs. In the United States, they are called FAANGs. I find both misleading. Both acronyms dismiss Microsoft, presumably because it is older than the others, but Microsoft is—and will remain—a major player of the digital economy, on a par with Apple and the others. The FAANG acronym includes Netflix, but the market capitalization of Netflix is one-third of that of Facebook, which itself is only about half that of Apple. Moreover, Netflix is now a major content producer, so I am not sure I see the point in comparing its business model to that of Facebook. I will therefore focus on the GAFAMs.

Everyone seems to have an opinion about the GAFAMs. Some think they are the greatest companies ever. Some think they are a threat to democracy. What everyone seems to agree on, however, is that these companies are fundamentally different, and that the old rules of capitalism simply do not apply to them. Is that really true?

There is no denying that internet companies are the stars of the market today. Table 13.1 lists the top ten global companies by market value in Spring 2018. Two facts stand out. First, eight out of ten are American companies, and the other two are Chinese. Europe and Japan are entirely missing (they are included in the data, they just don't make the cut). Second, the top six are internet technology companies.

TABLE 13.1

Top Ten Global Firms, Spring 2018

Company	Country	Market value ($ billion)
Apple	US	926.9
Amazon	US	777.8
Alphabet	US	766.4
Microsoft	US	750.6
Facebook	US	541.5
Alibaba	China	499.4
Berkshire Hathaway	US	491.9
Tencent Holdings	China	491.3
JPMorgan Chase	US	387.7
ExxonMobil	US	344.1

These companies are stars, undoubtedly. But there have always been stars in the economy. Are these stars different?

Carmen Reinhart and Kenneth Rogoff (2009) have famously shown that thinking "this time is different" is the shortest way to a financial crisis. In macroeconomics, there is no such thing as "this time is different." But, perhaps, matters could be different where the internet is concerned. There are some technological reasons to believe this time might be different. Internet firms can grow very quickly. It took Snapchat only eighteen months to reach the $1 billion valuation that it took Google eight full years to achieve, a feat that, on average, takes twenty years for a Fortune 500 company. Digital data can be used in ways that data stored on paper cannot. Learning models trained on very large, fine-grained data sets go further than traditional learning models. There is the potential for more knowledge creation, although here we need to recognize the fundamental difference between data and knowledge. A billion tweets are a lot of data but not necessarily a lot of knowledge.

I have a slightly more mundane take on the topic. I have noticed that people who are the most convinced that the GAFAMs are different are usually the people who know the least about these companies. Most of them repeat what they hear without taking the time to look at the data. Conversely, the more people know about these companies, the more they tend to describe them using relatively standard business concepts.

Understanding the GAFAMs matters for many reasons, but in particular when we seek to understand market concentration. These companies are very successful and innovative, of course, and they also control large shares of their domestic markets. I think it is hard to look at the growing concentration in US airlines, telecoms, and health care without thinking that these are negative trends for consumers and the economy as a whole. It is less clear how we should think about growing concentration in the GAFAMs' markets. Perhaps it's efficient, much like the Walmart-driven concentration in retail. Perhaps it's not fully efficient but a necessary cost of having large internet companies. At the very least, we should distinguish concentration as a result of the stars taking over the market from concentration driven by inefficient incumbents.

We thus need to understand whether these stars are different from those of the past. And more importantly, we need to understand if these star companies are going to create stellar performance in the economy as a whole.

In the next chapter, we will look at the lobbying and political influence of the GAFAMs. But before delving into their relatively new effort to flex their muscles in Washington, it's worth looking closely at them as businesses—specifically to interrogate two assumptions that allowed them to escape regulation for so long: first, that they are a special breed of company that mustn't be hindered by regulation, and second, that they are integral to the health of the US economy, and must therefore be treated with kid gloves.

The only way I know how to do that is by looking at the data. So, let us dig in.

The Business Models of the Stars

Let me start by discussing briefly the business models of these companies. Apple is a luxury manufacturing company. Google and Facebook are online advertising companies. Amazon is a marketplace and a retailer with a cloud service. Microsoft is a bit more diversified.

Apple sells iPhones. iPhones are desirable because they work well and because they are beautiful. They have become a status symbol, like Chanel bags or Hermès scarves. Apple also sells tablets and computers. Together, these three items account for 84 percent of Apple's revenues. But Apple is a luxury brand. It makes money with high margins, not just high volumes. The Korean company Samsung sells more smart phones than Apple does: its market share is 27 percent versus 24 percent for Apple, but Samsung's phones are relatively cheap.

An iPhone is to a smart phone what the Mercedes is to a car, except that Apple has a 24 percent market share, while Mercedes's market share is ten times smaller. Mercedes-Benz sold approximately 2.3 million cars worldwide in 2017 (a record year for the company). That's 2–3 percent of the global car market. Its revenues were about $120 billion and its profits about $13.5 billion, so its margin was around 10 percent. Apple sells about 220 million iPhones each year. Its consolidated revenues were about $230 billion in 2017, with $150 billion coming from iPhone sales alone. Its profits were around $50 billion, so its margin was above 20 percent. Its market value was more than ten times that of Mercedes. Apple, then, is a special kind of manufacturing company: it does luxury at scale. Another critical difference with other luxury manufacturing companies is that Apple develops a lot of software and services (iTunes, Apple Music, the App Store) that play a strategic role to support its manufacturing revenues. These services and software are used to attract and retain customers, and to create effective barriers to entry.

Google and Facebook earn most of their revenues from advertising: 88 percent for Google and 97 percent for Facebook. Their market shares are large. Together they collect about two-thirds of digital advertising expenditures. The ways in which they attract customers are different, however. Google helps people find stuff online. As of 2018, Google processes about 40,000 search queries per second worldwide, or 3.5 billion per day, or, if you prefer, 1.2 trillion searches per year. Google processes about two-thirds of global online searches, with Bing and Yahoo providing much of the rest. For internet searches initiated from mobile phones, Google's share is above 90 percent. Google does not get paid when you do a search. It only gets paid if you click on a paid link. You can immediately see why advertisers like this model: they only pay if you click. Moreover, their ads do not appear randomly but rather in response to your search, so there is a higher chance that you are actually interested in what they have to offer.

Facebook provides content that grabs your attention and then shows you a bunch of ads. Facebook's model is not so different from that of older media companies, newspapers, radios, and television networks. The main difference is in content and cost structure. Facebook does not *produce* any content. The content is you, your pictures and your videos, and your friends' pictures and videos. In a sense, you buy from yourself and Facebook takes a cut. That is a pretty smart business model. As CEO Mark Zuckerberg stated, "We provide the social technology. They provide the music." The other difference is that Facebook knows a lot about you, and your friends, and your family. As a result, Facebook can target its ads very precisely. That's what advertisers like. It's also what creates political risks for Facebook.

Microsoft has been around for longer than Google and Facebook. Perhaps for this reason, it also has a more diversified revenue stream. It derives significant income from Office, Windows, and Xbox, but also from its cloud services (Azure). Microsoft was the star of the 1990s. Its share price reached $55 in 2000. In 2009 it was down to $20, then increased to $25 in 2011. But it made a series of good business decisions, such as expanding its cloud business, and is now once again solidly among the stars. One important difference is that Microsoft is not a social media company. This could be considered a weakness, but it also reduces Microsoft's exposure to risks in that sector.

Amazon is an online retailer with a media business and a cloud service business. It is also a marketplace. In some respects, Amazon is quite different from the other four companies. Amazon has many employees, including blue-collar workers, and it does a significant amount of tangible investment. Amazon still has fewer employees than Walmart, but that's just because Walmart is so large. Amazon accounts for most of the growth in capital and research & development expenditures in the US retail sector over the past seven years. It is important to keep this fact in mind. We have discussed investment in Chapter 5. We have seen that investment and productivity growth have been weak, and that large and profitable businesses are largely responsible for the low ratio of investment to profits. Retail is an exception, as discussed in Chapter 2. By most accounts, it has remained quite competitive and productive.

Stars of Today, Stars of Yesterday

How do the GAFAMs compare to the stars of previous decades? We hear all the time that the market value of these companies is unprecedented. Apple was indeed the first company to pass the $1 trillion mark. But that's comparing Apples and Oranges (pun intended). These are current dollars, and in a booming stock market.

Is Apple's market value really unprecedented? No.

Table 13.2 contains the information we need to compare the GAFAMs to the previous cohort of stars. If you look at the data, the top five firms have typically accounted for about 10 percent of the total market value of US equities. In the 1960s, AT&T alone represented more than 6 percent of the market. Apple today is less than 3 percent. We are going to see that the GAFAMs are indeed different, but not in the way people think: they are . . . small!

Table 13.2 contains a lot of information, so let's unpack it slowly. It highlights some key facts regarding the star companies of each decade. We start in 1950, because this is when the Compustat database starts. For each decade, we compute the average market value of each firm, and we select the top five firms for the table (the top twenty firms for the figures below). Each column contains different pieces of information.

The rank is the rank by market value of equity. General Motors was the second largest firm by market value in the 1950s. At the time, the number of publicly traded companies was quite small, and GM accounted for 5.81 percent of total market capitalization. It employed 0.89 percent of civilian employment. GM was also buying a lot of inputs from other firms in the economy. On average its cost of goods sold (COGS in the table) was 1.22 percent of US GDP. Cost of goods sold is an accounting item that includes the intermediate inputs (car parts, steel, energy) as well as the wages of production workers. GM production wages were about 0.5 percent of US GDP and it bought approximately 0.72 percent of GDP in inputs. That means that GM was deeply integrated in the US economy.

At the bottom of each decade, I show averages or sums for the top five. The average operating profit margin (*Op. Inc. / Sales* in the table) of the stars of the 1950s was 20 percent. They paid 51.7 percent of their operating

TABLE 13.2
Seven Decades of Stars

Decade	Rank	Company	Profitability (%)		Taxes/Op. Inc.	MV/Emp ratio	Share of the Economy (%)		
			Op. Inc./Sales	Taxes/Op. Inc.			MV share	Emp share	COGS/GDP
1950s	1	AT&T	24.9	45.6		7.3	7.01	0.957	0.62
	2	General Motors	16.9	57.2		7.5	6.71	0.891	1.22
	3	ExxonMobil	16.8	38.2		24.7	5.70	0.231	0.57
	4	Dupont	28.7	59.7		39.0	5.55	0.142	0.16
	5	General Electric	12.7	57.9		8.0	2.98	0.373	0.47
		Average	20.0	51.7		10.8	27.95 Tot.	2.595	3.04
1960s	1	AT&T	30.9	44.6		7.4	6.40	0.869	0.56
	2	IBM	25.3	53.1		19.1	4.08	0.213	0.12
	3	General Motors	16.3	51.9		4.5	4.25	0.952	1.25
	4	ExxonMobil	13.5	43.0		14.5	2.98	0.206	0.69
	5	Texaco	12.9	23.3		20.9	1.88	0.090	0.25
		Average	19.8	43.2		8.4	19.59 Tot.	2.330	2.86
1970s	1	IBM	24.6	50.3		14.1	4.66	0.330	0.18
	2	AT&T	25.5	35.0		4.4	3.91	0.894	0.69
	3	ExxonMobil	17.5	66.6		15.6	2.46	0.158	1.03
	4	General Motors	9.2	46.4		2.5	2.20	0.873	1.31
	5	Eastman Kodak	24.1	47.5		12.6	1.72	0.137	0.10
		Average	20.2	49.2		6.3	14.95 Tot.	2.391	3.30

1980s	1	IBM	19.6	42.6	9.4	3.31	0.354	0.31
	2	ExxonMobil	9.8	44.5	15.8	2.08	0.132	1.14
	3	AT&T	12.8	18.7	4.4	2.10	0.472	0.85
	4	General Electric	11.5	33.5	4.6	1.48	0.320	0.42
	5	General Motors	4.3	11.3	1.5	1.05	0.710	1.21
		Average	*11.6*	*30.1*	*5.0*	*Tot.* *10.03*	*1.987*	*3.94*
1990s	1	General Electric	22.5	17.4	10.1	2.12	0.209	0.49
	2	Microsoft	39.0	35.5	93.6	1.28	0.014	0.01
	3	ExxonMobil	7.7	38.1	23.9	1.71	0.072	0.67
	4	Walmart	5.0	39.4	2.5	1.27	0.517	0.80
	5	Coca-Cola	23.1	31.7	55.2	1.34	0.024	0.05
		Average	*19.5*	*32.4*	*9.2*	*Tot.* *7.73*	*0.836*	*2.02*
2000s	1	ExxonMobil	13.0	48.2	41.1	2.51	0.061	0.88
	2	General Electric	23.8	10.3	10.5	2.35	0.223	0.44
	3	Microsoft	40.7	31.6	44.8	2.05	0.046	0.03
	4	Walmart	5.1	36.0	1.3	1.63	1.223	1.52
	5	Pfizer	32.0	16.3	20.5	1.47	0.072	0.02
		Average	*22.9*	*28.5*	*6.2*	*Tot.* *10.01*	*1.625*	*2.89*

(continued)

TABLE 13.2 (continued)

Decade	Rank	Company	Profitability (%)		MV/Emp ratio	Share of the Economy (%)		
			Op. Inc./Sales	Taxes/Op. Inc.		MV share	Emp share	COGS/GDP
2010s	1	Apple	29.6	25.8	41.8	2.54	0.061	0.24
	2	ExxonMobil	8.3	34.4	36.7	1.91	0.052	0.87
	3	Microsoft	32.8	18.4	23.0	1.68	0.073	0.07
	4	Alphabet	27.7	23.2	43.3	1.56	0.036	0.09
	5	Berkshire Hathaway	15.2	13.2	6.6	1.43	0.216	0.58
		Average	22.7	23.0	20.8	*Tot.* 9.11	0.438	1.84

Notes: Based on US-headquartered companies in Compustat. All quantities in percentage points. Cost of goods sold (COGS) adjusted for firm export shares. MV share is market value of equity divided by total US stock market value. Emp share is employment divided by total US civilian employment. MV/Emp ratio is ratio of market value share over employment share. AT&T COGS missing in 1950s, value input from 1960. Current names of firms are used for historical data (ExxonMobil, AT&T).

income in taxes (*Taxes / Op. Inc.*). Together, they accounted for 27.95 percent of the market value of listed companies, 2.59 percent of civilian employment (*Emp*), sourced inputs, and production labor for 3.04 percent of GDP (*COGS / GDP*).

Table 13.2 tells a fascinating story of how the economy has changed over time. The 1950s were dominated by manufacturing and petroleum. International Business Machines, better known as IBM, appears in the 1960s. GM drops out in the 1990s just as Microsoft and Walmart enter. Google (Alphabet) and Apple appear in the 2010s. To see Amazon and Facebook you need to zoom in at the end of the 2010s, as shown in Tables 13.1 and 13.3.

You might wonder why the banks are conspicuously absent in the 2000s. Citigroup is indeed a star in the early 2000s, but it crashes so badly in 2008 that its decade average barely makes the cut. JPMorgan Chase and Bank of America appear in the top ten in 2017, as shown in Table 13.3.

ExxonMobil is the only company that has remained in the top five for seventy years.* As the mother of the Princess of Parma reminds her daughter in Proust's *In Search of Lost Time,* "God in his bounty has decreed that you should hold practically all the shares in the Suez Canal and three times as many Royal Dutch as Edmond de Rothschild," and thankfully "nothing can alter the antiquity of blood, while the world will always need oil." ExxonMobil has changed a lot over time, however. Its employment weight has shrunk more than four times.

Do the GAFAMs Make Too Much Money?

Do the GAFAMs make excess profits? Let us focus on their profit margins. You can see in Table 13.2 that the pretax operating profit margins of the top twenty-five firms have typically been around 20 percent. Today's *pretax* margins are not out of line with historical norms. What has changed, however, is the average tax rate that these companies pay. AT&T used to have a profit margin of 25 percent, but it paid a tax rate of 45 percent. In the 2010s, Apple's margin was almost 30 percent and its tax rate was less than 26 percent. The after-tax margin has increased

---

* The FTC approved a merger between Exxon and Mobil in late 1999.

TABLE 13.3

Current Stars at the End of 2017

Rank	Company	Profitability (%)		MV/Emp ratio	Share of the Economy (%)		
		Op. Inc./Sales	Taxes*/Op. Inc.		MV share	Emp share	COGS/GDP
1	Apple	24.9	26.4	36.5	2.92	0.080	0.37
2	Alphabet	16.9	19.7	47.3	2.46	0.052	0.15
3	Microsoft	16.8	13.9	27.6	2.22	0.081	0.09
4	Amazon	28.7	35.0	5.2	1.90	0.367	0.42
5	Facebook	12.7	18.4	105.8	1.73	0.016	0.01
6	Berkshire Hathaway	30.9	25.4	6.7	1.65	0.245	0.70
7	Johnson & Johnson	25.3	15.4	14.5	1.26	0.087	0.05
8	JPMorgan Chase	16.3	19.1	7.5	1.23	0.164	0.08
9	ExxonMobil	13.5	-43.4	26.4	1.19	0.045	0.75
10	Bank of America	12.9	17.9	7.5	1.02	0.136	0.06
11	Wells Fargo	24.6	24.0	5.9	1.00	0.171	0.05
Average	1–5	20.0	22.7	18.8 *Tot.*	11.23	0.596	1.03
	GFAM (4)	17.8	19.6	40.8	9.32	0.229	0.61
	6–10	19.8	6.9	9.4	6.35	0.677	1.64
	Top 10	19.9	14.8	13.8	17.58	1.273	2.68

Notes: Based on US-headquartered companies in Compustat. All quantities in percentage points. COGS adjusted for firm export shares. MV share is market value of equity divided by total US stock market value. Emp share is employment divided by total US civilian employment. MV/Emp ratio is ratio of market value share over employment share. GFAM removes Amazon and does the calculations for the remaining four firms. *Tax rate as of 2016 because of tax changes in 2017.

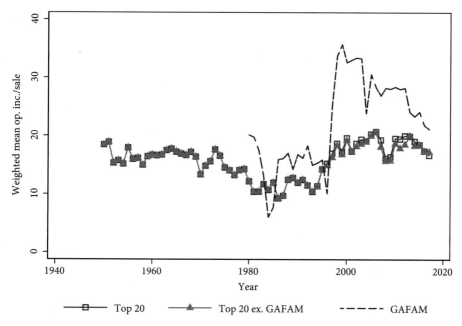

FIGURE 13.1 Pretax operating profit margins

dramatically. But is this a general phenomenon, or is this specific to the GAFAMs?

Figure 13.1 shows the profit margins of the top twenty firms in the United States (ranked by market value), the margins of the GAFAMs, and the margins of the top twenty excluding the GAFAMs. Operating margins have increased and settled at a higher level in recent years. The margins of the GAFAMs are significantly higher than those of the other top twenty firms. But the GAFAMs are not large enough to change the average much. The margins of the top twenty are rather similar with or without the GAFAMs. In all cases, we see the sharp increase in profit margins around 2000 that we have discussed earlier in the book. This increase happens with or without the GAFAMs.

The GAFAMs have extremely high profit margins, but so did many stars of the past. Their average profit margin in 2017 is 20 percent (Table 13.3), but the next five firms have an average margin of 19.8 percent. The profit margin of Apple was 25 percent in 2017, but IBM had the same margin in the 1960s and 1970s, and AT&T had a higher average margin for thirty years. The stars make money; that's why they are stars. But the stars of today are not making much more than the stars of the past. They just keep more of it.

Even more surprising—and contrary to many of the commentaries—there seems to be little new about the stock market value of the GAFAMs. The market value shares of the GAFAMs are not much higher than those of past stars. The GAFAMs account for 11.2 percent of the market cap of US stocks in 2017. In the 1980s, General Electric (GE), GM, IBM, AT&T, and Exxon accounted for 9.95 percent of the market. Apple might be almost 3 percent of the market, but IBM was more than 3 percent throughout the 1980s, and ExxonMobil was 2.5 percent in the 2000s.

What the data tell us here is that the assumption that tech firms are somehow thoroughly different from dominant companies of previous generations doesn't stand up.

This brings us to the second assumption—that the GAFAMs are so integral to the health of the US economy that they must be protected.

This is where we'll point out something that does set these new firms apart from their predecessors: they employ few people and interact little with the rest of the business sector. Actually, I should say the GFAM, because these points do not really apply to Amazon, as we shall see.

Why Footprints Matter

Let us now look at the footprints of the stars. Footprints are important in theory, because they affect the extent to which the performance of a company affects the performance of the whole economy.

A firm is deeply integrated when it buys many of its inputs from other firms in the economy. When a firm is deeply integrated, what is good for that firm tends to be good for the economy. The old saying, slightly restated in 1953 by Charles Wilson, GM's CEO, during confirmation hearings for Secretary of Defense, is true in that case: a star firm produces a star economy.

Box 13.1 explains why footprints matter. The punch line is that a star firm that does not interact with the rest of the economy matters less than a star firm that sits at the center of the economy.

Box 13.1. Inputs, Outputs, and Economic Footprints

A simple example illustrates why footprints matter (see Figure 13.2). Imagine two economies. Each has three firms. All firms produce output, and the GDP is the sum of their outputs. (We are using a simplified example in which relative prices do not enter.) In the first economy, firm 1 produces x_1 units and firm 2 produces x_2 units. Firm 3 produces q units, and total output is $x_1 + x_2 + q$. Let us use some simple numbers: $x_1 = 2$, $x_2 = 1$, and $q = 1$. GDP is equal to 4. Now suppose the productivity of firm 3 increases by 10 percent, from 1 to 1.1. What happens? GDP rises from 4 to 4.1, a 2.5 percent improvement. That's because firm 3 accounts for one-quarter of GDP, and its productivity increases by 10 percent. The impact on the economy is one-quarter of 10 percent. It's good but not great.

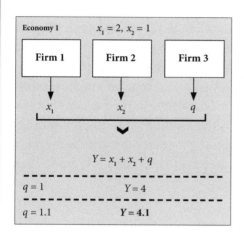 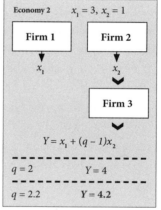

FIGURE 13.2 Why footprints matter

Now look at the second economy. In that economy, firm 2 produces intermediate inputs for firm 3. Firm 3 purchases x_2 inputs from firm 2 and turns them into qx_2 units of output. The value added of firm 3 is $qx_2 - x_2$ because it consumes the intermediate inputs. Let us imagine that $x_1 = 3$ and $q = 2$, so the starting value of GDP is still 4, the same as it was in the first economy. The GDP share of firm 3 is still one-quarter. So the second economy looks just like the first. But now imagine that firm 3 becomes 10 percent more productive. You can see that output increases by 5 percent.

That's twice as large as before. How is that possible? It's because the ratio of sales over GDP of firm 3 is now one-half. Even though its share of GDP is the same—and its share of market value would also be the same—it is now more integrated with the rest of the economy. As a result, improvements in firm 3 matter more in the second economy than in the first.

How should we measure the footprint of a company? It is difficult because it depends on the sector. In manufacturing, the cost of goods sold (COGS) is the right measure. Outside manufacturing, it does not work as well. In finance, it is useless. For lack of a better proxy, I will use employment. The correlation between the share of civilian employment and COGS/GDP in Table 13.2 is 86 percent. It's not perfect, but it's good enough for our simple analysis.

Figure 13.3 shows the employment share of the top twenty firms since 1950. The labor footprint of the stars has decreased over time. The recent pickup is only due to Walmart. We have already discussed the efficiency of the US retail sector. It is a particularly competitive and efficient industry. But if we exclude the retail sector, the footprint of the stars actually decreases from 4.5 percent to 2 percent over the past seventy years.

If we zoom in on the top five, the footprint shrinks even more dramatically. Table 13.2 shows that the employment share of the top five has decreased from 2.59 percent to 0.44 percent between the 1950s and 2010s, which is almost six times smaller.

Rise of the Recluse Companies

I define the *MV/Emp ratio* as the market equity weight of a company relative to its employment weight. To understand the idea, imagine a world where all workers are identical and all firms are equally productive and use the same capital to labor ratio. In such a world, firms would differ only by size, and size could be equivalently measured by number of employees, profits, or market values. Profits and market values would be directly proportional to the number of employees. The MV/Emp ratio would be 1 for all firms.

Of course, in reality, firms differ in the productivity and skill of their employees. Companies have high MV/Emp ratios when they create a lot

FIGURE 13.3 Labor footprint of the stars

of market value per employee. This can be because they are capital intensive, technologically advanced, and employ a highly skilled labor force.

When we focus on star firms, we select a group that is likely to have higher productivity than the rest of the economy. They may also hire more highly skilled employees than other firms, and they might use a high share of capital (machines, computers, software). We therefore expect the stars to have high MV / Emp ratios, and indeed this has always been the case. The average MV / Emp ratio for the top firms was between 7.5 and 15 from the 1950s to the 1980s.

Out of the GAFAMs, Amazon looks the most like a regular company. Its market value share is 1.9 percent in 2017, its employment share is 0.37 percent, so its MV / Emp ratio is 1.9 / 0.37 = 5.2, which is similar to General Motors in the 1950s and 1960s.

Starting in the 1990s, however, the MV / Emp ratio starts to increase dramatically. It is above 25 at Microsoft, Apple, and Google. If we look at the GFAM (minus Amazon), we see that these four companies account for 9.3 percent of the stock market but only 0.23 percent of employment.

That's an MV / Emp ratio of 40.8. The most extreme example is, of course, Facebook, with an MV / Emp ratio of 105.8. Facebook hires only highly skilled workers and builds everything in house. It buys essentially nothing from other firms.

Fading Stars

The notion that the biggest tech firms are somehow the pillars of the US economy is false on its face. The defining feature of the new stars is not how much money they make or how high their stock market values are. If we exclude Amazon, the defining feature of the new stars is how few people they employ and how little they buy from other firms. As Larry Page, co-founder of Google, said, "You don't need to have a hundred-person company to develop that idea."

Because their footprint is small, whatever happens to the GAFAMs does not matter a lot for the overall productivity of the US economy. If GM's productivity had doubled in 1960, people would have noticed the difference. Cars would have become cheaper, safer, and more fuel efficient, and the entire supply chain of GM consequently would have become more productive.* If Facebook's productivity were to double

---

* There might be a broader lesson here, but the analysis is preliminary. OECD researchers Dan Andrews, Chiara Criscuolo, and Peter Gal (2015) have studied frontier firms using harmonized cross-country data. They define global frontier firms as the top 5 percent of firms in terms of labor productivity or multifactor productivity levels within each two-digit industry in each year since the early 2000s. Global frontier firms are more productive by definition. They are also more capital intensive, larger, more profitable, and have more patents. They are also more likely to be part of a multinational group. They argue that the productivity slowdown of the past twenty years is not due to slower growth at the frontier but rather to an increasing productivity divergence between the global frontier and the rest. Between 2001 and 2013 average labor productivity at the global frontier grew at an average annual rate of 2.8 percent in the manufacturing sector and 3.6 percent in the market services sector, while the corresponding growth rate of all other firms was around 0.5 percent in both sectors. What they call frontier firms, however, are not GAFAMs at all. In their sample, the average revenue of "frontier" firms is around $40 million in manufacturing and $5 million in services.

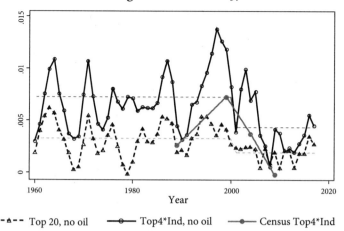

FIGURE 13.4 Contribution of stars to US growth

overnight, you would not notice much difference. The ads you see when you browse the app might be better targeted, but no other firm would become significantly more productive as a result.

German Gutiérrez and I (2019a) have studied the fifty-year history of the contribution of stars to overall economic growth in the US. Figure 13.4 shows that the superstars of today contribute less to productivity growth than their counterparts in previous decades: the contribution of super-star firms to US productivity growth has decreased by over 40 percent over the past twenty years.

We define superstar firms as the top twenty firms by market value in any given year ("economy-wide stars") or the top four firms by market value within each industry ("industry stars"). Stars—or any firm for that matter—can make two contributions to growth: they can increase the productivity of their current workers (*within contribution*), or they can be more productive in the first place and hire more workers (*realloca-tion contribution*). There are theorems along the lines of Box 13.1 that help us do the accounting correctly. We find that the within contribu-tion has collapsed while the reallocation contribution has become quite significant since the mid-1990s. Nonetheless, when we add them up, we get Figure 13.4: stars used to bring about seventy basis points of labor pro-ductivity growth each year (using the industry stars definition), but now it's only forty basis points.

Our results challenge the common wisdom about the stars of the new economy and shed light on the debate between Erik Brynjolfsson and Andrew McAfee (2014), who view digital technologies as "the most general purpose of all," and Robert J. Gordon (2016), who is skeptical about the impact of recent innovations. Our results are perhaps less surprising for students of history. History students are well aware of biased thinking that today is different—to paraphrase Reinhart and Rogoff (2009)—and that our current stars are exceptional. But there have always been star firms in the US economy, and they have always been large and productive. In our data, we find that today's stars are no match (so far) for yesterday's stars.

Ask More from the Stars

Facebook, Apple, Google, and Microsoft are smaller than the star companies of previous decades. When their productivity increases, it has less of an effect than a similar productivity increase at GM once had. Perhaps the battery life of your cell phone improves, perhaps your laptop runs a bit faster, perhaps you can more easily watch a movie in the subway. These welfare gains are meaningful, of course, and economic measurement has to take them into account. But they are not going to move the needle much as far as GDP or life expectancy is concerned.

If this conclusion sounds overly bearish, it is probably in reaction to the unwarranted hype that these companies have generated. There is no doubt in my mind that the GAFAMs are genuinely impressive companies, but so were GM, GE, IBM, and AT&T before them. They are not special and should be treated with the respect and circumspection other companies receive.

If there is one lesson that economic history teaches us, it is that great companies need to be challenged (and that one definitely applies to all the GAFAMs, Amazon included). We do not know for sure why productivity is slowing. Perhaps ideas are becoming harder to find, as Bloom et al. (2017) argue. But this book proposes that declining competition and rising barriers to entry have allowed incumbents to rest on their laurels. We need to bring in more competition. The problem, in the case of internet firms, is to find the right tools to do so.

CHAPTER 14

To Regulate or Not to Regulate,
That Is the Question

The FTC should tread carefully when reviewing Google, Facebook, Twitter or any other tech company, given the dynamism of our tech industry and the potential for making things worse through regulation.

JARED POLIS

IN 2012, at least thirteen members of the US Congress sent letters to the Federal Trade Commission concerning its investigation of Google. Some of the letters reflected the belief that, like banks too big to fail, one of the country's five biggest tech firms was too important to be investigated. US Representative Jared Polis, a Democrat from Colorado, voiced his concern "that application of anti-trust against Google would be a woefully misguided step that would threaten the very integrity of our anti-trust system, and could ultimately lead to Congressional action resulting in a reduction in the ability of the FTC to enforce critical anti-trust protections."

In the previous chapter we analyzed the business models and reach of these firms: Google, Amazon, Facebook, Apple, and Microsoft—the GAFAMs. I have argued that the stars of the digital economy are not as special as people think. Or, to be more precise, they are not special for the reasons that most people think. They are not the pillars of the US economy. Their profit margins and market values are in line with historical norms. What *is* new is that they have a smaller footprint in the real economy than previous vintages of stars. If we exclude Amazon, the defining feature of the new stars is how few people they employ and how little they buy from other firms.

In this chapter we look at the topics that make the GAFAMs controversial—lobbying, tax evasion, privacy, and antitrust—and the extent to which these issues do or do not create barriers to free entry. We will also analyze how big data is used and consider the not-so-obvious role of price discrimination.

The GAFAMs Go to Washington

Federal authorities, and Congress in particular, were originally somewhat gun-shy about trying to control the burgeoning tech industry. Lawmakers resisted calls to force online retailers to collect sales taxes and generally stayed out of the way while online startups like Amazon, Google, and Facebook took the first steps toward growing into the behemoths they are today.

Faced with a relatively low risk of serious interference from Washington, the largest tech firms did not follow the example of other major industries by building up a large lobbying presence in the capital. Amazon, founded in 1994, didn't begin spending money to lobby policy makers until 2005, and Google, founded in 1998, stayed out of the game until 2006. Founded in 2003, Facebook didn't begin investing in a heavy federal lobbying presence until 2013. Apple, in business since 1976, had a *de minimus* approach to lobbying until about 2014.

In the past decade, though, the GAFAMs have gone to Washington. They have rapidly increased their lobbying expenditures, investing about $50 million in 2017. They lobby about immigration, net neutrality, rules governing advertising, and company-specific issues.

Figure 14.1 shows that the GAFAMs' lobbying efforts are recent. The exception that proves the rule is Microsoft. In 1998, the DoJ brought antitrust charges against the software giant over its bundling of Internet Explorer with the Windows operating system, which, it was alleged, was a transparent effort to crush innovative start-up Netscape, which had created the Navigator web browser. The lawsuit took two years to settle and nearly ended with Microsoft being split up by a federal judge. As Figure 14.1 suggests, Microsoft's experience with the DoJ in the late 1990s seemed to convince the company of the importance of having a presence

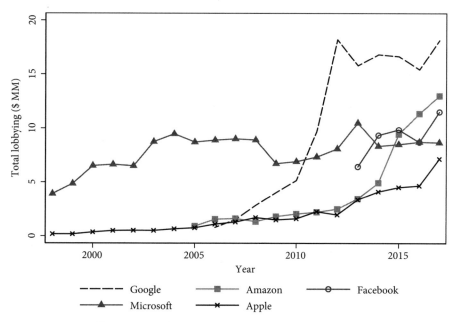

FIGURE 14.1 Lobbying expenditures. *Source*: Center for Responsive Politics

in Washington, DC, and its lobbying expenditures have been steady since then.

Why did the other GAFAMs suddenly feel the need to hire lobbyists? As we saw in Chapter 9, companies typically increase their lobbying efforts precisely because they feel threatened, or at least potentially threatened. As the GAFAMs' dominant positions became more obvious, and amid a string of scandals related to their treatment of users' data, they began to attract more regulatory scrutiny.

Amazon's lobbying increased after its acquisition of grocery chain Whole Foods. Facebook has been embroiled in a string of data privacy scandals, one of them involving the firm Cambridge Analytica. Waymo, Google's self-driving car unit, faces potential liability issues and other concerns. Google, Twitter, and Facebook are also involved in the targeting of their users by Russian agents during the 2016 campaign.

Generally, companies exert influence in Washington for one of four main reasons. The first two reasons are related to benefits they expect to receive thanks to their lobbying efforts. They want either to protect a privilege they already have or to convince policy makers to bestow one that they don't have yet. The other two reasons are related to costs they hope to avoid. Companies lobby to convince policy makers to lift an existing burden or to prevent them from imposing a new one.

We're going to start with an issue that is relevant to all corporations: taxes. Then we are going to focus on one particular benefit that tech companies currently enjoy: massive concentration and network effects. We'll also consider one burden they are anxious to avoid: new privacy protections for their users.

Do the GAFAMs Pay Their Taxes?

No, the GAFAMs don't really pay their fair share of taxes, but to be honest, neither do the other global firms. All top companies have been paying fewer taxes over time. Figure 14.2 shows the taxes paid by large firms relative to their operating income. Effective corporate tax rates have decreased over time. They were around 50 percent of operating income until 1980 and then decreased to less than 20 percent. The tax rate of the GAFAMs follows exactly the same path as the tax rate of the other leading firms. In case you are wondering, the massive decline in 2016 seen in Figure 14.2 is due to an anomaly in ExxonMobil reporting related to an oil price drop.

The issue of corporate income taxes is a rather complicated one. According to standard economic theory, it is a bad idea to tax corporate profits. It is usually more efficient to tax distributions to investors—interests, dividends, and capital gains—because corporate taxes are more likely to reduce investment.

That's in theory. What about in practice? The evidence is supportive of the standard argument, but not overwhelming. In general, researchers have found a negative impact of corporate taxes on investment, but the magnitude of the effects varies a lot across studies. Alan J. Auerbach (2002) provides a survey of these studies, and Simeon Djankov and co-authors (2010) look at more recent evidence. Nonetheless, there is some consensus among economists that corporate taxes should not be too high, and, more important, that they should be broad-based and free of loopholes.

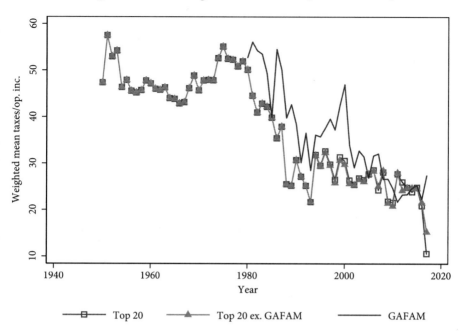

FIGURE 14.2 Corporate income tax rates. Total reported taxes over operating income.

In recent years, the main issue has been corporate tax evasion, which is legal for the most part but costly and inefficient nonetheless. According to research by Berkeley economist Gabriel Zucman, the US loses around $70 billion in tax revenue each year because corporations shift their profits to tax havens.* That is almost one-fifth of all corporate tax revenue. As Zucman explains, almost two-thirds of "all the profits made outside of the United States by American multinationals are now reported in six low- or zero-tax countries: the Netherlands, Bermuda, Luxembourg, Ireland, Singapore and Switzerland."

The GAFAMs do not seem to pay lower tax rates than other top companies. Large pharmaceutical, finance, and manufacturing companies engage in about as much profit shifting and tax evasion as the GAFAMs.

---

* See Gabriel Zucman's November 10, 2017, opinion piece in the *New York Times,* "How corporations and the wealthy avoid taxes."

There is one issue that is more prevalent with the GAFAMs: it is often harder to locate the profits. This is what makes the GAFAMs' tax issue politically explosive in Europe. One proposal is to compute taxes based on revenues instead of reported profits. If a company has high turnover in a particular country, it would pay more of its taxes to that country, even if it does not report high profits there.

In 2018, the US passed the Tax Cuts and Jobs Act (TCJA), which changed how international profits are taxed. It reduced the statutory corporate tax rate from 35 percent to 21 percent. This is not such a large change once you realize that tax breaks and loopholes had already reduced the effective rate much below 35 percent before 2018. The Institute on Taxation and Economic Policy showed that Fortune 500 companies paid an average federal tax rate of 21.2 percent between 2008 and 2015. But closing loopholes and lowering the statutory rate is probably a good idea.

The TCJA contains many provisions, and it is too early to tell how well it will work (see Chalk et al., 2018, for an early appraisal). It has, however, affected the way firms report and provision their taxes. Before 2018, firms had a choice: they could either provision their taxes on offshore earnings and include them in their headline taxes, or they could consider these earnings as perpetually reinvested outside of the US and not provision anything. Apple chose to provision taxes on a large fraction of its offshore earnings, which is why its headline tax rate appears relatively high. At the same time Apple lobbied hard to make sure it would never actually need to pay these taxes. The TCJA vindicated these efforts with a repatriation provision that taxes foreign earnings at a reduced rate of 15.5 percent, which is less than half of the rate used to provision the taxes. As a result, a large share of the taxes provisioned by Apple before 2018 will never be paid. All large companies engage in profit shifting, and most make use of tax havens to avoid paying taxes. But booking taxes that one does not expect to pay seems particularly disingenuous.

To wrap up our discussion of taxes, it is important to emphasize that corporate tax evasion represents a clear failure of public policy. Corporate tax evasion is mostly legal and could be reduced or even eliminated with a minimum of political willpower. Tax dodging by wealthy households, on the other hand, is mostly illegal and a more difficult problem to solve.

Is Concentration Required in the Digital Economy?

Information technology (IT) markets are highly concentrated. To understand the benefits of concentration to the GAFAMs, one must understand the principles of network economics. If we set aside political economy and lobbying, two economic forces can explain why and how a market becomes concentrated. The first explanation is that there are *economies of scale*: IT businesses have large fixed costs and then small marginal costs. This is an old idea, and not specific to IT. It also applies to pharmaceutical companies or aircraft manufacturers. Economies of scale might be stronger in IT because the marginal cost of information diffusion is often small or even zero, but that is an empirical question.

The second explanation—*network effects,* or *externalities* in the jargon of economics—is more specific to IT. The larger the network, the more members of the network have a chance to interact with each other. Reciprocally, people who are not on the same network cannot easily interact. Box 14.1 explains the basics of network economics.

Network externalities are a form of synergy. A positive synergy occurs when the sum is greater than the parts. When two firms merge, they might be able to reduce their costs by combining their IT systems, their human resource management, and other functions. They might create better products by combining their technologies.

Network externalities themselves come in two flavors: direct and indirect. The Facebook network is an example of a direct externality. We value Facebook directly because our friends are also on Facebook. In general, direct externalities arise when we derive utility from being in direct contact with another person on the network.

Indirect externalities arise when the presence of other users leads the network to offer services that we also enjoy. We do not care directly about being in touch with the other people on the network, but we share similar interests. A good example is the ecosystem of apps developed for an operating system, whether they be on a phone, a tablet, or a computer. In that example, we are not planning to interact directly with the other users. But when the number of users grows, developers have an incentive to build more apps, and we all benefit from them. At the end of the day, even though we do not value direct interactions with other users,

Box 14.1. Network Economics

Two concepts play a key role in the analysis of networks: economies of scale and network externalities.

The first is *economies of scale*. Consider an industry where consumers want to buy Y units of goods. To keep things simple, imagine that aggregate industry demand Y is inelastic: it does not depend on the *average* price of the goods. If $Y = 10$, for instance, consumers really want to buy 10 units of the good in total, although they would rather buy from the cheaper producers. There are N firms competing in the industry. They have the same marginal cost c. The outcome of competition and consumers' relative price elasticity is a markup m over the marginal cost and thus a price $p = (1 + m) \times c$. Since the firms share the same marginal cost and the same markup, they set the same price. We say that the equilibrium is symmetric. Each firm produces Y/N units and makes a profit mcY/N.

Let us denote by k the cost that any firm needs to pay to enter the industry, and let us assume free entry. Free entry means that new firms will keep entering the industry as long as they expect to recoup their entry cost. Under free entry, we must therefore have $mcY/N = k$, which means that the number of firms in the industry is given by $N = mY \times c/k$. The term c/k is the ratio of marginal cost over fixed cost. We say that economies of scale are large when fixed costs are large relative to marginal costs, that is, when c/k is small. Large economies of scale therefore imply a low value of N, and a concentrated industry. Note that this is true under free entry, so concentration does not imply rents. It simply reflects the fact that profits must be enough to cover entry costs.

The second concept is that of *network externalities*. Suppose you belong to a network with h other people. There is a positive network externality if the value you derive from the network, $u(h)$, is increasing in the number of users, h. Now suppose there are two networks and H people who are thinking about which network to join. Network 1 already has h_1 users and network 2 has h_2 users. Imagine that you are one of the $H - h_1 - h_2$ users who have not made up their mind yet. The values of joining network 1 and 2 are $u(h_1)$ and $u(h_2)$, respectively. If $h_1 > h_2$ and there are positive externalities, you realize that $u(h_1) > u(h_2)$. You are more likely, then, to join network 1. When your friend makes her decision after you, the numbers are $h_1 + 1$ versus h_2. She is even more likely to join network 1. All the remaining users will also choose network 1. Users of network 2 will notice the lack of popularity of their platform and, when given the chance, they will also switch. Absent any countervailing force network 2 will disappear, and network 1 will become a monopoly.

The main way networks can coexist is by differentiating their services. The key idea is to break the simple comparison of h_1 and h_2 by offering features that are valued differently by different groups of users, or by targeting different income groups. This is how the iOS and Android networks, or the Amex, Visa, and MasterCard networks, can coexist.

we still value their presence on the network. A network with few users would have too few apps to be attractive to us.

Most networks have a mix of direct and indirect externalities. For instance, search engines and GPS systems such as Waze become more precise and more reliable when more people use them.

It is often argued that positive synergies and network externalities are more prevalent today, in the intangible, digital economy, than before. The argument is then loosely used to justify high concentration and dominant positions. I think the argument is misleading, and the case for broad, positive synergies is weaker than most people realize.

Synergies exist in the new economy, but they also exist in the old economy. Leaders of the new economy, just like leaders of the old economy before them, tend to overestimate the positive externalities from their activities. Rana Foroohar, writing in the *Financial Times* about the gig economy (August 2018), mentions that several years ago, Travis Kalanick, the founder and former chief executive of the ride-sharing company Uber, told a group of business executives that we were heading toward a world in which "traffic wouldn't exist" within five years. Well, if recent experience in New York City is any guide, that is not happening. The average travel speed of cars in Midtown was 6.4 miles per hour in 2010. In 2017, it was 5 miles per hour, according to the Department of Transportation's Mobility Report.

Matias Covarrubias, Germán Gutiérrez, and I (2019) have studied the economies-of-scale hypothesis, and we have not found much support for it. Using detailed data from the US, we estimate the degree of returns to scale across various industries. We perform this analysis separately for the 1988–2000 period and then for the 2001–2016 period. We did not find evidence that returns to scale have increased significantly over the past thirty years. One model suggests that returns to scale are about the same today as they were in the past, and another model suggests they might be about 5 percent higher. Few industries show signs of returns to scale significantly above one.

There is also no reason to think that intangible assets are more likely to create positive externalities than tangible ones. Patents are a prime example of intangible assets. Many patents today, and most of the litigation surrounding them, come from patent trolls. They abuse the system and create negative externalities. Another example is market research and advertising, or marketing more generally. These have become more important in the digital economy, yet they contain a higher fraction of zero-sum activities than other types of research and development because the gains of one firm are directly related to the losses of another.

This is not to say that there are no examples of positive externalities in the digital economy. There are indeed increased possibilities of positive synergies in information sharing. Wikipedia is an amazing example. GitHub and Stack Overflow offer developers valuable online help and access to millions of pieces of code.* But the idea that the digital economy is full of positive synergies and returns to scale that can be achieved only through high concentration is misleading, to say the least.

What's the Trouble with Big Data?

Over the past decade, the GAFAMs have developed a large network advantage over potential competitors. They possess troves of data about

---

* Stack Overflow is a site where developers can ask for help from their peers. It has about 9 million users, 16 million questions, and 25 million answers per year. GitHub is at the heart of open-source software development. It is a code repository with around 25 million users and 50 million repositories. Microsoft announced in June 2018 that it would buy GitHub for $7.5 billion. The move was expected to help Microsoft compete against Amazon Web Services.

users that make it difficult or even impossible for rival startups to get a foothold in the marketplace. The collection of data also gives the GAFAMs opportunities to exploit their customers or suppliers.

As Cornell University professor Saule Omarova observed, "If Amazon can see your bank data and assets, [what is to stop them from] selling you a loan at the maximum price they know you are able to pay?"*

This highlights the growing issue of *price discrimination,* defined formally in Box 14.2. Is price discrimination in a market good or bad? The answer depends mostly on whether there is free entry in that market, or at least if the market is contestable. Price discrimination is efficient in the sense that it maximizes the total surplus of all transactions. When the firm has all the information, it can propose a price or a contract that is specific to each client and acceptable to each client. With efficient discrimination, as long as the transaction is economically viable, it will take place. Without discrimination, there are cross-subsidies, and some people can be priced out. The concern, however, is that a monopoly with full information can extract all the surplus. This is the fear expressed by Omarova. The key point here is that free entry becomes more important when firms increase price discrimination.

Platforms use a variety of tools to limit competition, and sometimes that involves *preventing* price discrimination. Nobel Prize–winning economist Jean Tirole (2017) emphasizes the role of price coherence, also called the "most favored nation" clause. That name is a metaphor that comes from international trade agreements. The idea is that a platform will prevent its merchants from offering lower prices outside the platform. Online booking services require that restaurants or hotels not offer cheaper prices on their own websites. Amazon imposes similar restrictions on its suppliers in many countries. American Express requires that a merchant not charge a higher price to consumers using their Amex cards even though Amex fees are often higher than those of other credit card companies. An important point here is that the extra costs are paid by customers who do *not* use the platform because the merchants are forced to charge everyone the same price. To understand why this

---

* Omarova is quoted in Rana Foroohar, "Banks jump on to the fintech bandwagon," *Financial Times,* September 16, 2018.

Box 14.2. Price Discrimination

Consider a market with two types of consumers, A and B, and one firm with production cost c. Consumers of type A value the good at $v_a > c$. Consumers of type B value the good at $v_b > v_a$.

First, let's look at the case of no price discrimination. If the firm cannot tell A from B, it must offer the same price to both. It has two choices. It could offer the price $p = v_a$, and all consumers would accept the offer and buy the good. Its profits would be $(v_a - c) \times (n_a + n_b)$ where n_a is the number of consumers of type A. But it could also offer the price $p = v_b$ and give up on the A consumers. Its profits would be $(v_b - c) \times n_b$. Giving up on A is a better strategy when $(v_b - v_a) \, n_b > (v_a - c) \, n_a$. The tradeoff is clear. On the left you have the extra profit from charging B a higher price. On the right you have the loss from not trading with A. The firm is more likely to give up on type A consumers when there are few of them (n_a is small) or when there is a lot of inequality ($v_b - v_a$ is high). When that happens, type A consumers are priced out, and that can be terribly inefficient and unfair.

Now we will consider the case of price discrimination. Imagine that the firm can tell A from B. It can then offer two prices, $p_a = v_a$ and $p_b = v_b$. There is no risk of type A being priced out. In that sense, price discrimination is efficient. On the other hand, the firm makes a killing: it extracts all the surplus from the consumers. This is why free entry is so important when firms can discriminate. With discrimination and free entry, the market is efficient, and the consumers end up with the surplus.

happens, imagine an economy in which half of the people are rich and enjoy using an expensive card with high merchant fees of 4 percent. The other half use a card with a 2 percent fee. If the merchants could pass on the fees, for a good worth $100 they would charge regular consumers $102 and rich ones $104. In both cases, they would net only $100 from each customer. If they are forced to offer the same price to all, they will charge everyone $103. On average they will still receive $100 net of fees, so they can stay in business. But now the poor and the rich both pay $103. And that is not the end of the story. The rich probably enjoy fancy rewards programs; otherwise, they would be less likely to buy the expensive card in the first place. What happens in this example, then, is that price coherence forces the poor to subsidize the rich.

What is the solution? You guessed it: free entry! With efficient price discrimination and free entry, we can have the best of both worlds. The combination of good information and free entry should lead to efficient markets with maximum consumer surplus.

This is an important lesson. Big data makes free entry more important than ever. Big data without free entry might be worse than no big data at all. If we cannot ensure free entry (or credible contestability), then we are better off restricting the ability of firms to gather data. And if we are going to let these firms use our data on a large scale, then we must ensure free entry. What is unacceptable in the current environment is the combination of big data with no meaningful contestability of markets.

One of the keys to market contestability in the digital age is giving people the property rights to their data. This is where competition and privacy become deeply intertwined.

Big Data and Privacy

Privacy and data protection issues have made the headlines. In 2015 Facebook claimed that it had put in place strict policies to restrict outsiders' access to personal information. Three years later, it disclosed that it had given dozens of companies special access to users' data. In over 700 pages of responses sent to Congress, Facebook acknowledged that it had shared its users' data with fifty-two hardware and software companies, many of them previously undisclosed. The new list includes Apple, Microsoft, and Amazon, as well as several Chinese companies, including Huawei. Facebook had been sharing data with device makers, mobile carrier AT&T, and chip designers such as Qualcomm.

A scoop from Douglas MacMillan and Robert McMillan in the *Wall Street Journal* (October 8, 2018) showed how Google kept secret knowledge of a glitch involving the private data of hundreds of thousands of Google+ users. A memo reviewed by the newspaper prepared by Google's legal and policy staff and shared with senior executives warned that disclosing the incident would likely trigger "immediate regulatory interest."

Perhaps they needn't have worried. US regulators have been painfully slow to address these problems, and the debate has migrated to the other side of the Atlantic. The European Union took a bold step in regulating online privacy when it passed the General Data Protection Regulation (GDPR). The GDPR, which took effect in May 2018, gives new rights to individuals and imposes new responsibilities on companies.

The GDPR restricts firms' ability to gather personal data without the consent of EU residents. People can ask to see the information gathered about them and require that the information be deleted. Firms have to limit their data collection and delete data that are no longer needed. The GDPR also contains the requirement that data custodians notify users promptly in the event of a breach.*

The GDPR is bold and ambitious. It is also a big mess. How could it be otherwise? It is the first effort to tackle an immensely important and complicated issue. One of the challenges for executives is that the legislation doesn't specify how regulators will assess compliance, making it difficult for companies to decide if they have made sufficient changes to their data policies or invested enough in upgrading their systems.

I was struck by the defensive reactions to this data privacy law that I heard in the US. Instead of acknowledging the issues and proposing improvements, many US commentators poked fun at the new regulation. I have heard countless lawyers complain that the GDPR's vague and imperfect definitions make compliance more difficult. In other words, they are complaining that by trying to protect the privacy of half a billion people the Europeans are making the jobs of a few hundred compliance officers more complicated. Seriously? This is not just silly, it is also a sign of weakness.

There are two ways to react when confronted by a daunting challenge. One is to sit down, procrastinate, and find excuses. The other is to try to do something, even if others complain that what you have done is not perfect. Everyone knows we need new data privacy regulations in the

---

* The GDPR requires companies to notify regulators of breaches within seventy-two hours. In the US there is no federal breach notification law. Instead, companies navigate a patchwork of state laws.

digital age. But the GDPR debate has US regulators and lobbyists in the role of the unhelpful complainers and EU members of Parliament in the role of the regulatory entrepreneurs. I would not have predicted such a reversal twenty years ago. It's unusual for Americans to stand on the sidelines and criticize instead of being midfield and playing.

Dealing with the GAFAMs

The issue of concentration in tech raises this question: Are the GAFAMs using their enormous scale to unfairly crush competition? Is it time to break them up? Or would that do more harm than good?

Let us start by saying that Google, Amazon, Facebook, and Apple in some sense owe their present success to the DoJ, which prevented Microsoft from monopolizing the internet in the late 1990s. It is therefore disingenuous to hear Google claim that antitrust enforcement is not needed. The beneficiaries of an open, competitive system often work to close the system and stifle competition once they are established (Rajan and Zingales, 2003). As successful firms grow large, they seek to alter the political system to their advantage and increase the cost of entry.

There are three ways to deal with the GAFAMs. These are not mutually exclusive and are ranked in order of controversy: limit their acquisitions, limit their exercise of market power, and break them up.

Limiting their acquisitions of small companies should be an obvious step at this point. With hindsight, it was arguably a bad idea to let Google buy Waze and DoubleClick, or to let Facebook buy Instagram and WhatsApp. These startups could have become real challengers. The key advantages of incumbents are their customer base and their financial resources. The key advantage of startups is that they are not held back by existing systems and are willing to make risky choices. In the case of the GAFAMs, another advantage of the incumbents is their understanding of the market. They are best positioned to understand before anyone else the potential of a startup. They can buy it early, before it becomes large enough to be noticed. This allows them to escape merger reviews. Generally, premerger notification is required if:

- ◆ either party to the proposed transaction has total annual net sales or total assets of at least $100 million and the other party has annual net sales or total assets of at least $10 million;

and

- ◆ as a result of the impending merger, the acquiring party will hold more than $15 million of the acquired party's stock and assets. An acquisition of another party's voting securities of less than $15 million also requires reporting if, as a result of the impending acquisition, the acquiring person will hold 50 percent or more of the voting securities of an issuer that has $25 million or more in annual net sales or total assets.

By buying their would-be competitors early, the GAFAMs exercise too much market power. These acquisitions need to be investigated and limited, but this is easier said than done. There are basically three ways to improve premerger notifications and merger reviews in the internet age.

One is to lower the threshold for notification and investigation. Germany has tried this approach recently, and the results are not encouraging. To be effective, the threshold needs to be quite low, and it captures many mundane acquisitions between medium-sized companies that do not cause any antitrust concern.

Another idea would be to use the price of the acquisition as an indicator, instead of the revenues of the target. Facebook paid around $20 billion for the messaging service WhatsApp. This was a shocking price considering that WhatsApp had very low revenues and fewer than fifty employees at the time. WhatsApp, however, had more than 450 million monthly active users, and Facebook knew better than anyone the threat this could pose to its own dominance. The price revealed the true economic importance of the acquisition and could have been used to justify an investigation. The problem with this approach is that acquisition prices, unlike revenues, can be manipulated. Firms could find ways to artificially lower the transaction price in order to avoid scrutiny.

A third potential improvement in merger review would be to allow the ex post control of some mergers. Ex post control has one particular advantage: it can rely on information about the competitive effect of a merger that was not available at the time of filing. On the other hand, ex post remedies are typically more costly because assets are already commingled. Ex post control also creates legal uncertainty. It is too early to tell which of these ideas, if any, will prove most practical, but it seems to me that the significance of an acquisition should depend on its price, and that ex post controls become more useful in a rapidly changing business environment.

The next option to discipline the GAFAMs is a bit more controversial. Limiting the exercise of the GAFAMs' market power directly targets their dominance in some markets. Although the US has been unwilling to follow this route, the EU has challenged market dominance by European companies as well as by American ones operating in Europe. Research by Yale economist Fiona Morton shows that European regulators have been more active in new areas of enforcement than American regulators. The European Commission's DG Comp has taken on a host of issues related to large tech firms, such as loyalty rebates, dominant positions in IT platforms, and others. Regulators in Germany and Brussels have begun investigating Facebook, Amazon, and Google for their market dominance and data-gathering activities.

To limit the excessive dominance of one network, such as Facebook, the authorities could require two features: interoperability (the ability to interconnect with other networks) and data portability (the ability to move one's data from one network to another). These features are quite similar to the ones that were imposed on Telecom firms in the past.

Regarding data gathering, regulators could impose a clause to let users opt out of horizontal tracking. Today Google and Facebook are the only companies able to track billions of users on millions of websites, whether the users like it or not. This is how they maintain their dominance in online advertising. An opt-out clause would allow users to decide whether or not they want to let Google and Facebook track them on other websites. Market forces are unlikely to lead to effective opt-out clauses, however. As Dina Srinivasan explains, "First, Facebook itself did not and does not allow consumers to opt-out of the new off-site tracking. Second, Facebook chose to ignore consumers' explicit requests, enacted via the browsers' Do No Track option, to not be tracked. Third, when consumers installed ad blockers to circumvent tracking and targeted advertising, Facebook responded by circumventing the users' installed ad blockers" (Srinivasan, 2019). An effective opt-out option is likely to require regulatory control. This would increase competition and consumer welfare.

The last option is to break up the GAFAMs. This is the most controversial option, and it would indeed be complicated. One issue is that the activities of the GAFAMs are more integrated than those of AT&T. In the case of AT&T, there was a clear distinction between long-distance service and the local infrastructure companies. It is not clear how a breakup of Amazon or Google would proceed. A breakup might seem like putting the cart before the horse. The priority should be to define privacy regulation and property rights over digital data and give customers effective opt-out clauses.

Antitrust regulation is likely to require more ex post control than in previous decades. Past acquisitions that have led to monopoly power are natural candidates for a breakup. Marketplaces also require strong remedies. In the case of Apple, many recent controversies center around its App Store, where prices are hidden, and rules are obscure and rife with conflicts of interest. Amazon is both a market (the online retail platform) and a market participant (with its own brands), and this situation also creates conflicts of interest.

Two Catch-22s

I see one reason for optimism and two catch-22s with the GAFAMs, all involving the use of data. The first catch-22 involves big data and free entry. As I have argued, big data can lead to powerful price discrimination. This can make markets more efficient, but it can also shift the entire surplus to the pockets of the monopolist. With big data, contestability becomes more important. The catch is that big data is in itself a barrier to entry.

The second issue involves economic footprints and privacy. As I have argued in the previous chapter, one reason the GAFAMs have not boosted the growth rate of the US economy is that their footprint is smaller than that of previous generations of star firms. This leads to the second catch-22. If they remain mostly as they are, their impact on growth will remain small and disappointing. If they branch out and increase their footprint, they could have a meaningful impact on aggregate productivity. But if they increase their footprint, the privacy issues worsen.

Google and Facebook are currently just large advertising machines. They disrupted many advertising firms and nearly all the newspapers. This does not create significant aggregate productivity, but it does create political and democratic issues. The same is true for Apple. The iPhone makes it more convenient to access digital content while traveling. It is nice, but if that's all it does, it will not move the needle of aggregate productivity. Moreover, the market for iOS apps is opaque, and conflicts of interest are pervasive.

To have a meaningful impact on economic growth, the GAFAMs or their siblings need to improve the markets that really matter: transport, energy, and health. If Google really helps to create a market for effective driverless cars, if Facebook really disrupts the banking system, if other digital technologies enable the efficient provision of health services, then we will see real, widespread benefits.

But here is the catch-22. In all these cases, privacy issues are paramount. In these new markets, the GAFAMs would have access to even more personal data, and data that are even more sensitive than what they can access today. If we already find it difficult to trust them with the data they have now, how will we feel about direct data feeds to private companies from our car or our health providers?

It is not hopeless, however. Technology can help solve the problems that it creates. For instance, artificial intelligence can also be used to fight off hackers and contain data breaches. Technology can make it easier and faster to assign blame for cyberattacks. Tech reporter Adam Janofsky notes that corporations are "using machine learning to sort through millions of malware files, searching for common characteristics that will help them identify new attacks. They're analyzing people's voices, fingerprints and typing styles to make sure that only authorized users get into their systems. And they're hunting for clues to figure out who launched cyberattacks—and make sure they can't do it again."*

---

* Adam Janofsky, "How AI can help stop cyberattacks," *Wall Street Journal*, September 18, 2018.

Competition can also help improve privacy, as Dina Srinivasan (2019) shows: "Facebook tried to renege on its promise not to track users in 2007, and again in 2010, but the market was competitive enough with adequate consumer choice to thwart Facebook's attempts." It was only after it acquired a monopoly position that Facebook could afford to disregard the privacy concerns of its users.

The good news is that the sharpest minds in policy circles are focused on this issue. The UK Chancellor of the Exchequer established a panel of experts in September 2018, led by a former chair of the Council of Economic Advisers, Jason Furman. This panel's influential report tackles some of the complex issues surrounding regulation of the digital economy and proposes a set of principles to guide policy decisions (Furman et al., 2019). Its policy recommendations emphasize "measures to promote data mobility and systems with open standards, and expanding data openness."

New technologies have the potential to revive productivity growth, but they have yet to deliver. The GAFAMs can be at the forefront of this push if we find a way to deal with the issue of data protection. We must ensure that big data does not present a barrier to entry, and we must make certain our privacy is protected.

CHAPTER 15

Monopsony Power and Inequality

> Masters are always and everywhere in a sort of tacit, but constant and uniform combination, not to raise the wages of labour above their actual rate.
>
> ADAM SMITH, *THE WEALTH OF NATIONS*

THERE ARE TWO TYPES of market power: monopoly and monopsony. Monopoly power is better known. A firm has monopoly power when it can charge a high price for its products because its clients have few other choices. It's easy to visualize, and we have discussed its implications.

A firm has monopsony power when it can exert market power on its employees and suppliers because they have few other places to sell their labor or their goods and services.

When I was in graduate school, monopsony power was deemed so irrelevant that the subject was dropped from the standard coursework. The modern models that we use to think about the economy do not include monopsony power. Monopsony was "so nineteenth century."

Much to my surprise, however, the topic has come back. There is evidence of growing monopsony power in several local labor markets across the US. And the pricing power of internet platforms—just like that of credit card companies—is also a form of monopsony, directed toward suppliers more than toward consumers.

Monopsony and monopoly have different sources but similar implications for the broad economy. Imagine a world where production requires only labor: one worker produces one unit of a good. Think about a monopoly charging a 50 percent markup over the wage. If the competitive wage is 1, then the price of the good is 1.5. If there are 100 workers in the economy, they produce 100 units of the good. The nominal GDP is $150, labor income is $100, and capital income is $50. Workers earn two-thirds of GDP, and capital owners earn one-third. But workers are also consumers. Each worker earns 1 but can only purchase 1/1.5, or 2/3 of a unit of the good.

Now imagine a monopsony. The price of the good is 1, but the wage is pushed down to 2/3 instead of 1 because workers have nowhere else to go. Notice that the outcome is exactly the same as before. Workers earn two-thirds of GDP and capital owners one-third. The worker can only buy two-thirds of the good, though in the perfectly competitive economy she would be able to buy a full unit.

At the aggregate level, therefore, monopsony and monopoly have the same implications for workers' standard of living. It does not matter whether firms mark up their prices by 50 percent or whether employers push down wages by 30 percent. In both cases the purchasing power of workers is 30 percent lower than it should be.

Labor Market Concentration

A few recent papers argue that monopsony power is coming back in the US labor market. The idea is relatively straightforward. If potential workers have the choice between only a handful of employers, then the employers have market power over the workers and can offer lower wages.

The first question, then, is this: how concentrated are labor markets? José Azar, Ioana Marinescu, Marshall Steinbaum, and Bledi Taska (2018) look at job vacancies posted online and collected by an analytics software company in 2016. They compute an index of labor market concentration using the Herfindahl-Hirschman index (HHI) for each commuting zone by six-digit federal Standard Occupational Classification codes. The average market has an HHI of 3,953, or the equivalent of 2.5 recruiting employers in the market. More than half of labor markets are highly concentrated with an HHI above 2,500—the cutoff in the DoJ/FTC guidelines we discussed in Chapter 2. Highly concentrated markets account for 17 percent of employment. When the authors consider other, plausible alternative market definitions, they find that the fraction of highly concentrated markets is never less than one-third.

The next question is whether concentration pushes down wages. It is difficult to measure, but recent papers suggest this might be the case. Economists Efraim Benmelech, Nittai Bergman, and Hyunseob Kim (2018) study the effect of local labor market concentration on wages using Census data over the period 1977–2009. They argue that local employer concentration has increased over time, and there is a negative relation between local employer concentration and wages. This is consistent with the idea that employers have monopsony power in concentrated labor markets. Moreover, they find the relation between labor market concentration and wages is more negative at high levels of concentration and when unionization rates are low. But wage growth is more tightly linked to productivity growth when labor markets are less concentrated.

Interestingly, they also find that concentration has increased in markets with greater exposure to import competition from China. These markets have become competitive on the product side, and we expect monopoly rents to have decreased. Unfortunately, the concentration might have triggered an increase in monopsony power, thus canceling some of the benefits of free trade. This is another example of the broad point that I made in the Introduction. There is a difference between domestic and foreign competition. Promoting domestic competition should be an absolute no-brainer. Foreign competition is more complicated and less clear-cut.

The literature on monopsony power is still in its infancy, and there is much more we need to learn. There is broad agreement that labor market power hurts workers. David Berger, Kyle F. Herkenhoff, and Simon Mongey (2019) estimate welfare losses from labor market power that range from 2.9 to 8.0 percent of lifetime consumption. There is no consensus, however, regarding the evolution of labor market concentration. Berger, Herkenhoff, and Mongey find that local labor market concentration has declined over the last thirty-five years despite the overall increase in national concentration. This brings us back to the issue that we discussed in Chapter 2. In Box 2.2 we showed that national concentration measures can differ from local concentration measures and give a misleading picture of the economy.

You might think that local labor market concentration matters less today because of online labor markets. Arindrajit Dube, Jeff Jacobs,

Suresh Naidu, and Siddharth Suri (2018) study exactly this issue. They examine one of the largest on-demand labor platforms, Amazon Mechanical Turk. Online platforms make it easier to search for a job, and one might have conjectured that they would lead to near-perfect competition. But the authors find a surprisingly high degree of market power, even in this large and diverse spot-labor market, suggesting that much of the surplus created by this online labor market platform is captured by employers.

Restricted Contracts

We have already seen how restrictive contracts are used by large hospitals to reduce competition in the health-care market. Similarly, large franchise employers use restriction in labor contracts to limit competition in the labor market. Princeton economists Alan B. Krueger and Orley Ashenfelter (2018) studied the role of covenants in franchise contracts that are commonly used by large firms, such as McDonald's, Burger King, Jiffy Lube, and H&R Block.

The covenants are meant to restrict the recruitment and hiring of employees from other units within the same franchise chain. In other words, the covenant prevents a McDonald's franchise in a particular location from poaching employees from another nearby location. Krueger and Ashenfelter find that almost 60 percent of major franchisors' contracts include these "no-poaching agreements" and that these agreements are more common for franchises in low-wage and high-turnover industries. They clearly decrease competition in the labor market and thus decrease wage growth.

The good news is that these labor market issues seem to finally be getting some attention. Twenty state attorneys general are looking into franchise noncompete hiring clauses in McDonald's franchise contracts based on Krueger and Ashenfelter's work.

Occupational Licensing

Geographic mobility has been declining for thirty years in the US. Workers are less likely to move between states and metropolitan areas now than they were in the past. There are several plausible explanations for this trend. One of them is the steady increase in the number of workers whose occupations require some sort of license or certification (Davis and Haltiwanger, 2014).

Morris M. Kleiner and Alan B. Krueger (2013) track the historical growth in licensing from a number of different data sources. They find that the share of the US workforce covered by state licensing laws grew fivefold in the second half of the twentieth century, from less than 5 percent in the early 1950s to 25 percent by 2008. State licenses account for the bulk of licensing, but if we add locally and federally licensed occupations, the share of the workforce that was licensed in 2008 reaches 29 percent.

The increase in licensing has two causes. The first is the growth in the number of employees in occupations that typically require a license over the last few decades. The field of health care contains many such occupations. But this only accounts for about one-third of the increase. At the same time, according to analysis from a 2015 report from the Council of Economic Advisers, there has been a large jump in the number of occupations that require licensing because of newly imposed licensing requirements. This expansion of licensing requirements across occupations explains two-thirds of the growth.

Licensing is always "officially" motivated by concerns for health, safety, and consumer protection. And sometimes it is legitimate. Often, however, it is the perfect way for incumbents to protect their rents. Indeed, they actively lobby for the extension of licensing requirements because they understand that these are efficient barriers to entry.

We have seen earlier that Europe has reduced barriers to entry in many industries. Some of that decrease was driven by a rollback of unnecessary licensing. There is still much illegitimate licensing in Europe, but at least the trend is in the right direction. Over the same period, however, the US has increased its licensing.

Inequality: The Rise of the Club Economy

There has been a large increase in inequality in the US economy, and there are many ways to account for it. For instance, we can look at the returns to education. They have increased over time. This implies that the earnings gap between educated workers (say, those with a college degree) and less-educated ones (say, high school dropouts) has increased over time.

We can look at the split of income between capital and labor. We have shown that the labor share has decreased while firms' profits and payouts have increased. The concentration of equity ownership is higher than that of human capital. When profits increase, they disproportionately benefit the few households with large equity portfolios. Concentration and market power therefore increase inequality.

Another way to break down the increase in inequality is to look at within-versus-between-firm inequality. Jae Song, David J. Price, Fatih Guvenen, Nicholas Bloom, and Till von Wachter (2019) use a massive, matched employer-employee database for the United States to analyze the contribution of firms to the rise in earnings inequality from 1978 to 2013. They find that one-third of the rise in the variance of earnings occurred within firms, whereas two-thirds of the rise occurred due to a rise in the dispersion of average earnings between firms.

However, this rising between-firm variance is not accounted for by the firms themselves but rather by a widening gap between firms in the composition of their workers. This compositional change can be split into two roughly equal parts: high-wage workers became increasingly likely to work in high-wage firms, and high-wage workers became increasingly likely to work with other high-wage workers. In other words, sorting increased and segregation rose.

They also find that two-thirds of the rise in the within-firm variance of earnings occurred within mega (10,000+ employee) firms, which saw a particularly large increase in the variance of earnings compared to smaller firms.

The Dangers of Monopsony Power

We have seen that there is a rise in monopsony power in the labor market. There is also the risk of a rise in monopsony power in online platforms. Large platforms have monopsony power with respect to their suppliers, even if they do not have much monopoly power on the consumer side.

Jeff Bezos once said that "there are two kinds of companies, those that work to try to charge more and those that work to charge less. We will be the second." And he was right: Amazon does not charge high prices to consumers. Amazon, however, uses the large scale of its operations to obtain rebates from its suppliers and delivery services, which increases its market power and makes it difficult for other firms to compete if they do not enjoy the same rebates. The macroeconomic implications of monopsony power are not so different from those of monopoly power. If a platform can push down the price at which it buys goods, the goods producers will have to reduce wages. Regulators should therefore make sure that rebates and other forms of monopsony rents do not become a barrier to entry in these markets.

Conclusion

Se vogliamo che tutto rimanga come è, bisogna che tutto cambi.

GIUSEPPE TOMASI DI LAMPEDUSA

"For things to remain the same, everything must change," explains Tancredi, the nephew of Prince Fabrizio Salina, as General Garibaldi's forces sweep through Sicily in Giuseppe di Lampedusa's novel, *Il Gattopardo* [*The Leopard*].* And so it is with free markets. Most of the issues that we struggle with are not new, but for markets to remain free, we must constantly adapt.

I have spent hundreds of hours researching and writing this book. You might have spent a few hours reading it, or, as I tend to do myself, jumping from figures to tables and reading the text only when the data look interesting.

At the very least, after so much work, we should have learned something. That is to say, we should have changed our minds about a few things. And we should have a few ideas to improve the current state of affairs.

I will not make a long list of policy recommendations. Instead, I am going to tell you what I learned, what surprised me, and what I took away.

What Surprised Me

I was surprised by how fragile free markets really are. We take them for granted, but history demonstrates that they are more the exception than

---

* The novel *The Leopard,* made into a film in 1963, takes place in 1860, toward the end of the Risorgimento and the wars of Italian Unification. Garibaldi captures the Kingdom of the Two Sicilies. Garibaldi wants a republic but has to settle for a constitutional monarchy under Victor Emmanuel II, the first king of the united Italy.

the rule. Free markets are supposed to discipline private companies, but today, many private companies have grown so dominant that they can get away with bad service, high prices, and deficient privacy safeguards. Only two decades ago, the United States was effectively the land of free markets and a leader in deregulation and antitrust policy. If America wants to lead once more in this realm, it must remember its own history and relearn the lessons it successfully taught the rest of the world.

Excessive concentration hurts individual consumers, true, but its impact spreads wider. Former defense secretary Robert Gates tells us in *Duty: Memoirs of a Secretary at War* (2014) that promoting competition among defense contractors was a real issue. In 2015 the Pentagon's acquisitions chief, Frank Kendall, explained that "one can foresee a future in which the department has at most two or three very large suppliers for all the major weapon systems that we acquire . . . The department would not consider this to be a positive development and the American public should not either." Rodrigo Carril and Mark Duggan (2018) study mergers among defense contractors to investigate how market structure impacts competition and costs. They find that market concentration in the defense industry has increased in the last three decades, leading to less competitive bidding and to more contracts that require the federal government to pay the contractor for all costs incurred, plus a markup.

I was surprised by the strength of the evidence in favor of competition. We have always known that competition lowers prices and increases real wages and standards of living. But the evidence also shows that competition is good for investment and suggests that it fosters innovation and productivity growth. In theory, however, competition can be excessive. We should expect, then, to find at least some industry at some time period in some country where competition has had a negative impact on innovation. But we find hardly any. Why is that? This is the story of the dog who did not bark. I have seen and discussed many papers showing that competition is good for growth (Buccirossi et al., 2013). I have not seen a paper that convincingly shows that protecting incumbents through patents, barriers to entry, or any other stratagem leads to an increase in productivity. It is highly unlikely that no researcher would have found this effect if it was in the data. The dog did not bark; that is the key piece of evidence. But why is it so difficult to find any such example? I think the answer is actually quite simple. The standard theory is incomplete because it ignores the political incentives of incumbents who lobby to weaken competition and erect barriers to entry. They often succeed for the wrong reasons, and this is why free markets are fragile. But in the rare instances in which their arguments have merit, their success is almost assured. As a result, the empirical distribution of industries is biased toward insufficient competition, and we almost never observe an industry on the wrong side of the innovation / competition curve.

I was surprised by the power and persistence of institutions beyond their original intent. It came to my attention when comparing Europe and the US. Having lived almost the same amount of time on each side of the Atlantic, I think that Europe faces deep challenges, probably deeper and more dangerous than the ones confronting the US. Moreover, European countries have not generally been at the forefront of good and innovative economic policies over the past thirty years. Yet EU competition policy has become stronger than US competition policy, and EU citizens are better off for it. It can all be traced back to the design of the Single Market, an institution that was heavily inspired by the best in class at the time. That's the irony. The reason EU consumers are better off than American consumers today is because the EU has adopted the US playbook, which the US itself has abandoned.

I was surprised by the extent and intricacies of American lobbying and campaign finance. They are at the same time visible and hard to pin down. They are hidden in plain sight but with enough noise to maintain plausible deniability. Institutions and interest groups create a dynamic ecosystem. Institutions shape the games played by lobbyists and are themselves influenced by political decisions. Economic inefficiencies are often embedded in overly complex institutions and sustained by continuous lobbying. The health-care system is a case in point. As a patient and especially as a parent of young children, I had naturally noticed the complexities, costs, and glaring inefficiencies of the system. But I did not fully comprehend the scale of the problem until I started putting the data together.

I was surprised by what I discovered about the internet giants. Like (almost) everyone, I use some version of Word to write documents, I have fond memories of my first MacBook, I remember the first time I saw the slick design of Google's home page, I order from Amazon, and I keep track of friends and family on Facebook, Instagram, and WhatsApp. Researching these firms, however, helped to clarify my thinking about exactly how they are special and how they are not. They are certainly fascinating companies but not nearly as influential in the economy as we might think. At least not yet. My big hope is that they can translate their ingenuity into things that matter more than tweets, targeted ads, and cute photos. But I am also convinced that they have become too entrenched and need a strong dose of competition.

Finally, I was surprised by the gap between economic research and policy. As economists we love to complain that if only politicians listened to us, economic policies would be more effective. There is some truth to that idea, but it is also too self-serving for my taste. First of all, as any economist who has had some policy experience will tell you, an economic adviser spends most of her time trying to kill obviously bad ideas and rarely gets the chance to advocate for good ones. Moreover, there is fairly strong evidence that economists fail to provide timely advice. The financial crisis of 2008 is an obvious example. Most financial economists failed to understand the risks before it was too late. The prevailing view at most academic conferences during the 2000s was that the finance industry was driving innovation and growth, and few economists questioned that narrative. Challenging the common wisdom is stimulating, but it is also risky. I wrote a paper in early 2008 to measure the efficiency of finance and, much to my surprise, I found that finance had not actually become more efficient. We discussed that idea in Chapter 11. This is probably one of my better-known papers, but it took seven years—and many rejections—to publish it (see Philippon, 2015).

There was a similar failure by economists to study and understand the growing concentration of many industries as it was happening. Today, of course, there is a flourishing literature on markups, competition, and concentration. But, with a few exceptions that I have highlighted in this book, none was prescient, and none challenged the status quo at a time when that would have been controversial and therefore useful.

The same issues occur in other areas of economics. Trade policy provides a good example. There is a wonderful *Trade Talks* podcast with Paul

Krugman that everyone should listen to.* Krugman explains how models of trade tended to lag behind developments in global trade. Before the 1980s most trade took place between rich nations and involved the buying and selling of items within the same industries. Standard models did not explain these patterns: they predicted trade of different goods between nations with different comparative advantages. New trade models based on specialization and returns to scale were developed to account for trade between rich countries . . . just in time for the rise of trade with poor countries that is well explained by the older, comparative advantage models. When the issue of trade and inequality became salient in the 1990s, trade models predicted small effects and economists argued there was not much to worry about . . . just in time for the entry of China into the World Trade Organization, which had a significant impact on employment and wages. With the China shock behind us, there is less to worry about as far as inequality is concerned, but this is not how the public sees it.

There is a lesson of humility here. It is not only because of misguided populism that economists have lost the trust of the public. It's also because we have often failed to challenge the consensus and to provide timely advice.

Taking Stock

My main argument in this book is that competition has declined in most US industries over the past twenty years. Here I would like to answer the trillion-dollar question: how much does this matter? To be more precise, suppose we could roll back the barriers to entry, undo the bad mergers, and somehow return to the level of competition we had in the late 1990s. How much better off would we be?

We are going to use a relatively simple model of the economy to answer that question. When economists talk about a "model," we mean a

---

* Trade Talks #66, December 2018. This podcast will convince you, whatever your political affiliations, that you can enjoy brilliant economic analysis in a nonpartisan way.

set of equations that represents how economic agents behave. Households work to make a living: they supply labor; they decide how much to save and what to buy, and they make consumption and saving decisions. Firms compete with each other to supply the goods and services that households and other businesses want to buy. They hire capital, labor, and intermediate inputs from other businesses. They understand that demand is elastic: they lose customers if they set their prices too high. All of these decisions can be written as mathematical objects. We can also incorporate the decisions of the government (taxes, spending, regulations) and the central bank (interest rates).

The virtue of a model is that we can compute the outcome of all these decisions. We call this outcome the *macroeconomic equilibrium*. The concept of equilibrium is important because the decisions are interdependent. Consider the labor market, for instance. Households supply labor, whereas firms hire labor. But firms hire labor because they expect to sell their products, which are bought by households using their labor income. Similarly, when we say that households save, we mean that they keep money in their bank accounts or that they invest in mutual funds. But banks and mutual funds are intermediaries, not end users. The savings eventually find their way into loans, bonds, and stocks. The return on these claims depends on the capital demand by firms. All these decisions are therefore interdependent. The practical implication is that if we want to understand the consequences of competition—or lack thereof—we need to keep track of what happens in all these markets at the same time. That's why we need a model.

Once we have the model, the key question becomes this: how large was the change in competition? Let's review the evidence. We saw that after-tax profits have increased by about 4 percentage points of GDP (Chapter 3). The labor share of income has decreased by about 6 percentage points of GDP (Chapter 6). When we compare the US with Europe, we find a relative markup increase of about 10 percent (Chapter 7). Some of it was due to EU markups going down in addition to US markups going up.

I am then going to feed into the model an experiment that is consistent with this evidence. Let us start from a situation that represents the 1990s. Markups are 5 percent over gross output, which means that firms add a 5 percent margin to the costs of labor, capital, and intermediate inputs. The economy has free entry, so these extra profits simply offset the cost of setting up and operating the businesses. I define the units so that GDP is $100 and total labor income is $65. The labor share is 0.65.

Now imagine that competition declines and that free entry is violated. Businesses can increase their margins from 5 percent to 10 percent. What happens then? The demand for capital, labor, and inputs decreases. Wages decrease too. The impact on employment depends on the willingness of households to continue working for lower wages. I use a conservative model in which households keep on working.* As a result, the main consequences of higher markups are lower wages, lower investment, and lower productivity, while employment stays about the same. Let us look at the numbers in more detail. Because of competition, GDP is only $95, that is, 5 percent lower. Labor income drops to $57. The new labor share is 57/95, which equals 0.6, and is in line with the evidence in Chapter 6. The capital stock decreases by 10 percent, which is also in line with the gap discussed in Chapter 4.

Let us put these numbers into perspective. US GDP is about $20 trillion. If we could make the economy as competitive as it was twenty years ago, the GDP would increase by 5 percent to $21 trillion. Employee compensation is about $11 trillion. In a competitive economy it would be 65/57×11, or $12.5 trillion. In other words, my calculations suggest that the lack of competition has deprived American workers of $1.5 trillion of income. This is more than the entire cumulative growth of real compensation between 2012 and 2018. The lack of competition has cost American workers six full years of growth. That is a large cost by any measure.

Another way to gauge the importance of the issue is to compare it to other policy proposals. As I am writing these lines, the US is entering the 2020 election cycle. I do not have the details of the proposals by the

---

* Formally, I use a low labor-supply elasticity—the so-called *Frisch elasticity*—of 0.1. In theory, since profits and payouts (dividends) increase while wages decrease, some households will rationally decide not to work as hard as before. If the Frisch elasticity was high, labor supply would decrease significantly, and this would amplify my results: it would lead to larger losses in GDP, consumption, and labor income.

various candidates, but I would be surprised if there is one that tops that number.

Returning to a high-competition economy will not be easy. Those who benefit from the lack of competition will fight to protect their vested interests. Let me offer a few principles to help you navigate the policy debate.

A Few Economic Principles for the Twenty-First Century

Principle 1: Free Entry, Always and Everywhere

A market cannot be free if it does not exist, so a monopoly is certainly better than a "zeropoly." Once a market exists, however, there is no reason to believe that the rents of the incumbent need to be actively protected, and many reasons to believe that they are usually too high. As a practical matter, fostering competition improves welfare. As I explain, the dog of excess competition did not bark.

If you believe in free markets, you need to be tough with everyone. American politicians and regulators have let regulations that restrict entry grow at the federal level and at the state level. We discussed the evidence in Chapters 5, 8, 9, and 15, but our data probably capture only the tip of the iceberg. Conservatives are right to argue that the US needs fewer regulations. I would simply qualify this idea as "regulations that hinder the entry or growth of small firms."

We also need to be tougher with incumbents, even the ones that we like. Today's monopolies are yesterday's startups. Successful firms are always both wonderful and excessive. Successful entrepreneurs are always part titan and part baron. Steve Jobs said he wanted to "put a ding in the universe." And he did. But that should not prevent us from keeping Apple's monopoly power in check. Competition and antitrust remedies are not punishments for moral wrongdoing—at least most of the time. They represent economic solutions that make the broader economic system more efficient. Firms have the right to try to beat their competitors and even to drive them out of business. Regulators have a duty to make sure they do not impede free markets. But no one should take it personally; it's just business.

Corollary 1: In an Efficient Market, the Marginal Firm Is Nearly Bankrupt

In a competitive market, the marginal firm should be on the brink of bankruptcy. This is the definition of free entry. Firms keep entering until they are not sure they will break even. Financial distress is not a bad sign and should never be used as an excuse for lax antitrust decisions. Moreover, bankruptcy is not liquidation. Distressed firms are usually reorganized. Bad policies follow almost invariably when temporary financial distress is used as an excuse to limit competition. The airlines used their financial distress as an excuse for concentration, and American skies became a large oligopoly.

Principle 2: Governments Should Make Mistakes Too

We live in a world where we tolerate data breaches from our banks, credit card companies, social media companies, email servers, and credit scoring companies. But in this world the idea that a regulator might make a mistake is unacceptable. When their cases are not perfect, regulators are pilloried by the press. It's no wonder they are shy. But they should not be. We are facing new issues that require new solutions. New solutions always involve mistakes, trial and error, and corrections. A zero-mistake approach to regulation is an approach to zero regulations. The courts should hold regulators to high standards, but overly laborious burdens of proof are not helpful.

In matters of economic policy in particular, perfect can be the enemy of the good. In a globalized world, we must also acknowledge the value of listening to regulators in several jurisdictions. Dieselgate is one of Europe's worst lobbying scandals. It exposed the deep corruption of European regulators by the car industry's lobbyists. Without the efforts of the California Air Resources Board and the US Environmental Protection Agency, Europeans would have suffered from higher levels of pollution, and the cheaters would not have been punished. But think about it: it is not by chance that Dieselgate was uncovered in the US, and it is not by chance that the General Data Protection Regulation was implemented in Europe. In both cases, domestic politicians and regulators had been captured, but foreign regulators had not.

Principle 3: Protect Transparency, Privacy, and Data Ownership

You cannot think about competition in health, finance, transport, and many other industries without thinking about data, information, and privacy. Over and over, we have seen that the way oligopolies maintain high prices and avoid outrage and crackdowns is by hiding their fees. That is true of banks, credit card companies, pharmaceutical companies, hospitals, insurers, and internet platforms. You need to know what you pay, and why you pay it. And if you do not pay, you need to know which part of you is being sold.

As daunting as they may seem, all these problems have solutions. I strongly believe that the economic issues discussed in this book can be fixed. For this to happen, however, the world badly needs US policy makers to take the field. It is therefore disheartening to see the US conspicuously absent from the most important regulatory debate of the twenty-first century, that of privacy and data protection. The Chinese government is pursuing policies that violate individual privacy rights and bear a growing resemblance to George Orwell's Big Brother. European policy makers are doing the best they can, but they are unlikely to succeed without active involvement from their US counterparts. To put it bluntly, solving the challenges of privacy and data protection requires a level of expertise that few institutions outside the US possess.

The economic challenges I have highlighted are universal. All countries need to face them. What sets the US apart is that it has more power and more responsibility. It has also lost its way more than other countries, perhaps because it started from a higher pedestal. This is not the first time a country has neglected what made it great in the first place. The Roman and Chinese empires lasted for centuries but fell apart when their leaders forgot the principles upon which the empires were built. The Siglo de Oro—the golden age of Spain—was brought down by nepotism, and by political and religious intolerance. The Dutch helped bring down the mighty Spanish empire and their republic became the foremost maritime and economic power of the seventeenth century, driven by creativity, entrepreneurship, and international openness. But they fell asleep at the wheel in trade, went to war with their neighbors, and allowed England to become the focal point of foreign investment and innovation. And the story goes on. Great powers rise, become complacent—or greedy—and fall.

The good news for the US is that this process, at least in historic terms, has only just begun, and the institutions that can arrest the fall remain in place. Yes, the US has neglected its free markets, but it has the opportunity to correct its mistakes. Yes, issues surrounding big data and privacy are difficult, but just as Europe has looked to the US in the past for ideas about improving competition, the US can now look to Europe to learn about protecting consumers' privacy.

And finally, yes, there is too much money in politics and too much pressure from special interests clouding the judgment of lawmakers and regulators. This may be the most intractable problem we face, if only because it has the potential to scuttle solutions to bring back free markets. But there are many examples of advanced economies governed by legislators who don't spend thirty hours every week dialing for dollars.

The US has overcome major challenges before. For more than a century, it has been at the leading edge of innovation, both private technological innovation and political and social innovation. US markets can and should regain their freedom.

Appendix

A. INDUSTRY CLASSIFICATION: NAICS AND ISIC

If I ask you: Who are Sears's competitors? You will quickly mention Walmart, Amazon, and a few others. But is that all? What are all the businesses that belong to the same industry? Economists and statisticians love to classify things. We classify firms into industries and industries into sectors. This appendix shows you what these names mean.

What is an industry? How do we classify firms across industries? We need to answer these basic questions if we want to study firms and industries. For instance, to compute the market share of a firm, we first need to figure out in what industry it operates (and then we need to worry about its physical location and such).

When we study the US, we will use the North American Industry Classification System (NAICS). It was developed jointly by the US, Canada, and Mexico in 1997 to replace the old Standard Industrial Classification (SIC) system. NAICS divides the economy into twenty sectors, and each sector is divided into industries. Table A.1 describes some important sectors of the US economy.

The goal of the classification is to group together economic units (factories, plants, stores) that have similar production processes. For instance, the NAICS *information* sector includes activities that transform and distribute information: broadcasting, publishing (books, newspapers, magazines), motion pictures, etc. The NAICS *professional, scientific, and technical services* sector covers activities where expertise (human capital) is the major input: lawyers, architects and interior designers, engineering services, advertising agencies, etc. The *manufacturing* sector is further divided into eighty-six industries at the four-digit level. *Retail* is divided into twenty-seven units and *professional services* into only nine.

Walmart is classified as retail. Its 2012-NAICS-3 code is 452 (general merchandise stores), and its NAICS-4 is 4529 (other general merchandise stores), which separates it from 4521 (department stores). Amazon

TABLE A.1.

NAICS Classification of Important Sectors of the US Economy

Selected Sector	Code	Definition	Example
Utilities	22	Generate, transmit & distribute gas, electricity, steam, water; sewage	22111 Electric power generation
Construction	23	Erect buildings & structures, repair & maintain	23731 Highway, street, and bridge construction
Manufacturing	31–33	Transform materials, substances, or components into new products	32541 Pharmaceutical and medicine manufacturing
Wholesale trade	42	Trade raw & intermediate materials, and goods for resale	42471 Petroleum bulk stations and terminals
Retail trade	44–45	Retail merchandise to the general public	44111 New car dealers
Transportation & warehousing	48–49	Transport passengers and cargo, store goods	481111 Scheduled passenger air transportation
Information	51	Distribute information and cultural products	51521 Cable
			51721 Wireless carriers
Finance & insurance	51	Create and trade financial assets and insurance products	52311 Investment banking and securities dealing
Professional services	54	Provide scientific & technical services to organizations	54181 Advertising agencies
Health care & social assistance	62	Provide health care and social assistance to individuals	62121 Offices of dentists

is also in retail, but its codes are 454 (nonstore retailers) and 4541 (electronic shopping and mail-order houses.)

Industry classification is difficult and imperfect. IBM started in computer manufacturing (334) but then moved toward professional services (541). In some databases, however, IBM's codes have been the same since 1950. How does NAICS deal with the fact that many large companies operate in different industries? Essentially, it splits them up. NAICS classifies establishments, usually in a single physical location: factory, mill, store, hotel, movie theater, airline terminal, etc. An establishment is the smallest operating unit for which records of inputs (number of employees, wages, materials, capital) and output are available. The output may be sold or provided to the parent company. NAICS is a rather advanced system. For instance, a shop located in a hotel is a separate establishment classified in retail, while the hotel itself is in accommodation. In transportation or in telecommunications, the establishments are the permanent branch offices, terminals, and stations. A company often owns several establishments and therefore appears in more than one NAICS industry. NAICS includes specific rules to deal with vertical integration (i.e., steel mills that make steel but also produce steel castings) and joint production (a car dealership that both sells and repairs cars).

Finally, when we compare the US with other countries, we use the International Standard Industrial Classification system (ISIC), organized by the United Nations. The principles underlying ISIC are similar to the ones of NAICS, and the US, Canada, and Mexico have tried to create NAICS industries that do not cross ISIC two-digit boundaries. Some differences remain, however, especially when we use granular definitions.

B. UNDERSTANDING REAL GDP GROWTH

Nominal GDP for the US measures the market value of goods and services in the current year, using current prices. The problem with nominal GDP is that the base level of prices is arbitrary. US nominal GDP was $19.5 trillion in 2017. That is, if you measure it in dollars. If you measured it in pennies, it would be 1,950 trillion pennies. That's a different number, but it obviously represents the same economic reality. We thus need to find a way to separate the concept of real GDP from that of GDP in some arbitrary unit of account.

Suppose that there are two goods, a and b. The quantity produced in year t are $q_{a,t}$ and $q_{b,t}$, the prices are $p_{a,t}$ and $p_{b,t}$. Nominal GDP is then:

$$Y_t = p_{a,t}\, q_{a,t} + p_{b,t}\, q_{b,t}.$$

If the same goods and services were sold at the same prices every year, we could use nominal GDP to make meaningful comparisons. But everything changes: prices change, some goods appear, and some goods disappear. We discussed the issue of new goods earlier, in Chapter 2. The idea of real GDP is to net out the effect of prices. Historically, there have been two ways to do it.

Fixed-Weight Real GDP

The traditional way to define real GDP has been to fix a base year and use prices from that year, year o. We can compute GDP in year t using prices from year o:

$$Y_{t,0} = p_{a,0} \, q_{a,t} + p_{b,0} \, q_{b,t}.$$

$Y_{t,0}$ is a measure of real GDP based on year o. It measures what GDP would have been in year t if all the prices had remained the same as in year o. It is what's known as a *Laspeyres index,* meaning that it uses a fixed set of prices, or *fixed weights*.

$Y_{t,0} / Y_0$ is a measure of real growth between year o and year t. This approach was used in the US until 1996. It is rather simple to explain, but it has one big drawback: the number you get for "real growth" depends on the arbitrary choice of the base year. For instance, the growth rate of the US economy in 1998 was 4.5 percent using 1995 as the base year, but 6.5 percent using 1990 prices, 18.8 percent using 1980 prices, and 37.4 percent using 1970 prices (Whelan, 2000). This problem is known as *substitution bias,* and it happens when there are large changes in relative prices over time.

Chained Indexes

The problem of using a base year is that its prices become obsolete. So why don't we use last year's prices instead? That is the basic idea of chained indexes:

$$Y_{t,t-1} = p_{a,t-1} \, q_{a,t} + p_{b,t-1} \, q_{b,t}.$$

This is the GDP this year using last year's prices, and we can compute the growth rate in year t as:

$$g_t^L = Y_{t,t-1}/Y_{t-1}.$$

The growth rate g_t^L is the Laspeyres growth with the previous year as base year. This is almost how growth is computed today. It is slightly more advanced because, if you think about it, when you compute growth between $t-1$ and t, you might want to treat $t-1$ and t in a more symmetric way. You can compute GDP at $t-1$ using t prices as $Y_{t-1,t} = p_{a,t} q_{a,t-1} + p_{b,t} q_{b,t-1}$. Then you can compute growth as:

$$g_t^P = Y_t/Y_{t-1,t}.$$

This is called a *Paasche index*. Both growth estimates are sensible, so why not use the geometric average? That is the method employed by the US Commerce Department's Bureau of Economic Analysis to produce the Fisher index of real growth:

$$g_t^F = \sqrt{g_t^L g_t^P}.$$

This is the headline number you hear about each quarter when the BEA releases its estimate of the growth rate of GDP.

C. REAL EXCHANGE RATES AND BALASSA-SAMUELSON

There are two types of exchange rates: a financial rate based on the foreign exchange (FOREX) market and a PPP rate based on local prices (International Comparison Program [ICP] PPP, or Big Mac PPP). Before we can compare prices around the world, we need to pause and think about how exchange rates are determined. The theory of purchasing power parity (PPP) says that, in the long run, the exchange rate adjusts in such a way that the law of one price (LOOP) holds for a basket of goods (see Chapter 7). What is the link between PPP and LOOP? The LOOP applies to individual goods (say, a pair of shoes), and PPP applies to the general price index (the price of a basket of goods). Clearly, if the LOOP holds for each good, then PPP will also hold for the basket of goods. Some prices might be off individually, but PPP might still work reasonably well for the average basket. So let's imagine a representative basket of goods sold in both Europe and the US. That would include food, cars, electronics, etc. If P_{US} is the cost of that basket in dollars in the US and P_{EU} is the cost of that same basket in euros in Europe, then the theory of PPP says that the euro / dollar exchange rate should gravitate toward the PPP rate:

$$E^{PPP} = P_{US} / P_{EU.}$$

Is there support for the PPP theory of exchange rates? It's the classic frustrating story of the half-empty glass. In the short term, exchange rates move for many apparently random reasons, largely unrelated to relative prices. And local prices are slow to adjust to changes in nominal exchange rates. PPP can only be a theory of exchange rates in the long run. Even then, the support is rather weak in the sense that the prices of similar baskets can remain substantially different for a long time.

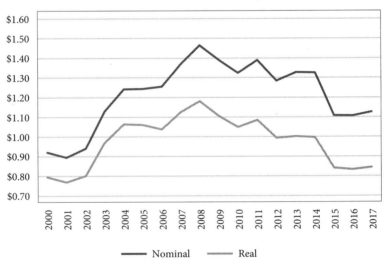

Nominal and Real Exchange Rates

FIGURE A.1 Nominal and real exchange rates. The real exchange rate (RER) is the ratio of the nominal rate to the PPP rate. When the RER rate is less than one, the euro is cheap. According to this view, the euro was somewhat expensive in 2007–2008, but has been cheap since 2015. Volatility is the sample standard deviation of the series.

Real Exchange Rates

There is support, however, for predicting the evolution of exchange rates: if a country is expensive, its currency tends to depreciate. To quantify deviations from PPP, we define the euro real exchange rate (RER) as:

$$RER = E^{MARKET} / E^{PPP}.$$

One way to state the PPP theory of exchange rates is that the real exchange rate should tend to 1 in the long run. Figure A.1 shows the nominal and real exchange rates of the euro against the dollar, i.e., the comparison between the US and EA19. E^{PPP} in 2017 is $1.33, and the market rate is $1.13. The RER is therefore 0.84. The theory predicts that the RER should increase—that is, the euro should appreciate over the next few years (or, equivalently, that the dollar should depreciate).

Notice that the RER is not much less volatile than the nominal exchange rate. The volatility of the market rate is $0.17, and it is 0.12 for the ICP-based RER. In the short term, movement in relative prices does not cancel much of the movements in financial rates.

The Balassa-Samuelson Effect

Wages are higher in rich countries, so local prices are higher. This circumstance is called the Balassa-Samuelson effect. Many goods are not traded internationally (haircuts, for example), and even the ones that are traded incur local distribution costs (labor costs and commercial real estate rents). The original figure from Balassa's 1964 paper shows that rich countries tend to have more expensive exchange rates than poor countries. Their prices are higher than one would predict based on the level of the market exchange rates. This is consistent with the haircut example that we used at the beginning of Chapter 7.

Angus Deaton and Alan Heston (2010) look at the same data forty-five years later and confirm the Balassa-Samuelson effect. In most emerging markets, the ratio of the market and PPP US dollar exchange rates is between 2 and 4, because nontraded goods and services are cheap in low-income countries even though the prices of tradable goods (machines,

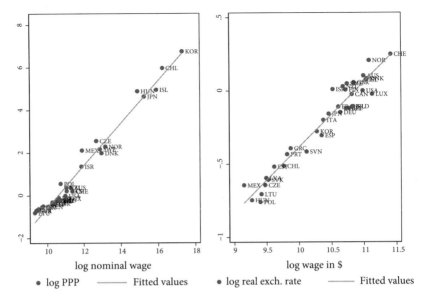

FIGURE A.2 Prices and wages in 2015. (*Left*): log (PPP) versus log (nominal wage). (*Right*): Variables are scaled by the FX exchange rate, so this graph plots log (RER) versus log (real wage).

etc.) are broadly similar. These differences mean that developing countries are richer on a PPP basis than on a market-rate basis. Incidentally, it means that the world appears somewhat less unequal when we view it from a PPP perspective.

Let us start by comparing prices and wages across various countries.

The first panel of Figure A.2 shows that, as expected, nominal prices and wages are proportional across countries: the slope of the lines in the left panel is one. In the second panel, we have the Balassa-Samuelson effect: real exchange rates are higher in countries where real wages are higher. On one hand, clearly, wages explain many of the differences in prices, as expected from basic pricing theory.

On the other hand, the data also show a great deal of variation in real exchange rates among countries with similar per-capita income. This is consistent with the Ferrari example given in Chapter 7, in which differences in markups explain differences in prices. It is worth noting that many issues arise when we use price indexes to compare costs of living across countries, as discussed in Deaton and Heston (2010). But these issues are most severe when we compare countries at different levels of income and development, or countries in very different climates, because many goods are consumed only in some places and not in others. For instance, the typical basket of food includes rice in Asia but not in Africa. That makes it hard to define a common basket and to compute the relative price index and apply the PPP approach. The relative importance of heating costs and air-conditioning costs are going to be very different for people living in Reykjavik, Iceland, and in Washington, DC. In this book, however, we focus on the comparison between the US and Europe, and we can assume that preferences and available goods are relatively similar.

More broadly, economists have shown that *pricing to market* is important. For instance, George Alessandria and Joseph P. Kaboski (2011) find that "deviations from the law of one price in tradable goods are an important source of violations of absolute PPP across countries . . . : at the U.S. dock, U.S. exporters ship the same good to low-income countries at lower prices. This pricing-to-market is about twice as important as any local non-traded inputs, such as distribution costs, in explaining the differences in tradable prices across countries."

D. QUALITY ADJUSTMENTS IN FINANCIAL SERVICES

Changes in the characteristics of the borrowers require quality adjustments to the raw measure of intermediated assets. For instance, corporate finance involves issuing commercial paper for blue chip companies as well as raising equity for high-technology startups. The monitoring requirements per dollar intermediated are clearly different in these two activities. Similarly, with household finance, it is more expensive to lend to poor households than to wealthy ones, and relatively poor households have gained access to credit in recent years. Using the Survey of Consumer Finances, Kevin B. Moore and Michael G. Palumbo (2010) document that between 1989 and 2007 the fraction of households with positive debt balances increased from 72 percent to 77 percent. This increase is concentrated at the bottom of the income distribution. For households in the 0–40 percentiles of income, the fraction with some debt outstanding goes from 53 percent to 61 percent between 1989 and 2007.

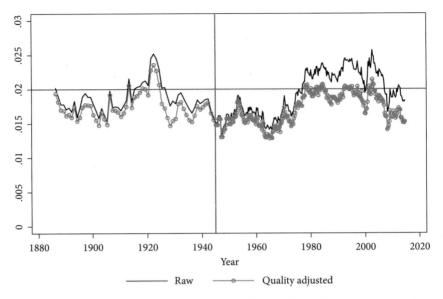

FIGURE A.3 Unit cost and quality adjustment. The quality-adjusted measure takes into account changes in firms' and households' characteristics. Data range is 1886–2015. *Source*: Philippon (2015)

Measurement problems arise when the mix of high- and low-quality borrowers changes over time.

I therefore perform a quality adjustment to the intermediated assets series, following Philippon (2015). Figure A.3 shows the quality-adjusted unit cost series. It is lower than the unadjusted series by construction, since quality-adjusted assets are (weakly) larger than raw intermediated assets. The gap between the two series grows when there is entry of new firms and when there is credit expansion at the extensive margin (that is, new borrowers). Even with the adjusted series, however, we see no significant decrease in the unit cost of intermediation over time, at least until very recently.

So, quality adjustments do not explain why finance is still expensive. Guillaume Bazot (2013) finds similar unit costs in other major countries (Germany, UK, France, Japan).

Glossary

abuse of dominance: The use of market power by a dominant firm in a way that harms competition, eliminates an existing competitor, or deters entry by new competitors. It is a complex and controversial idea, and its definition differs across jurisdictions. US regulators prefer to talk about monopolization.

adverse selection: A situation in which some market participants take advantage of private information that other participants do not have. The information can be about the true quality of a good (such as used cars), the true risk of an activity, or the true value of an asset. For instance, informed traders will try to sell their shares when they learn before anyone else that a company is in trouble. Markets can collapse when adverse selection is strong because everyone mistrusts the trading motives of everyone else.

anti-steering: A contractual arrangement that prevents firms from directing their clients toward some products. Credit card companies prohibit merchants from steering consumers toward cards with lower transaction fees. Hospitals prohibit insurers from steering patients toward cheaper health-care providers. In the mortgage market, on the other hand, anti-steering refers to a regulation that prevents lenders from steering borrowers into high-cost loans.

antitrust laws: The federal and state laws that promote competition and prevent monopolization. In the late nineteenth century, large companies organized as "trusts" to stifle competition. Antitrust deals mainly with mergers, cartels (price-fixing), and restrictive agreements (such as tie-ins or exclusive contracts). The three core antitrust laws in the US are the Sherman Act (1890), the Federal Trade Commission Act (1914), and the Clayton Act (1914). They are usually called *competition laws* or *anti-monopoly laws* outside of the US.

Balassa-Samuelson effect: The tendency for high productivity in tradable goods to raise wages in other sectors, leading to higher prices in the service sector in richer countries. It explains why, for example, haircuts cost more in Norway than in Indonesia.

barriers to entry: Obstacles that make it difficult for a new firm to enter the market. The barriers can arise from technology (critical assets), from regulations (such as licensing requirements), or from the strategic behavior of incumbents. See also ease of entry.

concentration: The equilibrium distribution of market shares resulting from the entry and growth of new firms versus the exit and mergers of existing firms. Concentration can be measured either as market share of top n firms (CRn, with $n = 4, 8 \ldots$), or with the Herfindahl-Hirschman index (HHI).

constant price GDP: See real GDP.

consumption of fixed capital (CFK): See depreciation.

cost of goods sold (COGS): An accounting item that refers to the direct costs of production. In manufacturing it includes the intermediate inputs (such as raw materials and energy) as well as the wages of production workers. It does not include R&D expenditures or the wages of administrators and researchers.

demand curve: A downward-sloping line showing the relationship between the price of a good or service and the quantity that buyers are able or willing to purchase at that price.

depreciation: The sum of wear and tear and obsolescence of the capital stock used in production; also called consumption of fixed capital (CFK).

diversification: A method of managing risk by investing in varied firms, industries, and countries; also the fancy name for not putting all your eggs in one basket.

duopoly: Oligopoly with two dominant firms.

ease of entry: An antitrust and merger-approval concept to gauge the ability of future competitors to impose meaningful constraints on a merged firm. It requires timeliness (less than two years to plan entry and have a significant market impact), likelihood (profitability under premerger prices), and sufficiency (adequate knowledge of the market and financial resources to withstand aggressive pricing by a merged firm).

economies of scale: A situation in which the average cost of production declines when production increases for a given good or service. The simplest example is that of a fixed cost: when output increases, the fixed cost is spread among more units and the average unit cost falls. See also network externalities.

economies of scope: Economies of scale applied to the diversity of goods and services. A simple example is a retail location offering more than one product, such as a gas station that also sells coffee.

efficiency (Pareto): A situation is Pareto-efficient (named for the Italian economist Vilfredo Pareto) when no single person or business can be made better off without decreasing the welfare of another. When an equilibrium is not Pareto-efficient, economists typically get agitated and try to fix it.

elasticity: The change in one variable in response to a unit increase in another variable. For instance, the elasticity of tax revenues is the percent increase in tax collections for a one percent increase in GDP.

elasticity of demand: The percent decline in the quantity of a good demanded in response to a one percent increase in the price of the good. If the elasticity is 2, consumers buy 20 percent fewer goods when the price increases by 10 percent.

endogeneity bias: When people are proactive and react to their environment, endogeneity bias is the result. For example, people go to see a doctor when they feel sick; companies invest when they are confident in the demand for their products; corporations lobby when they have something to ask for or when they feel threatened. Endogeneity makes correlations difficult—sometimes impossible—to interpret. It is the fundamental issue in empirical economics.

equilibrium: A situation that is stable for a period of time because the choices of economic agents are consistent with each other, and the budget constraints add up. A simple example of equilibrium is a market where the price adjusts so that supply equals demand. A complicated example is the labor market, where the unemployment rate depends on a large number of decisions by firms, workers, and consumers.

externality: A cost incurred or a benefit received by one who did not create or choose the cost or benefit. British economist Arthur Cecil Pigou argued that government should impose taxes to correct negative externalities, such as a carbon tax to address the problem of climate change. See also network externality.

fintech: Digital innovations in the financial services industry.

free entry: The ability of new firms to enter a market and begin producing and selling a product without interference from regulatory agencies or dominant firms.

gross domestic product (GDP): The total value of all the final goods and services produced within the borders of a country during a year. See also GDP per capita; nominal GDP; real GDP.

GDP per capita: Gross domestic product divided by population. For example, US GDP was $20.5 trillion in 2018. US population was about 327 million. US GDP per capita was therefore $62,700.

growth, real per capita: The growth of real GDP per capita. It is the starting point for analyzing changes in living standards. For instance, US real GDP increased by about 3 percent in the first quarter of 2019, as nominal GDP was up 3.8 percent and prices were up 0.8 percent. Since US population growth is around 0.7 percent, real per capita growth is about 2.3 percent. See also nominal GDP; real GDP.

Herfindahl-Hirschman index (HHI): A measure of market concentration, computed as the sum of the squared market shares of the firms competing in the particular market.

Horizontal merger: A merger between competitors at the same level of production and distribution of a good or service. It can have *unilateral effects* from the disappearance of competition between the products of the merged firms and *coordinated effects* from decreasing competition with other producers in the same market. See also vertical merger.

income: For households, the sum of labor earnings and capital income. For firms, see profit margin; profit rate.

Industrial Revolution: A rapid major alteration in an economy fueled by widespread advances in technology. The advances of the First Industrial Revolution were in mechanical production, beginning in Britain around 1780 with mechanized spinning and later iron manufacturing, fueled by coal and steam power. The Second Industrial Revolution was marked by advances in science and the mass production of goods (think of Ford's Model T). Around 1870, transportation and communication networks (railroad, telegraph) were expanded and utilities (gas, water, and electrical power) established. Major inventions included the telephone, fertilizer, and internal combustion engines. The Third Industrial Revolution was the Digital Revolution: semi-conductors (1950s), then mainframe computers, personal computers, and the internet. Many argue that we are entering a Fourth Industrial Revolution, with major advances in genetics, medicine, and artificial intelligence.

labor share: The share of GDP that accrues to labor instead of capital. The labor share is typically between 0.6 and 0.7, depending on the details of the calculation.

law of one price (LOOP): The hypothesis that identical goods should sell for the same price in different countries when the prices are expressed in units of the same currency. It is more likely to be true when shipping and distribution costs are small.

liquid asset: An asset that can be converted to cash without impacting its value.

lobbying: The attempt to influence a politician or a public official. It can be benign—sharing relevant information between businesses, regulators, and politicians—but it can also involve rent-seeking and even lead to corruption.

loss-leader pricing: The strategy of a firm that sells a product at a loss in order to attract customers and stimulate the sales of other, more profitable goods and services.

market power: The ability of a firm to raise its price over its marginal cost (the cost of producing the last unit sold). Market power increases the firm's profits at the expense of its customers but might be necessary to recoup sunk costs. Market power depends on the elasticity of demand and the nature of competition in the market.

market share: The ratio of a firm's revenues over the total sales in that market.

mergers and acquisitions: Legal transactions that lead to the consolidation of two or more entities. An acquisition is when one company buys another entity. The company becomes the new owner and the entity disappears. The acquisition can be friendly or hostile. A merger of equals happens when two firms of similar size combine forces. The shares of both companies are replaced by newly issued stocks of the joint company. See also horizontal merger; vertical merger.

merger review: Federal review of mergers and acquisitions between large firms. In the US, it is typically performed by the Department of Justice or by the Federal Trade Commission; in the EU, by the Directorate-General for Competition.

monopoly power: Monopoly power is a general term that refers to market power by a single firm, even when it has a few competitors. See and compare with pure monopoly.

monopsony power: A situation in which a buyer has market power, such as when a firm is the only large employer in a town.

moral hazard: A situation in which the provision of insurance or safety nets leads to reduced efforts or higher risk-taking behavior. For instance, unemployment or disability insurance can reduce individual incentives to work.

net asset value (NAV): The value of a fund's assets minus the value of its liabilities. A floating NAV fluctuates, whereas a fixed NAV does not.

net investment: Investment expenditures minus depreciation. Net investment measures the growth of the capital stock.

net present value (NPV): The value of future cash flows, discounted and adjusted for risk.

net sales: See revenues.

network externality: A form of synergy whereby the value of belonging to a network increases when the number of users on the network increases. It can lead to the emergence of a dominant firm.

nominal GDP: Gross domestic product expressed in local currencies (dollars, euros, yuan, etc.). It can be converted into the same currency (usually dollars) using exchange rates.

operating income: The basic measure of profits from operation, defined as sales (revenues) minus cost of goods sold (COGS) and selling, general, and administrative expense (SG&A). Just like earnings before interest and taxes (EBIT), it ignores taxes and interest payments. EBIT, however, also includes non-operating income.

payout rate: The ratio of the flow of dividends and share buybacks over the stock of capital.

predatory pricing: The strategy of a firm that sets low, unsustainable prices in order to drive its competitors out of business.

premerger notification: Application by the parties involved in a merger or acquisition for a formal review of the process by the Federal Trade Commission and Department of Justice.

price discrimination: The sale of identical goods or services at different prices to different customers.

product market regulation (PMR) index: A measurement of regulations in the market for goods and services, including regulatory barriers to firm entry and competition.

profit margin: A firm's profit over total sales, measured in percent.

profit rate: The ratio of income net of depreciation over the stock of capital at the beginning of the year.

purchasing power parity (PPP): A measurement tool to compare standards of living between countries by using the price of a common basket of goods and services. PPP can be used to define exchange rates and to compare real income per capita. The Big Mac index is PPP using the price of Big Mac sandwiches.

pure monopoly: A situation in which there is only one seller in a market, such as when a firm is the only supplier of a particular product in a particular location. Cases of pure monopoly are relatively rare.

real GDP: Gross domestic product adjusted for inflation.

regulatory capture: The influence or domination by industry or interest groups of the government agency intended to regulate that industry.

rent: A payment received by the owner of an asset in excess of the cost of reproducing or recreating that asset.

restricted contract: A contract between firms that encourages anticompetitive behavior. *See also* anti-steering.

revenues: The top line of the income statement of a firm. Also known as net sales.

skewness: A measure of the asymmetry of the probability distribution of a random variable around its mean. Symmetric distributions have a skewness of 0. Negative skewness means that the tail is fat on the left: large negative events are more likely than positive ones. Positive skewness means that the tail is fat on the right: large positive events are more likely than negative ones.

total factor productivity (TFP) growth: A measurement of the extent to which output expands for given levels of all inputs. It is the most important measure of technological progress and the key to sustainable growth.

Tobin's *q*: The ratio of the market value of a firm to the replacement cost of its capital stock.

unit labor cost: The average cost of labor per unit of output.

vertical merger: A merger that takes place between firms at complementary levels in the chain of production. See also horizontal merger.

vertical restraints: The restrictions agreed on by firms at different levels of the production and distribution process, as opposed to horizontal restraints between horizontal competitors. They include agreements on the maximum or minimum resale prices, agreements to accept returns of products, tying contracts where access to a product requires the purchase of another one, exclusive agreements not to buy from rivals, and so on. US courts have become more tolerant of such restraints over the past couple of decades.

REFERENCES

Acemoglu, D., D. Autor, D. Dorn, G. H. Hanson, and B. Price (2016). Import competition and the great US employment sag of the 2000s. *Journal of Labor Economics 34*(S1), S141–S198.

Alesina, A., and F. Giavazzi (2006). *The Future of Europe: Reform or Decline.* Cambridge, MA: MIT Press.

Alessandria, G., and J. P. Kaboski (2011). Pricing-to-market and the failure of absolute PPP. *American Economic Journal: Macroeconomics 3*(1), 91–127.

Alpert, A., D. Powell, and R. L. Pacula (2018). Supply-side drug policy in the presence of substitutes: Evidence from the introduction of abuse-deterrent opioids. *American Economic Journal: Economic Policy 10*(4), 1–35.

Al-Ubaydli, O., and P. A. McLaughlin (2017). RegData: A numerical database on industry-specific regulations for all United States industries and federal regulations, 1997–2012. *Regulation & Governance 11*(1), 109–123.

Andrews, D., C. Criscuolo, and P. N. Gal (2015). Frontier firms, technology diffusion and public policy. OECD Productivity Working Papers, no. 2, OECD, Paris, 1–38.

Ansolabehere, S., J. M. de Figueiredo, and J. M. Snyder Jr. (2003). Why is there so little money in U.S. politics? *Journal of Economic Perspectives 17*(1), 105–130.

Arayavechkit, T., F. Saffie, and M. Shin (2014). Capital-based corporate tax benefits: Endogenous misallocation through lobbying. Working paper, University of Pennsylvania.

Ashenfelter, O., and D. Hosken (2010). The effect of mergers on consumer prices: Evidence from five mergers on the enforcement margin. *Journal of Law and Economics 53*(3), 417–466.

Ashenfelter, O., D. S. Hosken, and M. Weinberg (2011). The price effects of a large merger of manufacturers: A case study of Maytag-Whirlpool. NBER Working Paper No. 17476, National Bureau of Economic Research, Cambridge, MA, October.

Auerbach, A. J. (2002). Taxation and corporate financial policy. In *Handbook of Public Economics,* ed. A. J. Auerbach and M. Feldstein, vol. 3, 1251–1292. New York: Elsevier.

Autor, D. H., D. Dorn, and G. H. Hanson (2016). The China shock: Learning from labor-market adjustment to large changes in trade. *Annual Review of Economics 8*(1), 205–240.

Autor, D., D. Dorn, L. Katz, C. Patterson, and J. Van Reenen (2017). Concentrating on the fall of the labor share. *American Economic Review 107*(5), 180–185.

Azar, J. A., I. Marinescu, M. I. Steinbaum, and B. Taska (2018). Concentration in US labor markets: Evidence from online vacancy data. NBER Working Paper No. 24395, National Bureau of Economic Research, Cambridge, MA, March.

Azoulay, P., B. Jones, J. D. Kim, and J. Miranda (2018). Age and high-growth entrepreneurship. NBER Working Paper No. 24489, National Bureau of Economic Research, Cambridge, MA, April.

Bajgar, M., G. Berlingieri, S. Calligaris, C. Criscuolo, and J. Timmis (2019). Industry concentration in Europe and North America. OECD Productivity Working Papers, no. 18, OECD, Paris, January.

Baker, R. B., C. Frydman, and E. Hilt (2018). Political discretion and antitrust policy: Evidence from the assassination of President McKinley. NBER Working Paper No. 25237, National Bureau of Economic Research, Cambridge, MA, November.

Baker, T., and B. G. C. Dellaert (2018). Behavioral finance, decumulation and the regulatory strategy for robo-advice. Research Paper 18-19, Institute for Law and Economics, University of Pennsylvania, July.

Basu, S., J. G. Fernald, N. Oulton, and S. Srinivasan (2003). The case of the missing productivity growth. *NBER Macroeconomics Annual 18*, ed. M. Gertler and K. Rogoff, 9–63.

Baumgartner, F. R., J. M. Berry, M. Hojnacki, D. C. Kimball, and B. L. Leech (2009). *Lobbying and Policy Change: Who Wins, Who Loses, and Why.* Chicago: University of Chicago Press.

Bazot, G. (2013). Financial consumption and the cost of finance: Measuring financial efficiency in Europe (1950–2007). Working Paper, Paris School of Economics.

Bekkouche, Y., and J. Cagé (2018). The price of a vote: Evidence from France 1993–2014. CEPR Discussion Paper No. 12614, Centre for Economic Policy Research, London, January.

Benmelech, E., N. Bergman, and H. Kim (2018). Strong employers and weak employees: How does employer concentration affect wages? NBER Working Paper No. 24307, National Bureau of Economic Research, Cambridge, MA, February.

Berger, A., R. Demsetz, and P. E. Strahan (1999). The consolidation of the financial services industry: Causes, consequences, and implications for the future. *Journal of Banking and Finance 23*(2), 135–194.

Berger, D., K. F. Herkenhoff, and S. Mongey (2019). Labor market power. NBER Working Paper No. 25719, National Bureau of Economic Research, Cambridge, MA, March.

Bergman, M., M. Coate, M. Jakobsson, and S. Ulrik (2010). Comparing merger policies in the European Union and the United States. *Review of Industrial Organization 36*(4), 305–331.

Bergstresser, D., J. Chalmers, and P. Tufano (2009). Assessing the costs and benefits of brokers in the mutual fund industry. *Review of Financial Studies 22*(10), 4129–4156.

Bertrand, M., M. Bombardini, R. Fisman, and F. Trebbi (2018). Tax-exempt lobbying: Corporate philanthropy as a tool for political influence. NBER Working Paper No. 24451, National Bureau of Economic Research, Cambridge, MA, March.

Besley, T., and A. Case (2003). Political institutions and policy choices: Evidence from the United States. *Journal of Economic Literature 41*(1), 7–73.

Birnbaum, J. H. (1992). *The Lobbyists.* New York: Times Books.

Blanchard, O. (2003). Comment on Basu et al. *NBER Macroeconomics Annual 18,* ed. M. Gertler and K. Rogoff, 64–71.

Blanes i Vidal, J., M. Draca, and C. Fons-Rosen (2012). Revolving door lobbyists. *American Economic Review 102*(7), 3731–3748.

Blonigen, B. A., and J. R. Pierce (2016). Evidence for the effects of mergers on market power and efficiency. NBER Working Paper No. 22750, National Bureau of Economic Research, Cambridge, MA, October.

Bloom, N., C. I. Jones, J. V. Reenen, and M. Webb (2017). Are ideas getting harder to find? NBER Working Paper No. 23782, National Bureau of Economic Research, Cambridge, MA, September.

Bombardini, M., and F. Trebbi (2011). Votes or money? Theory and evidence from the US Congress. *Journal of Public Economics 95*(7–8), 587–611.

Bombardini, M., and F. Trebbi (2012). Competition and political organization: Together or alone in lobbying for trade policy? *Journal of International Economics 87*(1), 18–26.

Bork, R. (1978). *The Antitrust Paradox.* New York: Basic Books.

Brynjolfsson, E., A. Collis, W. E. Diewert, F. Eggers, and K. J. Fox (2019). GDP-B: Accounting for the value of new and free goods in the digital economy. NBER Working Paper No. 25695, National Bureau of Economic Research, Cambridge, MA, March.

Brynjolfsson, E., and A. McAfee (2014). *The Second Machine Age.* New York: W. W. Norton.

Buccirossi, P., L. Ciari, T. Duso, G. Spagnolo, and C. Vitale (2013). Competition policy and productivity growth: An empirical assessment. *Review of Economics and Statistics 95*(4), 1324–1336.

Bundestags-Drucksache (2013). Parliamentary paper no. 17/12340.

Byrne, D. M., J. G. Fernald, and M. B. Reinsdorf (2016). Does the United States have a productivity slowdown or a measurement problem? *Brookings Papers on Economic Activity* (Spring), 109–182.

Carree, M., A. Günster, and M. P. Schinkel (2010). European antitrust policy 1957–2004: An analysis of commission decisions. *Review of Industrial Organization 36*(2), 97–131.

Carril, R., and M. Duggan (2018). The impact of industry consolidation on government procurement: Evidence from Department of Defense contracting. NBER Working Paper No. 25160, National Bureau of Economic Research, Cambridge, MA, October.

Case, A., and A. Deaton (2015). Rising morbidity and mortality in midlife among white non-Hispanic Americans in the 21st century. *Proceedings of the National Academy of Sciences 112*(49), 15078–15083.

Case, A., and A. Deaton (2017). Mortality and morbidity in the twenty-first century. *Brookings Papers on Economic Activity* (Spring), 397–467.

Cette, G., J. Fernald, and B. Mojon (2016). The pre-Great Recession slowdown in productivity. *European Economic Review 88*, 3–20.

Chalk, M. N. A., M. Keen, and V. J. Perry (2018). The tax cuts and jobs act: An appraisal. IMF Working Paper No. 18/185, International Monetary Fund, August.

Chalmers, J., and J. Reuter (2012). Is conflicted investment advice better than no advice? NBER Working Paper No. 18158, National Bureau of Economic Research, Cambridge, MA, June, rev. September 2015.

Combe, E. (2010). Les vertus cachées du low cost aérien. In *Ouvrage Innovation Politique 2012.* Fondapol-PUF.

Corrado, C., D. Sichel, C. Hulten, and J. Haltiwanger, eds. (2005). *Measuring Capital in the New Economy,* Studies in Income and Wealth, vol. 65. Chicago: University of Chicago Press.

Council of Economic Advisers (2016). Benefits of competition and indicators of market power. CEA Issue Brief, Obama White House, April.

Covarrubias, M., G. Gutiérrez, and T. Philippon (2019). From good to bad concentration? U.S. industries over the past 30 years. *NBER Macroeconomics Annual 34,* ed. M. S. Eichenbaum, E. Hurst, and J. A. Parker.

Crawford, G. S., O. Shcherbakov, and M. Shum (2018). Quality overprovision in cable television markets. *American Economic Review 109*(3), 956–995.

Crouzet, N., and J. Eberly (2018). Intangibles, investment, and efficiency. *AEA Papers and Proceedings 108*, 426–431.

Cunningham, C., F. Ederer, and S. Ma (2018). Killer acquisitions. Working paper, August 28. http://dx.doi.org/10.2139/ssrn.3241707.

Darolles, S. (2016). The rise of fintechs and their regulation. Financial Stability Review 20, 85–92, Banque de France, April.

Davis, S. J. (2017). Regulatory complexity and policy uncertainty: Headwinds of our own making. Working paper, January. http://www.policyuncertainty.com/media/Davis_RegulatoryComplexity.pdf.

Davis, S. J., and J. Haltiwanger (2014). Labor market fluidity and economic performance. NBER Working Paper No. 20479, National Bureau of Economic Research, Cambridge, MA, September.

Deaton, A., and A. Heston (2010). Understanding PPPs and PPP-based national accounts. *American Economic Journal: Macroeconomics 2*(4), 1–35.

Decker, R., J. Haltiwanger, R. Jarmin, and J. Miranda (2014). The role of entrepreneurship in US job creation and economic dynamism. *Journal of Economic Perspectives 28*(3), 3–24.

Decker, R. A., J. Haltiwanger, R. S. Jarmin, and J. Miranda (2015). Where has all the skewness gone? The decline in high-growth (young) firms in the U.S. Working Papers 15–43, Center for Economic Studies, U.S. Census Bureau.

de Figueiredo, J. M., and B. K. Richter (2014). Advancing the empirical research on lobbying. *Annual Review of Political Science 17*(1), 163–185.

de Figueiredo Jr., R. J. P., and G. Edwards (2007). Does private money buy public policy? Campaign contributions and regulatory outcomes in telecommunications. *Journal of Economics and Management Strategy 16*(3), 547–576.

DellaVigna, S., R. Durante, B. Knight, and E. La Ferrara (2014). Market-based lobbying: Evidence from advertising spending in Italy. CEPR Discussion Paper No. 9813, Centre for Economic Policy Research, London, February.

Dellis, K., and D. Sondermann (2017). Lobbying in Europe: New firm-level evidence. ECB Working Paper No. 2071, European Central Bank, June.

De Young, R., D. Evanoff, and P. Molyneux (2009). Mergers and acquisitions of financial institutions: A review of the post-2000 literature. *Journal of Financial Services Research 36*(2), 87–110.

Djankov, S., T. Ganser, C. McLiesh, R. Ramalho, and A. Shleifer (2010). The effect of corporate taxes on investment and entrepreneurship. *American Economic Journal: Macroeconomics 2*(3), 31–64.

Djankov, S., R. LaPorta, F. Lopez-de-Silanes, and A. Shleifer (2002). The regulation of entry. *Quarterly Journal of Economics 117*(1), 1–37.

Dolfen, P., L. Einav, P. J. Klenow, B. Klopack, J. Levin, L. Levin, and W. Best (2019). Assessing the gains from e-commerce. NBER Working Paper No. 25610, National Bureau of Economic Research, Cambridge, MA, February.

Drechsler, I., A. Savov, and P. Schnabl (2017). The deposits channel of monetary policy. *Quarterly Journal of Economics 132*(4), 1819–1876.

Dube, A., J. Jacobs, S. Naidu, and S. Suri (2018). Monopsony in online labor markets. NBER Working Paper No. 24416, National Bureau of Economic Research, Cambridge, MA, March.

Duso, T., K. Gugler, and B. Yurtoglu (2011). How effective is European merger control? *European Economic Review, 55*(7), 980–1006.

Duval, R., D. Furceri, B. Hu, J. T. Jalles, and H. Nguyen (2018). A narrative database of major labor and product market reforms in advanced economies. IMF Working Paper No. 18/19, International Monetary Fund, January.

Economides, N. (1999). U.S. telecommunications today. In *IS Management Handbook,* ed. Carol V. Brown, 7th ed., 191–212. Boca Raton, FL: CRC Press, Taylor and Francis Group.

Egan, M., G. Matvos, and A. Seru (2016). The market for financial adviser misconduct. NBER Working Paper No. 22050, National Bureau of Economic Research, Cambridge, MA, February.

Elsby, M., B. Hobijn, and A. Sahin (2013). The decline of the U.S. labor share. *Brookings Papers on Economic Activity* (Fall).

Evans, W. N., E. M. J. Lieber, and P. Power (2019). How the reformulation of OxyContin ignited the heroin epidemic. *Review of Economics and Statistics 101*(1), 1–15.

Faccio, M., and L. Zingales (2017). Political determinants of competition in the mobile telecommunication industry. NBER Working Paper No. 23041, National Bureau of Economic Research, Cambridge, MA, January.

Feenstra, R. C., and D. E. Weinstein (2017). Globalization, markups and U.S. welfare. *Journal of Political Economy 125*(4), 1040–1074.

Feinberg, R. M., and K. M. Reynolds (2010). The determinants of state-level antitrust activity. *Review of Industrial Organization 37*(3), 179–196.

Flandreau, M. (2001). The bank, the states, and the market: An Austro-Hungarian tale for Euroland, 1867–1914. OeNB Working Paper 43, Oesterreichische Nationalbank, Vienna.

Foncel, J., V. Rabassa, and M. Ivaldi (2007). The significant impediment of effective competition test in the new European merger regulation. In *The Political Economy of Antitrust,* ed. Vivek Ghosal and Johan Stennek, 349–367. Bingley, UK: Emerald Insight.

Fouirnaies, A., and A. B. Hall (2014). The financial incumbency advantage: Causes and consequences. *Journal of Politics 76*(3), 711–724.

Furman, J., D. Coyle, A. Fletcher, P. Marsden, and D. McAuley (2019). Unlocking digital competition. Report of the Digital Competition Expert Panel. UK Government Publishing Service, March.

Gates, R. M. (2014). *Duty: Memoirs of a Secretary at War.* New York: Knopf.

GBD 2016 Healthcare Access and Quality Collaborators (2018). Measuring performance on the Healthcare Access and Quality Index for 195 countries and territories and selected subnational locations: A systematic analysis from the Global Burden of Disease Study 2016. *Lancet 391*, 2236–2271.

Gerber, D. J. (1998). *Law and Competition in Twentieth Century Europe.* Oxford: Clarendon Press.

Goldin, C., and L. F. Katz (2008). Transitions: Career and family lifecycles of the educational elite. *American Economic Review 98*(2), 363–369.

Goldschlag, N., and A. Tabarrok (2018). Is regulation to blame for the decline in American entrepreneurship? *Economic Policy 33*(93), 5–44.

Gordon, R. J. (2016). *The Rise and Fall of American Growth.* Princeton: Princeton University Press.

Greenwood, J., and J. Dreger (2013). The transparency register: A European vanguard of strong lobby regulation? *Interest Groups & Advocacy 2*(2), 139–162.

Greenwood, R., and D. Scharfstein (2013). The growth of finance. *Journal of Economic Perspectives 27*(2), 3–28.

Grossman, G., and E. Helpman (1994). Protection for sale. *American Economic Review 84*(4), 833–850.

Grossman, G. M., and E. Helpman (2001). *Special Interest Politics.* Cambridge, MA: MIT Press.

Grullon, G., J. Hund, and J. P. Weston (2018). Concentrating on q and cash flow. *Journal of Financial Intermediation 33*, 1–15.

Grullon, G., Y. Larkin, and R. Michaely (forthcoming). Are U.S. industries becoming more concentrated? *Review of Finance.*

Gutiérrez, G., C. Jones, and T. Philippon (2019). Entry costs and the macroeconomy. NBER Working Paper No. 25609, Cambridge, MA, National Bureau of Economic Research, February.

Gutiérrez, G., and T. Philippon (2017). Investment-less growth: An empirical investigation. *Brookings Papers on Economic Activity* (Fall).

Gutiérrez, G., and T. Philippon (2018a). How EU markets became more competitive than US markets: A study of institutional drift. NBER Working Paper No. 24700, National Bureau of Economic Research, Cambridge, MA, June.

Gutiérrez, G., and T. Philippon (2018b). Ownership, governance and investment. *AEA Papers and Proceedings 108*, 432–437.

Gutiérrez, G., and T. Philippon (2019a). Fading stars. NBER Working Paper No. 25529, National Bureau of Economic Research, Cambridge, MA, February.

Gutiérrez, G., and T. Philippon (2019b). The failure of free entry. Working paper.

Guzman, J., and S. Stern (2016). The state of American entrepreneurship: New estimates of the quantity and quality of entrepreneurship for 15 US states, 1988–2014. NBER Working Paper No. 22095, National Bureau of Economic Research, Cambridge, MA, March.

Hamm, K. E., and R. E. Hogan (2008). Campaign finance laws and candidacy decisions in state legislative elections. *Political Research Quarterly* 61(3), 458–467.

Haskel, J., and S. Westlake (2017). *Capitalism without Capital.* Princeton: Princeton University Press.

Higham, S., and L. Bernstein (2017). The drug industry's triumph over the DEA. *Wall Street Journal,* October 15.

Hirshleifer, J. (1971). The private and social value of information and the reward to inventive activity. *American Economic Review* 61(4), 561–574.

Holburn, G. L. F., and R. G. Vanden Bergh (2014). Integrated market and non-market strategies: Political campaign contributions around merger and acquisition events in the energy sector. *Strategic Management Journal* 35(3), 450–460.

Hölscher, J., and J. Stephan (2004). Competition policy in central eastern Europe in the light of EU accession. *JCMS: Journal of Common Market Studies* 42(2), 321–345.

Hortaçsu, A., and C. Syverson (2015). The ongoing evolution of U.S. retail: A format tug-of-war. *Journal of Economic Perspectives* 29(4), 89–112.

Huckshorn, R. J. (1985). Who gave it? Who got it? The enforcement of campaign finance laws in the states. *Journal of Politics* 47(3), 773–789.

Hyatt, H. R., and J. R. Spletzer (2013). The recent decline in employment dynamics. *IZA Journal of Labor Economics* 2(5).

Hylton, K. N., and F. Deng (2007). Antitrust around the world: An empirical analysis of the scope of competition laws and their effects. *Antitrust Law Journal* 74(2), 271–341.

Jayachandran, S. (2006). The Jeffords effect. *Journal of Law and Economics* 49(2), 397–425.

Jones, C. (2017). Discussion: Long-term growth in advanced economies. Presentation at the ECB Sintra Forum on Central Banking, European Central Bank, June 28.

Jovanovic, B., and P. L. Rousseau (2001). Why wait? A century of life before IPO. *American Economic Review* 91(2), 336–341.

Kalemli-Ozcan, S., B. Sorensen, C. Villegas-Sanchez, V. Volosovych, and S. Yesiltas (2015). How to construct nationally representative firm level data from the ORBIS global database. NBER Working Paper No. 21558, National Bureau of Economic Research, Cambridge, MA, September.

Kang, K. (2016). Policy influence and private returns from lobbying in the energy sector. *Review of Economic Studies 83*(1), 269–305.

Khan, L. M. (2017). Amazon's antitrust paradox. *Yale Law Journal 126*(3), 710–805.

Kleiner, M. M., and A. B. Krueger (2013). Analyzing the extent and influence of occupational licensing on the labor market. *Journal of Labor Economics 31*(S1), S173–S202.

Kroszner, R. S., and T. Stratmann (2005). Corporate campaign contributions, repeat giving, and the rewards to legislator reputation. *Journal of Law and Economics 48*(1), 41–71.

Krueger, A. B. (2017). Where have all the workers gone? An inquiry into the decline of the U.S. labor force participation rate. *Brookings Papers on Economic Activity* (Spring).

Krueger, A. B., and O. Ashenfelter (2018). Theory and evidence on employer collusion in the franchise sector. NBER Working Paper No. 24831, National Bureau of Economic Research, Cambridge, MA, July.

Krugman, P. (1998). It's baaack: Japan's slump and the return of the liquidity trap. *Brookings Papers on Economic Activity 2*, 137–187.

Kumar, S. (2016). Relaunching innovation: Lessons from Silicon Valley. *Banking Perspectives 4*(1), 19–23.

Kwoka, J. (2015). *Mergers, Merger Control, and Remedies*. Cambridge, MA: MIT Press.

Kwoka, J. (2017a). A response to the FTC critique. Working paper, April 6. https://papers.ssrn.com/sol3/papers.cfm?abstract_id=2947814.

Kwoka, J. E. (2017b). U.S. antitrust and competition policy amid the new merger wave. Research report, Washington Center for Equitable Growth, July 27. https://equitablegrowth.org/research-paper/u-s-merger-policy-amid-the-new-merger-wave/.

Kwoka, J., and L. J. White (2014). *The Antitrust Revolution*, 6th ed. Oxford: Oxford University Press.

Leech, B. L., F. R. Baumgartner, T. M. La Pira, and N. A. Semanko (2005). Drawing lobbyists to Washington: Government activity and the demand for advocacy. *Political Research Quarterly 58*(1), 19–30.

Leucht, B. (2009). Transatlantic policy networks in the creation of the first European anti-trust law. In *The History of the European Union*, ed. W. Kaiser, B. Leuchter, and M. Rasmussen, 56–73. London: Routledge.

Leucht, B., and M. Marquis (2013). American influence on EEC competition law. In *The Historical Foundations of EU Competition Law*, ed. K. K. Patel and H. Schweitzer. Oxford: Oxford University Press.

Lewis, B., A. Augereau, M. Cho, B. Johnson, B. Neiman, G. Olazabal, M. Sandler, S. Schrauf, K. Stange, A. Tilton, E. Xin, B. Regout, A. Webb, M. Nevens, L. Mendonca, V. Palmade, G. Hughes, and J. Manyika (2001). U.S. productivity growth, 1995–2000. McKinsey Global Institute, October.

Lucca, D., A. Seru, and F. Trebbi (2014). The revolving door and worker flows in banking regulation. NBER Working Paper 20241, National Bureau of Economic Research, Cambridge, MA, June.

Lyon, S. G., and M. E. Waugh (2018). Redistributing the gains from trade through progressive taxation. *Journal of International Economics 115*, 185–202.

Mahoney, C. (2008). *Brussels versus the Beltway: Advocacy in the United States and the European Union*. Washington, DC: Georgetown University Press.

Mathews, A. W. (2018). Behind your rising health-care bills: Secret hospital deals that squelch competition. *Wall Street Journal*, September 18.

McGrath, C. (2006). The ideal lobbyist: Personal characteristics of effective lobbyists. *Journal of Communication Management 10*(1), 67–79.

Meyer, B., and J. Sullivan (2018). Consumption and income inequality in the United States since the 1960s. *VOX*, January 15.

Miller, M. H. (1998). Financial markets and economic growth. *Journal of Applied Corporate Finance 11*(3), 8–15.

Mishak, M. J. (2016). Drinks, dinners, junkets, and jobs: How the insurance industry courts state commissioners. Center for Public Integrity, October 3.

Monnet, J. (1978). *Memoirs*. London: Collins.

Moore, K. B., and M. Palumbo (2010). The finances of American households in the past three recessions: Evidence from the Survey of Consumer Finances. FEDS Working Paper No. 6, Finance and Economics Discussion Series, February.

Mullainathan, S., M. Noeth, and A. Schoar (2012). The market for financial advice: An audit study. NBER Working Paper No. 17929, National Bureau of Economic Research, Cambridge, MA, March.

Olley, G. S., and A. Pakes (1996). The dynamics of productivity in the telecommunications equipment industry. *Econometrica 64*(6), 1263–1297.

Olson, M. (1971). *The Logic of Collective Action: Public Goods and the Theory of Groups*. Cambridge, MA: Harvard University Press.

Papanicolas, I., L. R. Woskie, and A. K. Jha (2018). Health care spending in the United States and other high-income countries. *JAMA 319*(10), 1024–1039.

Perrone, M., and B. Wieder (2016). Pro-painkiller echo chamber shaped policy amid drug epidemic. The Center for Public Integrity, December 15.

Peters, R. H., and L. A. Taylor (2016). Intangible capital and the investment-q relation. *Journal of Financial Economics 123*(2), 251–272.

Philippon, T. (2015). Has the US finance industry become less efficient? On the theory and measurement of financial intermediation. *American Economic Review 105*(4), 1408–1438.

Philippon, T., and A. Reshef (2012). Wages and human capital in the U.S. finance industry: 1909–2006. *Quarterly Journal of Economics 127*(4), 1551–1609.

Philippon, T., and A. Reshef (2013). An international look at the growth of modern finance. *Journal of Economic Perspectives 27*(2), 73–96.

Pierce, J. R., and P. K. Schott (2016). The surprisingly swift decline of US manufacturing employment. *American Economic Review 106*(7), 1632–1662.

Pigou, A. C. (1932). *The Economics of Welfare,* 4th ed. London: Macmillan.

Piketty, T., and E. Saez (2006). The evolution of top incomes: A historical and international perspective. *American Economic Review 96*(2), 200–205.

Pinkham, R. (1999). European airline deregulation: The great missed opportunity? *SAIS Europe Journal* (1 April).

Rajan, R. G., and L. Zingales (2003). *Saving Capitalism from the Capitalists.* New York: Crown Business.

Reinhart, C. M., and K. S. Rogoff (2009). *This Time Is Different: Eight Centuries of Financial Folly.* Princeton: Princeton University Press.

Renkin, T., C. Montialoux, and M. Siegenthaler (2017). The pass-through of minimum wages into US retail prices: Evidence from supermarket scanner data. Working paper, November.

Ritter, J. R. (2019). Initial public offerings: Updated statistics, April. https://site .warrington.ufl.edu/ritter/files/2019/04/IPOs2018Statistics-1.pdf.

Robinson, J. (1952). The generalization of the general theory. In *The Rate of Interest and Other Essays.* London: Macmillan.

Schreyer, P. (2002). Computer price indices and international growth and productivity comparisons. *Review of Income and Wealth 48*(1), 15–31.

Schuur, J. D., H. Decker, and O. Baker (2019). Association of physician organization–affiliated political action committee contributions with US House of Representatives and Senate candidates' stances on firearm regulation. *JAMA Network Open 2*(2), e187831.

Sen, A. (1982). *Poverty and Famines: An Essay on Entitlement and Deprivation.* New York: Oxford University Press.

Shapiro, C. (2018). Antitrust in a time of populism. *Journal of Industrial Organization 61,* 714–748.

Snyder, J. (1989). Election goals and the allocation of campaign resources. *Econometrica: Journal of the Econometric Society 157*(3), 637–660.

Snyder, J. (1992). Long-term investing in politicians; or, give early, give often. *Journal of Law and Economics 35*(1), 15–43.

Song, J., D. J. Price, F. Guvenen, N. Bloom, and T. von Wachter (2019). Firming up inequality. *Quarterly Journal of Economics 134*(1), 1–50.

Srinivasan, D. (2019). The antitrust case against Facebook: A monopolist's journey towards pervasive surveillance in spite of consumers' preference for privacy. *Berkeley Business Law Journal 16* (1), 39–101.

Stigler, G. J. (1971). The theory of economic regulation. *Bell Journal of Economics and Management Science 2*(1), 3–21.

Stratmann, T. (1998). The market for congressional votes: Is timing of contributions everything? *Journal of Law and Economics 41*(1), 85–114.

Stratmann, T. (2019). Campaign finance. In *The Oxford Handbook of Public Choice,* ed. R. D. Congleton, B. Grofman, and S. Voight, vol. 1, 415–432. New York: Oxford University Press.

Stratmann, T., and F. J. Aparicio-Castillo (2007). Campaign finance reform and electoral competition: Comment. *Public Choice 133*(1–2), 107–110.

Syverson, C. (2004). Market structure and productivity: A concrete example. *Journal of Political Economy 112*(6), 1181–1222.

Syverson, C. (2017). Challenges to mismeasurement explanations for the US productivity slowdown. *Journal of Economic Perspectives 31*(2), 165–186.

Tabakovic, H., and T. G. Wollmann (2018). From revolving doors to regulatory capture? Evidence from patent examiners. NBER Working Paper No. 24638, National Bureau of Economic Research, Cambridge, MA, May.

Tirole, J. (2017). *Economics for the Common Good.* Princeton: Princeton University Press.

Tripathi, M., S. Ansolabehere, and J. M. Snyder (2002). Are PAC contributions and lobbying linked? New evidence from the 1995 lobby disclosure act. *Business and Politics 4*(2), 131–155.

Tseng, P., R. S. Kaplan, B. D. Richman, M. A. Shah, and K. A. Schulman (2018). Administrative costs associated with physician billing and insurance-related activities at an academic health care system. *JAMA 319*(7), 691–697.

Valletta, R. G. (2016). Recent flattening in the higher education wage premium: Polarization, skill downgrading, or both? NBER Working Paper No. 22935, National Bureau of Economic Research, Cambridge, MA, December.

Vassalos, Y. (2017). Le pantouflage financier à la commission européenne. *Savoir / Agir* (3), 49–57.

Vita, M., and F. D. Osinski (2018). John Kwoka's *Mergers, Merger Control, and Remedies:* A critical review. *Antitrust Law Journal 82*(1), 361–388.

Welch, W. P. (1980). The allocation of political monies: Economic interest groups. *Public Choice 35*(1), 97–120.

Whelan, K. (2000). A guide to the use of chain aggregated NIPA data. FRB Working Paper, US Federal Reserve Board, June.

Zeitz, D. (2009). Overview of microeconomic reforms undertaken by EU member states based on the MICREF database. Joint Research Center, European Commission. Luxembourg: Publications of the European Community.

Zingales, L. (2017). Towards a political theory of the firm. *Journal of Economic Perspectives 31*(3), 113–130.

Zucman, G., T. Tørsløv, and L. Wier (2018). The missing profits of nations. NBER Working Paper No. 24701, National Bureau of Economic Research, Cambridge, MA, June, rev. August.

Acknowledgments

Many people and institutions have helped make this book possible.

Olivier Blanchard has been my teacher, mentor, and friend for the past twenty years. He has taught me to respect facts and theories equally, to keep an open mind and a healthy skepticism of fads and fashions, and to challenge the common wisdom when it appears to be wrong.

New York University has been a wonderful place to learn about economics and finance, and the Stern School has provided the support and flexibility that I needed to complete this project.

Many friends and colleagues have helped me develop the ideas presented in these pages. I would not have been able to write this book without the talent and energy of Germán Gutiérrez. Janice Eberly and Chad Syverson have discussed my papers on several occasions and provided the most helpful critical comments one can hope for. Bo Cutter was one of the first to suggest the idea of a book and has a special talent for asking the right questions.

I owe a great deal to Gerard Anderson, Matilde Bombardini, Nicolas Crouzet, Thomas D'Aunno, Francesco Franco, John Kwoka, Irene Papanicolas, Lasse Pedersen, and Francesco Trebbi, who read and commented on early drafts of various chapters.

I have had the chance to learn from my wonderful co-authors Maryam Farboodi, Callum Jones, Virgiliu Midrigan, Roxana Mihet, and Laura Veldkamp.

I have also benefited greatly from the insights of Ariel Burnstein, Luis Cabral, Gilbert Cette, Emmanuel Combe, Chiara Criscuolo, Jan De Loecker, Robin Döttling, Tomaso Duso, Rana Foroohar, Xavier Gabaix, Bob Hall, Erik Hurst, Seema Jayachandran, Sebnem Kalemli-Ozcan, Thomas Piketty, Howard Rosenthal, Tano Santos, Fiona Scott Morton, Dina Srinivasan, Johannes Stroebel, Jonathan Tepper, Jean Tirole, Nicolas Véron, David Wessel, Luigi Zingales, and Gabriel Zucman.

I am grateful to Ian Malcolm and Mark Steinmeyer, who saw promise in my early ideas, to Rob Garver and Katherine Brick, who edited my dry and technical prose, to the team at Harvard University Press for their professionalism, and to the Smith Richardson Foundation for its support. Abhishek Bhardwaj and Matias Covarrubias provided invaluable assistance and feedback.

Index